SAIGŌ TAKAMORI

SAIGŌ TAKAMORI:
THE MAN BEHIND THE MYTH

CHARLES L. YATES

KEGAN PAUL INTERNATIONAL
London and New York

First published in 1995 by
Kegan Paul International Limited
UK: P.O. Box 256, London WC1B 3SW, England
USA: 562 West 113th Street, New York, NY 10025, USA

Distributed by

John Wiley & Sons Limited
Southern Cross Trading Estate
1 Oldlands Way, Bognor Regis
West Sussex, PO22 9SA, England

Columbia University Press
562 West 113th Street
New York, NY 10025, USA

Copyright © Charles L. Yates 1995

Set in 11½ on 12½ Garamond
by Intype, London

Printed in Great Britain by TJ Press, Padstow, Cornwall

ISBN 0 7103 0484 6

British Library Cataloguing in Publication Data

Yates, Charles L.
    Saigo Takamori: Man Behind the Myth
    I. Title
    952.025092

    ISBN 0–7103–0484–6

US Library of Congress Cataloging in Publication Data

Yates, Charles L.
    Saigo Takamori: the man behind the myth / Charles L. Yates.
        235pp.   21cm.
    Includes bibliographical references and index.
    ISBN 0–7103–0484–6
    1. Saigo, Takamori, 1828–1877.   2. Statesmen–Japan–Biography.
I. Title.
DS881.5.S2Y38   1994
952'.025'092–dc20
    [B]   93–45592
                                                                      CIP

CONTENTS

ACKNOWLEDGEMENTS

The idea of a critical biography of Saigō Takamori originated in a seminar conducted by George M. Wilson at Indiana University in 1978. Our purpose in that seminar was to examine the applicability in historical writing of the psycho-biographical method developed by Erik Erikson. Though I eventually lost interest in the Erikson approach, the challenge of interpreting Saigō stayed with me. I did the first systematic reading for the dissertation on which the present work is based in Marius B. Jansen's seminars at Princeton University between 1980 and 1982.

Over the years since then, I have become indebted to many people, and I cannot hope to thank them all here. Professors Wilson and Jansen, as my principle advisors when I was in school, have helped me in ways too numerous to describe, or even to remember. My other mentors at Indiana University and Princeton, each of whom contributed to my intellectual development in unique and invaluable ways, include George Elison, Lynn Struve, Philip West, Leo Ou-fan Lee, Martin Collcutt, Sheldon Garon, and Richard Bowring. I owe a special debt to my classmates at Princeton, particularly Constantine Vaporis, Bob Wakabayashi, Barbara Brooks, Kazuko Furuta, and David Noble, for the many hours of lively and productive discussion we shared. And I am equally indebted to James McClain and Peter Nosco, who shared the little room in the Shiryō Hensanjo at the University of Tokyo with Constantine and me in 1985 and 1986, and who gave freely of their time and their insight as the first drafts of my dissertation took shape. Likewise I must thank Carol Gluck, Helen Hardacre, Irokawa Daikichi, and Hayami Akira, all of whom were unflagging in their encouragement and moral support as my dissertation gradually took shape at Princeton.

In Japan, besides those already mentioned, I am most heavily indebted to Arima Manabu, my research advisor at Kyushu University in Fukuoka. Professor Arima spent many long hours with me, discussing not only my evolving ideas, but the whole broad tapestry of early modern and modern Japanese history. His insights enabled me to avoid many pitfalls, and saved me incalculable amounts of time. More recently, Mitani Hiroshi of the University of Tokyo at Komaba has been extremely helpful to me in introducing me to new circles of colleagues in Japan, and in discussing interpretive problems with me constructively. The argument of the present work has benefitted tremendously from the insights provided to me by Professor Mitani and his associates in the Modern Japanese History Seminar (Kindai Nihon Kenkyūkai), particularly Saitō Osamu, Fukuchi Atsushi, Matsuda Kōichirō, Murase Shin'ichi, Suzuki Jun, Tanimoto Masayuki, Furuta Kazuko, Sugiyama Shinya, Hirota Teruyuki, Sakamoto Takao, and Bill Steele. All of these people were my teachers, and all of them have left their marks on my work.

At the Historiographical Institute (Shiryō Hensanjo) of the University of Tokyo, I was generously assisted by Professors Kanai Madoka and Ono Masashi. At Princeton, I incurred a tremendous debt to Ms. Soo-won Kim of the Gest Oriental Library. Ms. Kim cheerfully ordered numerous titles for me and never failed to let me know when the library acquired something she thought might be of value to me. Other libraries at which I spent considerable time include those of Kyushu University, Kagoshima University, Kagoshima Prefecture, Fukuoka Prefecture, and the Historiographical Institute in Tokyo. In addition, I spent many useful hours in the collection of the Reimeikan, Kagoshima's prefectural museum, and the Saigō Nanshū Kenshōkan, whose special exhibits on Saigō's life and times add a sense of reality to the often dry picture emerging from the literature. To the staffs of all these institutions, I express my gratitude.

My research was supported in the United States by university fellowships from Princeton in 1980–81, 1981–82, 1983–84, and 1986–87. In Japan, I received a Japan Foundation Language Fellowship for 1982–83, a GARIOA/Fulbright Kyushu Area Grant for 1984–85, and a further Fulbright grant provided by the Japan-United States Education Commission for 985–86. My thanks go to all who were instrumental in securing those grants for me,

Acknowledgements

but in particular I must thank Ms. Caroline A. Matano-Yang of JUSEC in Tokyo, and the members of the GARIOA/Fulbright Kyushu Alumni Association, who raised the money for my Kyushu Area Grant and looked after me faithfully during my year in Fukuoka.

Several of my colleagues at Earlham College have read the manuscript, in whole or part, and made helpful comments. I am especially indebted to Dan Meerson, Steve Heiny, and Jackson Bailey. My wife Deb also has read and commented on the entire manuscript.

Finally, I must express deep gratitude to Owen D. Mort, Jr. for his unflagging material and moral support throughout my years of study, and to my parents, whose confidence in me was at times greater than my own. In the same vein, my thanks go to many others not involved directly in my work, including Amy B. Wood, my brother Ken, and numerous friends who encouraged me even though they had no idea what I was doing.

Needless to say, while my debts to all these people and institutions are heavy and irredeemable, all responsibility for the content of this study, in particular any errors of fact or judgement, is mine.

CONVENTIONS EMPLOYED IN THE TEXT

Japanese terminology

I have followed the customary practice of giving Japanese names with the surname first, and I have referred to individuals consistently by their surnames, except where that might be confusing. In those cases, I have used the most common given name.

For Japanese words, I have used the English equivalent when it was less cumbersome to do so, and I have used the more familiar terms such as shogun, daimyo, and samurai without italics or diacritical marks, as if they were English words. The same applies to well known places such as Tokyo or Kyoto, but not the less familiar ones.

For more specialized terminology, I have introduced each word or phrase by giving an English equivalent first, followed by the Japanese term in parentheses, italicized and with diacritics. In subsequent usage, I have retained the diacritics, but not the italics.

All translations are my own.

Dating

On January 1, 1873, the Japanese government adopted the Gregorian calendar, replacing the lunar calendar by which the Japanese had reckoned dates ever since the seventh century. Under the lunar calendar, this event took place on the third day of the twelfth month of the fifth year of Meiji. The lunar calendar divided the year into twelve months, each of which had either twenty-nine or thirty days. Since this system did not reflect the movement of the cosmos accurately, discrepancies accumulated, and it was necessary occasionally to insert a thirteenth intercalary month to make the end of the year fall in the right place.

The Gregorian calendar makes dating more convenient, but there is a problem with expressing dates in a narrative that overlaps the transition from one system to the other. Most Western scholars simply convert all dates to Gregorian. I have dated events according to the calendar in use in Japan at the time. Prior to January 1, 1873, dates are lunar; after that, they are Gregorian. This approach is somewhat awkward, but it has the advantage of providing the reader with the dates as they appear in Japanese primary and secondary sources.

All dates are expressed in the form: year/month/day. Lunar dates give the year that corresponds to the traditional Japanese era. Intercalary months are marked by a lower case 'i' before the number of the month. Thus, the Japanese adopted the Gregorian calendar on 1873/1/1. which bore the lunar date 1873/12/3, with 1873 corresponding to the fifth year of the Meiji era. If the month had been intercalary, the date would read 1873/i12/3.

There are a number of helpful works available for converting lunar dates to Gregorian. For the period 1848 to 1872, the most convenient by far is *Bakumatsu ishinishi jiten*, edited by Konishi Shirō (Tokyo: Shin jinbutsu ōraisha, 1983), pages 334–59. For dates prior to 1848, consult Paul Y. Tsuchihashi, *Japanese Chronological Tables from 601 to 1872 A. D.* (Tokyo: Sophia University Press, 1952).

Abbreviations

I have used the following abbreviations for works cited frequently in the notes. For multi-volume works, citations indicate volume numbers with Roman numerals and page number with Arabic numerals, separated by a colon.

Diss	Charles L. Yates, 'Restoration and Rebellion in Satsuma,' Princeton doctoral dissertation.
DSZ	*Dai Saigō zenshū*, 3 vols.
Kenshi	*Kagoshima kenshi*, 7 vols.
OTden	Katsuda Magoya, *Ōkubo Toshimichi den*, 3 vols.
OTM	*Ōkubo Toshimichi monjo*, 10 vols.

OTN   *Ōkubo Toshimichi nikki*, 2 vols.
SHKJ   *Shimazu Hisamitsu kō jikki*, 3 vols.
STden   Katsuda Magoya, *Saigō Takamori den*
STZ   *Saigō Takamori zenshū*, 6 vols.
Inoue   Inoue Kiyoshi, *Saigō Takamori*, 2 vols.

INTRODUCTION:
Saigō Takamori: Image and Reality

Every year, Japan's public television network, NHK, airs a year-long mini-series based on a multi-volume historical novel, presenting a one-hour episode each Sunday evening. For those who cannot manage to sit through all of the weekly episodes, there is a condensed version of six to eight hours that airs in December, after the screening of the last regular episode. Since its inauguration over twenty years ago, the annual NHK historical series has become a regular fixture in the lives of many Japanese, and one hears discussions of it at social gatherings, in bars, and even on commuter trains.

The series for the 1990 season was based on a ten-volume work by the widely read novelist Shiba Ryōtarō, titled *Tobu ga gotoku* ('as if to fly').[1] Shiba's main focus in the novel is on the early development of Japan's domestic politics, and on the emergence in that context of widespread discontent toward the policies of the Meiji government among the samurai class, leading eventually to a series of armed rebellions between 1874 and 1877.

The central character in *Tobu ga gotoku* – both the novel and the television series – is Saigō Takamori, the samurai from Kagoshima who played a major role at several stages in the turbulent events leading to the Meiji Restoration of 1868, and then died in 1877 while leading the last great rebellion against the same government he had done so much to create. If we are to accept the judgement of Ivan Morris, Saigō's only biographer in English to date, he was among the most important men of his own time, and remains today among Japan's most beloved national heroes.[2]

1

Like most Japanese historical fiction, Shiba's original novel is most fundamentally a character study, an examination of the interplay between personalities and circumstances in a dynamic historical context. In the hands of NHK's script-writers, it has become a portrait of Saigō, and of his lifelong relationship with his boyhood friend Ōkubo Toshimichi, who was himself probably the most important figure in the early consolidation of the Meiji government, and certainly one of the most sagacious politicians Japan has ever produced.[3] Ōkubo died less than a year after Saigō, murdered by several former samurai who had not been able to get to Kagoshima in time to take part in Saigō's rebellion, and who held Ōkubo responsible for provoking the rebellion, and thus also for causing Saigō's death.[4]

The NHK mini-series always attracts a large audience, but judging from the impressions I gained while in Japan during 1990, the series for that year was more popular than usual, and it would be difficult to say whether that was because of Saigō Takamori's prominent place in it, or because of Nishida Toshi-yuki, the well-known and much-liked actor who portrayed him. No doubt it was some combination of both. Nishida's performance was very engaging – sensitive, thoughtful, and thought-provoking, and clearly based on a good deal of research into his character – and that in itself may have accounted for much of the success of the series. At the same time, the popularity of the series as a depiction of Saigō Takamori serves to remind us of the remarkable and undiminished power this man seems to exert on the Japanese imagination, even now, over a century after his death, when so many Japanese know nothing more about him than his name and one or two of the more conspicuous details of his life.

It is interesting enough in its own right that so many Japanese still *do* know Saigō's name and something about the big events of his life, because most of them have long since forgotten most of his contemporaries. Why should this one man stand out so prominently, in a period that had more than its share of remarkable men and women, and more than the usual concentration of memorable events? The simplest answer is that, as many Japanese have told me, Saigō has a special appeal for them because he embodies the essence of what it means to be Japanese. This makes sense, but it really does little more than suggest that for most Japanese, the image of Saigō is more important than the reality. And as that implies, what one encounters in the current

Japanese view of Saigō is actually a curious blend of fact and fancy.

Most Japanese would be quick to agree that Saigō is among the most important men in their country's history, but most of them actually know little about the historical man, beyond a vague awareness of his involvement in two of the most important episodes in the first decade of the Meiji period. One of those is the controversy over the 'proposal to punish Korea' (*seikanron*), a policy disagreement that split the Meiji government in late 1873. The other is the Satsuma rebellion (*seinan sensō*), the massive samurai uprising that broke out in Kagoshima early in 1877 and engaged tens of thousands of rebel and government troops in a series of terrible battles in southern Kyushu before it was finally suppressed in the autumn of that year.

Scholars of Saigō in Japan, professional and amateur alike, have argued about these two episodes almost from the moment they ended, giving the impression that scarcely anything else is more important than Saigō's place in them, but acting as if the reason for that overwhelming importance were self-evident. Perhaps to them and to their audience it is; to an outsider, it is not. Many other people of equal or greater importance in Meiji history were involved in both episodes, and the fundamental historical significance of both, as I have argued elsewhere, has little to do with Saigō himself, but rather with their character as domestic power struggles in the process of creating a centralized government for Japan.[5] Yet to my knowledge, no one has argued this point in Japan, or has even noticed that there is a point to argue, leading to the suspicion that the business of defining Saigō's place in events is more urgent than that of understanding the events themselves. Why should this be so?

Oddly enough, the man who bears the name Saigō Takamori in the minds of most Japanese actually has never existed except in the Japanese imagination, while the man named Saigō Takamori who actually did exist in Japan between 1827 and 1877 remains largely unknown, not just in the popular mind, but even in the minds of many of Japan's professional historians. The man of the popular imagination, called Great Saigō (*Dai Saigō*), is a superhuman figure; in the popular mind, this figure truly 'bestrode Japan like a colossus,' as Ivan Morris puts it,[6] and would have been fully capable of the remarkable historical legacy attributed to the Great Saigō. The historical Saigō, on the other hand, unquestionably impressed many of his contemporaries,

3

especially with the force of his personality, but never actually 'bestrode' anything, and certainly never assumed the proportions of a colossus. The man in the myth, as it were, has little to do with the man in the historical record. These two aspects of Saigō are so far apart and so mutually incompatible: how do we account for such a discrepancy?

Figuring out Saigō's place in Japanese history ought to be a relatively straightforward process of examining the primary evidence, weighing it against interpretations based on it in the secondary literature, and then finding one's own way to the conclusions that seem most clearly warranted. In the simplest of terms, that is what I have tried to do in the present study. Yet it is surprising to discover how difficult this rather routine task seems to have proven for the several generations of Japanese who have studied Saigō since his death. This difficulty is all the more perplexing in light of the fact that Japanese scholars routinely have no trouble reaching impressively solid and persuasive conclusions about other aspects of their past. For some reason, when most Japanese scholars go in search of Saigō he eludes them, and they end up producing little other than more or less imaginative rehashes of the same old formulaic controversies they had initially set out at least to avoid, if not actually to resolve.

There is nothing mysterious about the historical record on Saigō. Certainly there are not as many primary materials as one would like.[7] And there are places in those materials where one must use deduction to fill gaps. There are thoughts left unfinished or unsaid, statements that can be taken more than one way, even a few small contradictions, but for the most part, the evidence is direct and unambiguous. In any case, one could say these things about practically any body of historical data; the evidence is never complete, and using deduction to fill in the gaps is the essence of the historian's work. The biggest problem is that there is not enough explicit evidence to produce clear and unassailable conclusions about Saigō's involvement in the two episodes identified above: the 1873 debate on Korea policy and the 1877 rebellion in Satsuma. But even there, as I hope to show in the following narrative, it is not difficult to use what evidence there is to form conclusions that are not only reasonable but also consistent with the whole record.

In other words, it is not for lack of evidence, or of the capacity to evaluate it effectively, that scholars in Japan have had such difficulty producing a picture of Saigō that a majority of them and their readers could accept.[8] Something else is going on here. Saigō's image is getting in the way; Dai Saigō is obstructing the search for Saigō Takamori.

I think the 1990 mini-series on NHK attracted a large audience in part because so many people were eager to have another look at that image, to test the Saigō in their own imaginations against the one on the television screen, and to see whether the fit between the two would be emotionally satisfying. If the fit were good, then the audience would stay with the series to the end; if the fit were not so good, the audience would shrink steadily and drift away to other programming. Again, all the indications are that it was the former that occurred: the audience stayed, eager for more, right to the bitter end, and then stayed around for the eight-hour condensation as well. All of this suggests not only that a great many Japanese today still have vivid images of Saigō in their minds, but also that those images are quite important to them, and that what matters most about those images is not their literal truth but their affective value.

What Saigō did in history, then, is probably not really very important for most Japanese, whether they be scholars or lay people. What he does in their imaginations – how he helps or hinders the creation and maintenance of satisfying self-images – appears to be crucial. To perform this sort of function well, Saigō needs to be less a verifiable and irreducible historical datum than simply a blank slate, an empty vessel that one can fill with whatever details one finds most important at the moment, but that one also can empty out and refill with new contents whenever the need arises. Saigō seems to perform these functions supremely well, and that, more than anything else, explains why he has continued for so long to have such a firm hold on the Japanese imagination. It also explains why he has proven so elusive to scholars searching for the Saigō of literal historical truth, and why there have been so many different and irreconcilable depictions of him over the years. How should one go about making sense of these phenomena?

One good way to get a better fix on Saigō's place in the Japanese imagination is, of course, to start with the historical Saigō and assemble as complete and accurate a picture of him as the surviving evidence permits, and that is what I have tried to do in the bulk of the present study. Another way, however, is to think of him in Carol Gluck's terms, as an example of the 'stressed part' in ideological discourse.[9]

Carol Gluck has made a major contribution to the understanding of ideology with her argument that ideological discourse is governed by its own rules of grammar, and that these rules function, as in language, to generate consistent meanings out of a diversity of expressions. Gluck identifies three parts in an ideological statement: a 'stressed part,' which appears at the heart of every variation of the statement; an 'unstressed part,' which she calls the 'dependent clause,' and which modifies the stressed part and may change from one variation to the next; and an 'unarticulated part,' which is never stated but always assumed, and which Gluck equates with 'deep social meanings' which 'enabled ideological expressions to 'make sense' in the context in which they were articulated.'[10]

For example, consider the passage: 'I wish I was in the land of cotton; old times there are not forgotten. Look away, look away, look away, Dixie Land.' Here, the stressed part is 'Dixie' (a synonym for 'the South,' in such expressions as 'the South's gonna rise again'). The unstressed part is contained in the references to 'the land of cotton' and 'old times there,' and serves to clarify what is meant by the term 'Dixie.' The unarticulated part, which is the real punch line in the statement and the original reason for the formulation, is the entire system of social and ethical values associated with the slave-owning plantation culture of the South, *and* the affective responses associated with them.

The statement speaks of the South, but it is about a way of life associated with the South, and about the identity one acquires by living life in that way, according to those values. Thus, while the statement appears to do no more than point nostalgically to the world of those values, its real effect is to evoke a deep and powerful emotional response. As evoked by the statement, that emotion is in soft focus; it is fuzzy, not crisp and clear, and it is essential that it remain fuzzy. Its power, deriving importantly from that very fuzziness, is such as to motivate all sorts of actions that would be impossible to provoke with a clear and logical discursive statement about the value of Southern culture. Emotion is usually a more potent motivator than thought; and emotion can motivate more people, more effectively, when expressed vaguely, so that it can be associated with a wider variety of referents, than when spelled out with precision. That is simply because a fuzzy statement, without clear boundaries, is accessible to a broader array of personal needs and tastes.

Like such terms as 'Dixie' or 'the South,' Saigō Takamori has appeared over and over again as the central image in a bewildering variety of ideological formulations, not about Saigō himself, though that is how it looks, but rather about what it means to be Japanese. The 1990 NHK television series is such a statement, as is Shiba Ryōtarō's novel, and other fictionalized treatments of Saigō's life and times. The famous statue in Ueno Park, portraying Saigō as a humble commoner with his faithful dog, constitutes another such statement, and this, incidentally, helps to explain why so many writers have begun their accounts of Saigō by talking about the Ueno monument.[11] Many of the methodical studies of Saigō by professional historians are also little more than ideological formulations, and that explains why Saigō scholars have such a hard time reaching agreement about his historical meaning. Their representations of him are predicated on and seek to validate disparate unarticulated meanings, and it is actually the differences among these meanings, rather than disagreements about Saigō himself, that spark and sustain the controversies.

In other words, different scholars need to fill the empty vessel of Saigō's image with different contents, in order to realize different self-images, and so naturally they will always disagree about the portrayals of Saigō that result. To be sure, this sort of appropriation of Saigō for ideological purposes is not always obvious, and in some cases it is simply not there, but nowhere is it easier to recognize than in Meiji period wood block prints (*nishiki-e*) depicting the major events in which he was involved.[12]

Like the 1990 television series, and the historical novel on which it was based, these prints were intended for mass consumption. Thus, like the series and the novels, they are more concerned with Saigō's image than with his reality. And because they speak to widely felt needs – otherwise they would not have sold well, and would not have appeared in such profusion for as long as they did – they show us not only how the image works in the popular mind, but also what the image is. Finally, because we can compare the Saigō of these prints with that of, say, the NHK mini-series, we can also get some clues as to how images of him have changed over the generations since 1877.

Unlike the older and better known woodblock prints of the Tokugawa era, most of which have long since been appropriated by collectors and museums, these late Meiji prints are still not difficult to find, on the shelves of art dealers, as one would expect, but also in surprising numbers among the other odds and ends at flea markets, where they are still comparatively inexpensive. Most of those devoted to Saigō give us frozen moments of time, like movie stills, from either the Korea debate or the Satsuma rebellion. Some show scenes from other moments in his life, such as his unsuccessful suicide attempt with the monk Gessho in 1858, or his leadership of Satsuma troops in the various battles of the Meiji Restoration era, between 1864 and 1869. Less common, but ultimately more fanciful and fascinating, are the portrayals of Saigō in various scenes from *after* 1877, returning alive to Japan from a place of hiding somewhere abroad, or returning from the dead as an avenging spirit or as a portentous astral phenomenon.[13]

Colorful, lurid, and sensational, all of these prints tell us, usually in readily comprehensible terms, not what Saigō did or what befell him, but what was on the minds of average people in Japan during the late Meiji period, and what the majority of them wanted the predominant image of Saigō to be. And they tell us these things not only in the details of their content, but also in the way they consistently repeat certain motifs and conventions.

One feature of these prints that is surprisingly consistent is their composition. Nearly all of them are triptychs, and in most examples Saigō appears in the center panel, dominating a scene defined by a semicircle of supporting characters that fans out toward the left and right borders. When Saigō appears in one side panel or the other, the artist nevertheless identifies his location as the center of gravity, by arranging the circle of supporting figures so as to guide the eye and the attention to wherever he is. Thus, Saigō is not only at the center of the composition; he is at the center of the action as well, and whatever he is doing determines what the print is actually about, regardless of what particular historical event it purports to show us.

Another feature of these prints that is quite consistent is their flamboyant and melodramatic portrayal of both the characters and the action. Many of them look less like representations of historical episodes than like those moments on the *kabuki* stage when the action is frozen into a brief tableau, with all attention centered on the dramatic pose (*mie*) of the central character. No doubt this effect is quite deliberate, for one can imagine the better prints bringing the viewer to much the same sort of emotional peak achieved by the mie in kabuki. In fact, many of the nishiki-e are not scenes from history at all, but from the kabuki stage, where the big events of Saigō's life, like those from other decisive periods of Japan's past, have been reduced to starkly polarized dramas – of rewarding good and punishing evil (*kanzen chōaku*) or of the conflict between duty and feeling (*giri/ ninjō*) – according to formulas that never fail to appeal to popular taste.[14]

In many nishiki-e, Saigō and those around him are dressed in Western-style military uniforms, resplendent with gold epaulets, brocade sashes, and flashy medals, and most of the characters in a typical scene have full beards and mustaches.[15] Both the uniforms and the facial hair were popular in Japan in the middle of the Meiji era, during the period of avid cultural borrowing in the 1880s, and many prominent Japanese, including those who appear in these prints, such as Ōkubo Toshimichi, Itagaki Taisuke, and others, did grow beards, and did dress often in military uniforms. Like them, Saigō owned Western-style uniforms, so we may presume that he wore them occasionally.[16] However, there is no indication that he ever had a beard. On the contrary, the evidence suggests that soon after 1868 he shaved his head, and ended up looking more like a Buddhist monk than like a politician or a military leader. Thus the image of him in the popular mind during the Meiji period was a fabrication born in the minds of print designers, and the question then is where they got their ideas.

No verifiable photograph of Saigō is known to exist; the 1883 lithograph by the Italian artist Edouardo Chiossone, probably the most accurate representation of him, is actually a composite of the features of his brother Saigō Tsugumichi and his cousin Ōyama Iwao, designed by Chiossone on the advice of people who had known Saigō personally. From time to time over the years, a previously unknown photograph has turned up, and for a while people have believed that it represents Saigō, but sooner or later the true identity of the person in the picture is always established.

One of the first people to be widely mistaken for Saigō on the basis of photographs was a samurai from Kagoshima named Nagayama Yaichirō, who commanded a battalion of Satsuma troops in the rebellion of 1877. In the pictures of him that survive, he appears as a tall, slender man, cutting a trim and dashing figure in wide-brimmed hat, long coat, tailored pants, and high-top boots, and sporting a stylish beard and mustache. The most remarkable thing about this photograph is not that it might actually be a representation of the corpulent Saigō, but rather that Nagayama bears a striking resemblance to Erroll Flynn. For some Japanese Saigō is very much the sort of character in history that Erroll Flynn defined for American culture in his films.[17]

Without doubt, nishiki-e designers portrayed Saigō as a tall, slender man with a full beard because of Nagayama's portrait, and the widespread but mistaken belief that it actually represented Saigō. What is most fascinating, however, is that even after the man in the photographs was identified as Nagayama, printmakers went on showing Saigō in a full beard, as if the risk of misrepresenting him were nothing compared to the risk of disappointing audiences who had come to think of him as tall, slender, and bearded.

In the end, no doubt, it is much better that we do not have a verified photograph of Saigō, at least as far as the producers of ideological formulations are concerned. Such an explicit and incontrovertible bit of data would be a great inconvenience for people who need to have Saigō vague and malleable. An empty vessel, after all, does not bear a label listing its exact contents, and that is the effect a proven photograph of Saigō almost certainly would have on his otherwise empty and infinitely exploitable image. The only other late Tokugawa (*bakumatsu*) figure who has captured the popular imagination in Japan as decisively as Saigō is Sakamoto Ryōma, the low-ranking samurai from the domain of Tosa, and it may be that Saigō has remained more popular than Sakamoto as an exploitable image in part because there are a number of good photographs of the latter to keep our imaginations in check as to how he looked.[18]

The Saigō of the nishiki-e prints is manifestly an elaborate cliche, more than anything else, a complicated and carefully interwoven skein of meanings reduced to simple images, whose function is to establish the significance of the historical events in which he is portrayed, and to make that significance seem to be not just the most plausible of alternatives, but in fact the only possible alternative. The attitude he adopts most frequently is a combination of grim determination and righteous defiance, as if he were Martin Luther, unflinchingly declaiming, 'Here I stand.' Whether he sits in the midst of fellow council members in 1873, staunchly determined to go to Korea and settle the dispute between that country and Japan, or kneels on the ground at the end of the rebellion in 1877, surrounded but unperturbed by swarms of bullets from government rifles, and calmly prepares to plunge the knife into his belly, he always appears solidified by the power of moral rectitude, an immovable object against which even irresistible force eventually will prove unable to prevail. As if to reinforce this emphasis on his moral energy, others in the scene often appear less as independent participants than as mere stage decorations, polarized like iron filings along the lines of righteous force radiating from Saigō.

Needless to say, most of the events portrayed in nishiki-e never happened, or at best did not happen as they are shown. For example, during the week or so that the council of state argued Korea policy in 1873, Saigō attended only one meeting to defend his position; he was not present when the decisions were made, as some nishiki-e prints suggest. Likewise, many of the other figures portrayed in nishiki-e representations of that event were not only not present at the time, but in some cases were not even members of the government. In the same manner, most portrayals of Saigō's suicide show him on the battlefield, surrounded by his loyal followers, who look on as he enacts the *seppuku* ritual. One particularly imaginative depiction shows him in a small boat at sea, with ominous lightning crackling above a squadron of Western-style warships in the distance – the imperial flotilla closing in for the kill – while two of his loyal followers look on. In reality, there were no naval battles during the Satsuma rebellion, and most of the ships used to deploy troops and supplies against the rebels were Western vessels on loan to the Meiji government. In fact, there is no evidence that Saigō committed suicide at all. Rather, he was decapitated by a subordinate after a bullet gored his abdomen and thigh, opening a wound from which he would have died quickly in any case.

But then it scarcely matters whether these prints represent anything factual or not. Like the newspaper accounts they were often based on, it is not their primary purpose to tell the truth. All of them together – not just those depicting Saigō but also all those showing the many details of Meiji Japan's progress into the modern day – constitute an elaborate and ongoing conversation which late nineteenth-century Japanese had with themselves about who they were. As Carol Gluck has shown, that conversation contained a variety of propositions about different aspects of Japanese life. Saigō is only one of them, one among many.

As fashions in Japan changed and modernization proceeded apace, the nishiki-e eventually disappeared, along with most of the vivid images portrayed in them. But it is interesting that,

11

unlike the steam engines and the gas lights on the Ginza and the thoroughly modern men and women going about their business in all sorts of settings, Saigō did not vanish when the nishiki-e went out of fashion. He found other media in which to appear, but the essential point is that he continued to appear – in newspaper essays, novels and short stories, biographies, and kabuki plays, and then later also in television productions, feature films, and mass market periodicals for both the high brow and the low. He has even appeared in comic books, and in advertising layouts for everything from food, alcohol, and drugs to travel services and office machines.[19]

And so he continues to appear today, over and over again. The stream of new writing about him has yet to diminish, even though it has been flowing steadily now for over a century.[20] What all of this suggests, among other things, is that the controversies about Saigō have endured not because they cannot be resolved, but rather because to resolve them is not the point. The image of Saigō retains all of its power today, as in the past, because ordinary Japanese are not done with it yet, and still find it useful. They continue to rediscover it, and to fill it and refill it with ever new contents, always in answer to their needs at the moment.

But this man of images of whom I have been speaking is not Saigō Takamori; it is Dai Saigō, the Last Samurai, the gentle giant from Kagoshima. Behind the image there is a man, and it is on his life that the following study is focused. When the story of his life is told, we can come back to the image, and see whether we can determine what there is to learn from a comparison of the two.

In the chapters that follow, I examine the major phases of Saigō's life: his early development in Kagoshima, his initiation to politics in the 1850s, the further growth of his thought during two periods of exile, his involvement in the Meiji Restoration process from 1863 through 1869, his participation in national and local government reforms after 1868, and his final years, down to the Satsuma rebellion. Several aspects of my treatment of Saigō are depatures from what has been customary hitherto.

First, I argue that an understanding of Saigō's intellectual development during his exile between 1859 and 1863 is crucial for a full interpretation of his behavior in the later part of his life.[21] Second, I suggest that Saigō's political ambitions were all essentially satisfied after 1868, and that his only remaining desire of any consequence was to go into retirement. One implication of this claim is that Saigō was drawn back into government in 1871 largely against his will and against his better judgement. Third, I propose to understand both the Korea policy debate of 1873 and the Satsuma rebellion of 1877 chiefly as power struggles within the Meiji government, erupting as members of the loose coalition that had effected the Meiji Restoration sorted themselves out and determined which of several conflicting political agendas would predominate. Fourth, as a consequence of the above point, I also contend that both of those episodes were caused by and symptomatic of the process of Japan's political centralization, and that they both would have occurred more or less in the same way whether Saigō had been involved in them or not.

These four claims and their implications lead my evaluation of Saigō's place in Japanese history toward a twofold conclusion: first, he probably did not want Japan to invade Korea, but hoped instead to achieve a mutually agreeable negotiated relationship between the two countries; and second, he probably had little or nothing directly to do with the outbreak of the Satsuma rebellion, but rather was drawn into it by the entailments of his personal beliefs only after it was underway. To ask whether Saigō was or was not culpable in either of these two episodes may be of passing interest in some narrow sense, but ultimately, I conclude, it is to ask the wrong question; it is to frame the issues in an unproductive way, and thus to miss the point.

The Saigō I have found in the historical record is not a very good match for any of the images of him that have been current in Japan since his death, although he resembles some more than others. There is much circumstantial evidence that may influence the details of any Saigō portrayal, but I have tried to avoid it, so that the Saigō I have reconstructed emerges almost entirely from the hard evidence. I think he fits that evidence better than most other portrayals, and he seems more plausible as a real person than they do. As a Westerner, I must remain a sojourner in Japanese culture, not a native. Thus while the Japanese may see Saigō imperfectly through emotional or ideological veils, there are other obstructions that block my view just as effectively. Yet being an outsider also has its advantages. My portrayal of Saigō is not influenced by any need to create a satisfying image of myself as a Japanese.[22] Consequently, I have no need to take a position on his moral significance for the emergence of contemporary Japan. My Saigō is neither as villainous as his detractors

13

in Japan would like him to be, nor as virtuous as his apologists would insist. I have no quarrel with those who would condemn Saigō or consecrate him, and who might take me to task for not choosing sides, but my project is not the same as theirs. In the first place, Saigō's historical significance does not lie in such one-sided attributions; in the second, I simply think that the passing of such value judgements is beyond the limits of the historian's competence.

· 1 ·

Saigō's Childhood in Satsuma,
1827–59

During the first three decades of his life Saigō passed from the sheltered provincial anonymity of his childhood in the city of Kagoshima into his first period of political exile in the Amami islands. At the beginning of this period, he was but an unknown vassal of the Shimazu family, and probably content to be nothing more. By the end of it, his name was well known among the politically thoughtful and active throughout Japan, and he had earned more notoriety than he may have wanted. To tell the story of how he got from one extreme to the other, we need to begin with a survey of the environment in which he grew up, and how it came to be what it was at the time he entered it.

The setting:
Satsuma, 1185–1851

Satsuma, the hereditary domain of the Shimazu family, occupied what is today Kagoshima Prefecture, in southern Kyushu.[1] It first came under Shimazu rule in 1196. In that year Minamoto Yoritomo, the founder of Kamakura period rule, appointed his ally Koremune Tadahisa as governor of an estate (*shōen*) known as Shimazu-shō.[2] To mark his accession to local control, Koremune took the name of this estate as his surname, establishing the Shimazu family. In the late sixteenth century, taking advantage of fluid political conditions prevailing throughout Japan at the time, and conquering their neighbors one by one in brilliant military campaigns, the Shimazu came close to dominating all of Kyushu, but in 1587 they were overwhelmed and pushed back to the southern tip of the island by Toyotomi Hideyoshi, who

15

confined them to the provinces of Satsuma and Ōsumi.³ Tokugawa Ieyasu confirmed these holdings when he came to power in 1600, and in 1609 he approved the extension of Shimazu hegemony southward into the Amami and Ryūkyū island groups.⁴ Shimazu dominance of these territories continued until the abolition of all the daimyo domains (*han*) by the Meiji government in 1871. Thus the Shimazu controlled roughly the same lands without interruption for nearly seven hundred years. In the process they established traditions of forceful leadership and continuity of rule that had no equal in Japanese history.

Those traditions were reinforced by Satsuma's geographical isolation. Farther from the centers of power in Kyoto and Edo than any other han, and walled off even from the rest of Kyushu by rugged mountains, Satsuma evolved into a world apart, and its people came to view themselves as both separate from and superior to their countrymen. They identified themselves not with other Japanese, but with the fiercely independent ancient inhabitants of southern Kyushu, known as *Hayatō*. They developed their own customs and mores, and the Satsuma dialect, like those in other remote parts of Japan, became almost a separate language, effectively unintelligible outside the domain's borders. The distinguished military history of the Shimazu, based on dramatic achievements at the end of the sixteenth century both in Kyushu and in Korea, further reinforced this sense of superiority. By the beginning of the Tokugawa period there were no people more proud or aloof than those of Satsuma, particularly the members of its samurai class, who were more numerous as a proportion of the whole population than those of most other han. Most of them, moreover, were rural samurai (*gōshi*) and though they were at the bottom end of the samurai status hierarchy within Satsuma,⁵ they shared the pride of their higher ranking fellows in the castle town, and their routine presence in every village and hamlet in the han helped to keep even the lowliest of Satsuma's peasants constantly aware of the pride the han's elite took in their traditions and in themselves.

For the most part, the men who headed the Shimazu family through thirty successive generations were strong and capable leaders, and they were blessed with a territory whose sub-tropical climate and volcanic soil allowed for a wide variety of agricultural products, and therefore provided a compartively secure basis for their revenue. Other things being equal, they ought to have enjoyed consistently secure economic foundations for their rule.

However, confronted with bewildering social and economic change during the seventeenth and eighteenth centuries, Satsuma fell prey to the combination of bad luck and bad planning that plunged nearly all daimyo domains into heavy indebtedness. By the early nineteenth century, despite several attempts at reform, Satsuma found itself burdened with the largest debt in the country, a total of some five million *ryo*.[6] As a result, Satsuma's leaders faced a painful dilemma.

The new realities of late Tokugawa Japan had already created a world that would have been unrecognizable in many ways to those who had established the Tokugawa order in the seventeenth century, but Satsuma had changed less than any other part of Japan, and the han's leaders in 1600 would have felt comfortably at home in the Satsuma of 1800. Without sweeping administrative reform, however, Satsuma could not hope to survive, either economically or politically, and reforms on the scale required would also necessitate profound institutional change. That change, in turn, would alter traditional social relations, and would threaten the values they represented. In effect, political and economic survival could be won only through the obliteration of traditional social identity, because the customs and values threatened by institutional reform embodied the whole system of symbols by which Satsuma's people had defined and maintained their sense of themselves for over half a millenium. Beginning in the late eighteenth century, an atmosphere of crisis developed in Satsuma, growing out of the conflict between the obvious need for change as a means to economic and political survival and the loss of social identity such change would bring about. The sense of crisis was exacerbated, moreover, by long-standing social tensions that had evolved out of Satsuma's rigid status system and the disparities of economic and political enfranchisement it enforced. These tensions were brought to the fore and deepened profoundly by a series of political confrontations in the late eighteenth and early nineteenth centuries.

The first such confrontation unfolded during the administration of Shimazu Shigehide, the twenty-fifth of Satsuma's rulers (*hanshu*), who came to power in 1755. Like many of his ancestors, Shigehide was possessed of great energy, a lively intellect, and a determination to reform his administration. The measures he instituted – most notably the creation of a monopoly on cane sugar production in the Amami islands – did make some temporary headway against Satsuma's fiscal problems. However, his administrative policies cut to the heart of traditional social relations and values, abolishing some practices and altering others beyond recognition. High ranking samurai became more powerful under Shigehide, while those at the lower end of the hierarchy sank further into impoverishment and humiliation than they had ever been before. As a result, Shigehide was hated by most of his subjects, and none more so than his own son Narinobu, who despised him both for the severity with which he extracted revenue from the peasants, and for the dissension he had caused in the samurai class through his inequitable treatment based on rank.

Consequently, when Narinobu succeeded Shigehide and assumed power in 1787, he set out to undo everything his father had done. Narinobu appointed new administrators, many of them from the lower ranks of samurai who had been so ill-treated by Shigehide. These men purged Shigehide's high-ranking administrators and systematically reversed the reforms they had carried out under his direction. Motivated less by rationality than by righteous indignation, Narinobu's measures had more in them of revenge than of reform, and they presented Shigehide with a challenge to his self-esteem, if not to his symbolic authority, that he could not ignore indefinitely. In 1808, invoking his authority as Narinobu's father and the eldest male in the Shimazu family, he intervened. He forced Narinobu into retirement, and ordered penalties ranging from simple dismissal and demotion, through house arrest and exile, to suicide for over a hundred of Narinobu's followers, in what is known as the Bunka purge (*Bunka hōtō jiken*).

Narinobu was succeeded by his son Narioki who, acting under the guidance of Shigehide, ordered a third series of reforms. Like their forerunners, these had little effect until 1827, when Shigehide and Narioki assigned comprehensive authority for all aspects of reform to a low-ranking but exceptionally capable bureaucrat named Zusho Hirosato. Zusho had begun life as a member of the *koshōgumi*,[7] the lowest ranking and largest of the castle town samurai status groups, but had risen to prominence through diligent service and sagacious courting of political favor. The policies he put into effect, known as Satsuma's Tenpō reforms, eventually proved successful.

Centered on the further rationalization of the Amami sugar monopoly, but including also the development of new cash crops and markets both locally and nationally, Zusho's reforms began

18

with the simple repudiation of the han's five million ryō debt, and ended with a comprehensive review of the system of stipends and military service among Satsuma's samurai. Zusho also expanded direct trade with Chinese merchants. Such trade had been routine in Satsuma since well before the beginning of the Tokugawa era, even though it was illegal after about 1640. Satsuma conducted it not only through the Ryūkyū islands and out of secluded inlets along Satsuma's coast, but even directly under the noses of the Tokugawa officials in Nagasaki. By the start of the 1840s, Satsuma was not only out of debt, but was running a substantial surplus, which Narioki devoted chiefly to the modernization of han military forces. By the time Commodore Perry sailed into Edo Bay in 1853, Satsuma's economic vigor and military strength were unmatched anywhere in Japan, and over a century of economic crisis had been brought to an end.

Zusho's triumph was complete, but it was not without cost. Like most other reforms in Tokugawa Japan, Zusho's placed the heaviest part of the burden on those least able to bear it. Already accustomed to giving up over half of what they produced even at the best of times, Satsuma's peasants now had to surrender even more, and they were required to spend all of their free time in the cultivation of special cash crops like lacquer and rapeseed oil. Under the regulations governing sugar production, the people of the Amami islands were effectively enslaved. Forbidden to produce anything but sugar, and obliged to purchase necessities with credit based on the amount of sugar they produced, they lived near starvation most of the time, and the penalty for hoarding or attempting to sell sugar privately was death. In the same way, the reform of the stipendiary system drove Satsuma's lower samurai further into poverty, while Zusho and his associates in the upper strata grew wealthy through bribery, land speculation, and rake-offs.

The tensions produced by these disparities led to a second confrontation, which came to a head in 1849, when Narioki learned that a group of samurai favoring the succession of his eldest legitimate son Nariakira had contrived a plot to murder a number of high ranking han officials connected with the reform, including Zusho himself. The chief target of this scheme was Narioki's concubine, Okada Yura, who had been attempting to persuade Narioki to name their illegitimate son Hisamitsu as his successor. Nariakira's supporters believed that Yura had arranged for the poisoning of several of his children, presumably in order

19

to undermine his candidacy as Narioki's successor by depriving him of heirs, and the arrogance of this assault on the legitimate succession was more than some of his supporters could abide. It is not clear whether these men actually did plan to kill Yura, Zusho, and others, but that made no difference to Narioki. Like his grandfather Shigehide, he carried out a sweeping attack on suspected enemies, ordering varying degrees of punishment for some fifty men, in what came to be known as the Kaei purge (*kaei hōtō jiken*) or, in reference to its primary focal point, the Yura disturbance (*Yura sōdō*).

Then, in 1851, before he could capitalize on whatever benefits this purge might have yielded, Narioki abruptly retired in favor of Nariakira, and brought the matter to a close. Ostensibly this sudden change of heart was a response to pressure from officials of the Tokugawa government (*bakufu*) in Edo. This pressure was orchestrated by Nariakira's supporters there, including not only the Fukui hanshu Matsudaira Shungaku, head of a Tokugawa collateral house, but also the most powerful man in the bakufu itself, the elder (*rōjū*) Abe Masahiro. In fact, since Nariakira had told Abe about Satsuma's illegal trade, it it probable that Narioki chose to retire rather than face official sanctions for condoning the systematic violation of one of the bakufu's most cherished prohibitions. Zusho did not fare so well; evidently hoping to protect Narioki, he took responsibility for the illegal trade upon himself and committed suicide.

Nariakira's accession marked the dawning of a new day for Satsuma. Raised in Edo, close to his great-grandfather Shigehide, he shared the latter's energy, intelligence, and determination. He also shared Shigehide's passion for Western learning, and he meant to conduct reforms that would do more than just revive existing social and economic relations. Like others in mid-nineteenth-century Japan, Nariakira was convinced that the country must open itself to intercourse with the West if it hoped to survive, much less compete, in the wide world of international power politics to which Japan was about to be unwillingly introduced by Commodore Perry. Nariakira's reforms, the fourth set of major new policy changes since Shigehide, were devoted to the establishment of Western industrial technology in Satsuma, and to the complete reorganization of Satsuma's military forces according to Western models, trained in Western techniques, and equipped with Western weapons. His social policies were equally radical, calling for the easing of hitherto inflexible status distinctions within the samurai class, and the opening up of administrative office to all with ability and imagination. After so many years of hardship, the people of Satsuma had ample reason to rejoice in the accession of Nariakira. But if they greeted his arrival with celebration, they had not forgotten what they regarded as the morally intolerable and abusive practices of his predecessors, and these were wounds that would prove to be a long time in healing.

Of particular importance was the resentment felt by the koshōgumi, who had been at the bottom of the status scale in the castle town throughout the Tokugawa period, and from whose ranks had come the majority of the victims in both the Bunka and the Kaei purges. Traditionally, these men had filled the lowest administrative posts in the han bureaucracy, where they gained a great deal of practical experience but enjoyed little prestige or influence. Many of them never received official appointments, and were obliged to spend their time either in scholarship or in idleness. Never far from poverty, they were often forced to take up various forms of cottage industry to make ends meet. Because of their experience at the level where policy was transformed into practice, they understood the han's administrative problems better than anyone else, or at least they believed they did. Their work placed them in frequent contact with the peasants, and so they saw at first hand the hardship caused by the policies of those in power. Their exclusion from positions of responsibility, however, made it impossible for them to apply what they knew. Only during Narinobu's brief tenure had any of them risen high enough to make policy, and these men were the first to die when Shigehide struck back in 1808. Zusho, like his patron Shigehide, excluded them from power, and it was they who paid the highest price under his stipendiary reform in the 1840s, and Narioki once again found most of his victims in 1849–50 among the koshōgumi. Thus the members of this group had good reason to see themselves as a special class of victims, even though there is no direct evidence that they did so.

Among the most famous of Kagoshima's koshōgumi was Ōkubo Toshimichi, and to judge from surviving records, the experiences of his family offer an example that was not uncommon.[8] At the time of the Kaei purge, Ōkubo was serving as a copyist in the han records office. Narioki removed him from his post and ordered him into house arrest. His father was exiled, and the entire family was placed under close scrutiny. In the

Bunka purge, Ōkubo's grandfather had been among those humiliated by dismissal and domiciliary confinement on Shigehide's orders.[9] Three successive generations in a single family thus had suffered at the whim of the han's rulers; misfortune on such a scale could not have been coincidence, and therefore could not have failed to leave a deep impression, not only on the Ōkubo household, but on their friends and neighbors as well.

Among those neighbors were a number of young men who would later rise to prominence in Satsuma, including Saigō Takamori. Perhaps most intriguing, when young samurai in Satsuma came together in the 1850s to form an activist group, a surprising number of them bore surnames that had already appeared on the lists of victims in both the Bunka and the Kaei purges.[10] In short, there is considerable reason to suspect the development of a bitter factional polarization among Kagoshima samurai, based primarily on status inequalities, with the high-ranking titled families (*monbatsu*) on one side and the low-ranking koshōgumi on the other. This polarization, together with the passionate animosities it generated, endured from the time of Shigehide's first reforms into the early decades of the Meiji era, and exerted an important influence of the politics of Satsuma throughout.

To sum up, then, over the course of roughly a century, Satsuma had sunk steadily deeper into debt, while its people, faced with growing insecurity in both economic and social terms, clung ever tighter to their traditions. A series of reforms under Shigehide, Narinobu, and Narioki had turned the han administration first one way and then another, but with little lasting effect until the years of Zusho's leadership in the 1830s and 1840s. Yet in spite of his fiscal success, his social policies only worsened feelings of factional resentment that had already begun to emerge when Shigehide came to power. If the people of Satsuma could finally feel comparatively secure under the enlightened leadership of Nariakira, they likewise could not readily forget the suffering his predecessors had put them through for generations.

Then, as Nariakira set about the work of reform once again, the future not only of Satsuma but of Japan itself came into question, with the arrival of the aggressive Westerners and their demands for trade and free intercourse. It was into this uneasy world of economic crisis and social conflict that Saigō Takamori was born, early in the final month of 1827.

The life of a young samurai:
Kagoshima, 1827–44

Regardless of variations in detail resulting from individual taste and temperament, all Japanese who value the image of the Great Saigō share the belief that he was the perfect embodiment of the ideal samurai. He was stoic, gentle, and fearless, a master of martial arts and a brilliant military leader. His intellectual powers, and the scholarly originality he achieved through them, were second only to his military abilities, and he was a master of all of the important intellectual currents of his time, including Zen Buddhism and both of the dominant traditions of Neo-Confucian thought. He was physically imposing: larger than life, exceptionally strong, and in complete control of his body. His character was likewise flawless: he was scrupulously faithful to his ethical code, obedient to those above him in status and benevolent toward those below, and he always placed his duty to others above his own needs. And, in the best hagiographical tradition, he came by all of these qualities early in his childhood, and exhibited them all consistently throughout his life. Two things are noteworthy in this image of Saigō. The first is that it tells us more about what Japanese today understand the ideal samurai to be than it does about what the real samurai of traditional Japan may have been. The second is that, except for a few comparatively unimportant details, practically nothing about it can be verified from existing evidence.

Most of the information on Saigō's childhood is anecdotal, and of limited value at best. According to the biographical tradition, Saigō was a quiet boy who was bullied frequently by other children because he lacked the bravado deemed appropriate for a samurai's son.[11] When he was thirteen, he got into a quarrel with a boy from another part of Kagoshima and received a sword cut in his right arm. Because the wound did not heal properly, the arm became stunted. Saigō is said accordingly to have renounced the study of martial arts in favor of scholarship.[12] Whether this story is true or not, it fits with the more general impression one gets from surviving evidence, that Saigō was quiet by nature, and that contrary to the popular impression, he had little taste either for warfare or for the self-image of a warrior.[13]

Saigō's family belonged to the koshōgumi, and he grew up in Kajiyamachi, a section of Kagoshima reserved for members of that status group. This part of Kagoshima is well known because it was the boyhood home of some of Meiji Japan's most prominent leaders, including Ōkubo Toshimichi, Tōgō Heihachirō, Saigō's younger brother Tsugumichi, and his cousin Ōyama Iwao. Like many other koshōgumi, the Saigō family was poor. During Saigō's early childhood, they are said to have supplemented their income by making umbrellas, and the infant Saigō helped with the shaving of the struts.[14] The family also supplemented its income through agriculture, a practice that seems to have been fairly common among lower ranking samurai. Saigō's oldest surviving autograph is a letter acknowledging a loan of 100 ryō, which was used to purchase the right to cultivate a small parcel of land, presumably in order to sell the produce for cash.[15]

Saigō was the first of seven children – four boys and three girls – and the most widely repeated story of his youth tells how all seven of them had to crowd together under a single quilt in the winter.[16] All of them were robust of build and healthy, but of the four brothers, only one lived to old age. Kichijirō, the second son, died in the fighting between imperial and Tokugawa supporters in the Tōhoku campaign of 1868, and Kohei, the youngest of the boys, died with Saigō in the Satsuma rebellion of 1877. The survivor was Shingō, better known as Tsugumichi. All three daughters married into low-ranking samurai families, but the surviving record tells us nothing noteworthy about them.

Little is recorded of Saigō's parents. His father served in the han accounting office and is said to have been gentle and modest, hard working and widely respected. Like his eldest son, he had a reputation as a formidable sumo opponent.[17] He was also employed by the family of Akayama Yukie, a high-ranking samurai who committed suicide on Narioki's orders in the Bunka purge of 1849- 50. He was present when Akayama took his life, and brought the dead man's bloody undergarment home to the young Saigō. If we may believe the biographical tradition, the latter vowed then and there to devote his life to the cause of righteousness.[18] Perhaps it strains credibility to suggest that a comparatively naive and sheltered youth of barely twenty should discover his mission in life on beholding the bloody garments of a suicide victim, yet even if Saigō did not become a political radical on the spot, it is likely that he found it difficult to forget the ghastly souvenir and it may indeed have made a lasting emotional impression on him.

Ōkubo Toshimichi's family probably influenced Saigō's development as much as his own did.[19] Ōkubo's father and grandfather are both reputed to have been men of great intelligence and imagination, and were established scholars to whom the sons of many Kagoshima samurai came for education. Saigō learned Wang Yang-ming Confucianism from Ōkubo's father, and practiced Zen meditation for a time under the guidance of the father's mentor, a monk named Musan. Saigō and Ōkubo also spent time together in other ways, becoming involved in an informal reading circle, where they met with other youths from the neighborhood to discuss the writings of the Sung Neo-Confucianist Chu Hsi. We can only speculate about the influences this group of young men may have exerted on Saigō's intellectual development, but the personal ties they formed were to have greater significance later on.

Overall, what probably influenced Saigō most was the example of the Ōkubo family's sad fate at the hands of both Shigehide and Narioki. Likewise, Saigō's boyhood friendship with Ōkubo is probably more important as the basis for their adult interaction than for any lasting impact Ōkubo may have had on him when they were young. It would be difficult to find two people less alike than these two. The habitually thoughtful and taciturn Saigō and the quick-witted and articulate Ōkubo no doubt made an interesting pair, and ultimately it was their differences of temperament rather than their similarities of belief that would decide the fate of their relationship, even if their constant interactions could have provided the basis for a close friendship. The same thing must be said of the reading circle in which both men took part. It proved important in the long run less as a seedbed for significant political thought than as merely the first regular association of a group of youths who later emerged as Satsuma's young samurai activist group, the Seichūgumi.

Another important influence on Saigō's early development came from the *gōjū kyōiku*, Satsuma's unique system of neighborhood education for lower samurai.[20] Under this system, all boys of koshōgumi rank had to spend their days together from the age of six until they either got married or went into han service, between their late teens and early twenties. Every day from sunrise until sunset they worked, practiced martial arts, exercised, and learned reading and writing together, under the guidance of older boys from the same neighborhoods. In effect, they educated themselves, along lines laid down in han regulations. The system socialized them and taught them their values, and the primary punishment for deviance from established norms was public humiliation or ostracism. Emphasis was on cooperation, and the mastery of such traditional Confucian values as loyalty, obedience, duty, honor, propriety, and righteousness. As a formal educational institution, the gōjū kyōiku no doubt left much to be desired, but we should not underestimate its potential power as a socializing mechanism.

No doubt the gōjū kyōiku had a telling impact on Saigō's development, but other events in his youth probably left deeper marks. In the final months of 1852, both of his parents died, leaving him responsible for the welfare of six siblings, an aged grandmother, and a new wife, whom Saigō had married earlier the same year. Saigō's stipend was scarcely adequate to support so many, and to make matters worse, his father had left him a debt worth 200 ryō.[21] Two years later, after Saigō had left Kagoshima to accompany Nariakira to Edo, his wife divorced him and returned to her family. He subsequently observed that there had never been a more bitter time in his life than these years.[22]

These examples and others like them shed interesting light on some aspects of Saigō's development during the first two decades or so of his life, and together they give us a picture that is generally consistent with his behavior later on. Unfortunately, most such details are unverifiable, so it is difficult to say how much is fact and how much is embellishment added later in the development of the biographical tradition. There are some things we can say with a degree of confidence, by way of comparison with the ideal picture outlined at the beginning of this section.

Saigō was never a man of many words, and while his disposition was generally very even, he was also capable of violent outbursts of temper. He spent much of his life in military service, but his reputation as a great military man has little basis in fact. He certainly knew which end of a sword to pick up, but he had neither the taste nor the talent to become the master swordsman some say he was. Judging from the record, what he valued most about being a samurai was the emphasis it obliged him to place on personal character, and the opportunity it gave him to die a solitary and honorable death in the service of some noble cause. It may be that Saigō overestimated the importance of the samurai's obligation to sacrifice his life when circumstances called for it, and spent his life searching for a suitable place to die, but we should not let the very real possibility of a preoccupation with glorious death blind us to the full array of other factors influencing Saigō's development and outlook.

Just as Saigō was not a great warrior, he was not a remarkable scholar either. He read avidly in works that captured his imagination, and he knew his Confucian classics as well as any of his peers, but he had few original ideas, and he tended to be at his best when advocating the ideas of others. Repeatedly throughout his life he worked as a teacher, and he was very effective at persuading others to accept his point of view. However, that point of view usually consisted of ideas Saigō had adopted from others, and his effectiveness as a persuader had less to do with his intellectual originality or his rhetorical abilities than with his powerful physical presence and the sincerity of his convictions.

Saigō's impact on history, in other words, probably resulted more from his emotional qualities than from his intellectual or military brilliance. His emotions and their effects on his behavior no doubt owe much to his inborn temperament and the impact of his early environment, things that are now completely beyond our ability to evaluate. However, the sources of his mature outlook are somewhat easier to identify, because we can compare surviving documents with the events of his life and trace connections. We can test what he said against what he did, in other words, and this is especially so during the third decade of his life and later, because the documentary record increases abruptly. We begin to see the development of Saigō's mature outlook from the time he entered public service.

The emergence of the public man:
Satsuma, 1844–54

Unlike most of his friends, who began their public careers as tea servers in the castle, Saigō started out in the countryside, among the peasants. In 1844 he was appointed as copyist's assistant (*kakiyaku tasuke*) to the district magistrate (*kōri bugyō*), a man named Sakoda Taji'emon.[23] For the next ten years, Saigō made regular trips through the districts under his charge in order to observe conditions and to gather information for the annual collection of the land tax (*nengu*). In the process he developed a detailed and sophisticated first-hand knowledge of what peasant life involved, and these experiences gave him a lifelong interest in rural administration. During his years in the countryside, Saigō's views were also influenced importantly by Sakoda, who fostered in him a concern for the welfare of the peasants and a firm belief in fair and equitable administration.

Though little is known of Sakoda, he must have been a man of strong convictions himself, and he must have taught Saigō as much by example as by precept. In 1849, five years after Saigō became his assistant, he resigned his post in protest at the refusal of senior han officials to lessen taxes in the wake of a bad harvest. On the wall of his lodging, he left the following verse:

> Insect, insect
> do not cut off the roots of the crops;
> cut them and you too will wither and fall.[24]

In other words, to treat the peasants harshly is to interfere with their productive capacity; that will reduce revenue and imperil the solvency of the han, which in turn will endanger the livelihood of the samurai themselves. This story is apocryphal, but it appears throughout the biographical tradition. Yet whether the episode actually took place or not, it conveys clearly the rather sentimental view of the peasantry that Saigō learned during his years of service in the countryside, and that penchant for sentimentality toward the peasants and impatience with harsh administration is borne out by evidence of a more reliable kind.

Not long after he assumed power in 1851, Nariakira called for suggestions from his subordinates on how to improve han administration, and Saigō is said to have replied with a series of strongly worded memorials.[25] According to the biographical tradition, these memorials so impressed Nariakira that he decided to take Saigō to Edo with him in 1854. In fact, no such documents survive, but a memorial of this type does exist for 1856, two years after Saigō's arrival in Edo. In that year another rural official suggested to Nariakira that a new cadastral survey of the entire han would reveal significant increases in production resulting from land reclamation and improved farming methods. Nariakira asked Saigō for his views on this proposal and the reply, composed when Saigō was twenty-nine, gives us the earliest surviving statement of his views on the theory and practice of rural administration.[26]

Saigō began this memorial by pointing out that in the last major cadastral survey, during the Kyōhō era (1716–36), han officials encouraged the peasants to report increases in production

28

by promising that they could keep any gains made since the last survey. When the assessment was complete, however, the han government appropriated all reported gains. In Saigō's view, this act not only betrayed the trust of the peasants, but also demonstrated to them that the officials who dominated their lives were deceitful. On top of this, Saigō added, senior han officials were widely known to practice skimming routinely. As a result of such irregularities, tax collection was thrown into chaos, and the peasants fled to other han. Even when Satsuma officials brought them back and gave them new livestock and equipment, they preferred to abscond again rather than remain at the mercy of such corrupt administration.

From these events Saigō concluded that there would be little point in conducting land surveys when official corruption and loss of confidence had rendered the entire institutional framework dysfunctional. In order to create favorable conditions for a land survey, abuses would have to be eliminated, benevolent and virtuous administration restored, and the trust of the peasants regained. In Saigō's view, the way to achieve all of these goals was to return to the customs of the past.

The leading cause of official corruption was not greed, Saigō believed, but loss of self respect. The solution, therefore, was to repair the self image of the administrator, who in 1856 was usually a gōshi. Since these quasi-samurai were at the bottom of the status hierarchy in the han, they would probably respond favorably to any measure that improved their status. Saigō suggested a return to the terminology that had been in use when the gōshi had first come into being, as that would recall a time when their prowess in Satsuma's battles had gained them considerable prestige. Moreover, those who distinguished themselves through virtuous administration should be allowed to reside in the castle town for a generation. As these proposals indicate, for Saigō the way to eliminate all abuses in administration was simply to restore the pride and the morale of the samurai administrators. Men who respect themselves, contended Saigō, will behave respectably.

It is important to notice that Saigō said nothing in this 1856 memorial, or in any of his later statements on rural administration, about the rights of the peasants, nor did he ever suggest that they were anything other than the social inferiors of their samurai masters. He felt genuine sympathy for their hardships, of course, but it was a sympathy predicated on something other

29

than a belief in their inherent right to a comfortable life. What was most importantly at stake in mistreatment of the peasants was not peasant welfare, but samurai integrity. If samurai integrity were restored, abuse of the peasants would stop automatically, as would all other abuses.

The author of this memorial is a man who knows a great deal about the routine details of rural administration, and who believes that the best formula for enlightened and effective government is the traditional combination of virtuous officials and obedient subjects. The model for Saigō's vision of a just world lies in the patterns of the past; by implication, then, it is change that invites trouble. Such a conservative attitude seems odd in a man who so enthusiastically supported Nariakira's reform programs, and the sweeping changes they called for, but not if we assume that Saigō supported Nariakira because he believed his lord was about to restore the society of Satsuma to the supposed ethical purity of its past.

Also clear in this memorial is Saigō's belief in the moral superiority of the samurai. That superiority for him is a given, and so it should be taken as a first premise in the making of policy. Moreover, when administration becomes corrupt, it is that same superiority more than anything else that is placed in peril. In the same way, while peasant hardship is certainly not desirable, it is deplorable more because of what it says about the moral decay of the samurai than because the peasants have any inherent right to be protected from hardship.

The values Saigō expressed in this memorial of 1856 did not change much over the remaining twenty years of his life, and his behavior during those two decades exhibits a contradiction that we can see implied here for the first time. It takes the form of a tendency to miss the finer points of a problem and commit himself to opposing principles. Convinced that legitimacy and justice lay in the precedents of the past, Saigō embarked on a career whose aim was to restore that past, but whose consequences made any return to it impossible. Moved emotionally by the plight of the peasants, he looked for solutions in the samurai class, when it would have been difficult to improve the lot of either one without worsening that of the other. We will see this pattern again and again. The reasons for it are impossible to identify, but its effects are unmistakable. One of the basic themes of Saigō's life was his unfortunate habit of trapping himself between mutually exclusive commitments.

Prior to this memorial of 1856 there is little to tell us what Saigō believed. Three letters survive from the first thirty years of his life, and one of them is the promissory note mentioned earlier. In a letter of 1853, Saigō indicated that he was aware of the startling events brought on by Commodore Perry's arrival at Edo, and he speculated on what Satsuma's leaders were likely to do about it. His chief interest was in what effects the American overture to Japan might have on the balance of power in Satsuma's politics.[27] But by the time he wrote this letter, he was about to enter the world of startling events himself, for in the first month of 1854, at the age of twenty-seven, he left Kagoshima for the first time and followed his hanshu Nariakira to Edo.

This was a major turning point in his life, for several reasons. First, it took him out of the narrow provincial world of Kagoshima and plunged him into the wide-open society of Edo. Second, it marked the beginning of his brief but decisive association with Nariakira. Third, it introduced him to national politics, and to the world of political intrigue. However he may have felt about what befell him after 1854, he would never be able to return to the simple naivete of his earlier life.

The making of a national reputation:
Edo, Kyoto, and Kagoshima, 1854–59

Between 1854 and 1859, Saigō's understanding of the world expanded dramatically, and four men played decisive roles in the process. First there was Nariakira, who gave Saigō frequent personal instruction and introduced him to the political issues of the time. Next was Fujita Tōko, the outspoken ideologue of Mito han. Third was Hashimoto Sanai, the samurai advisor to the hanshu of Fukui. And finally there was the Kyoto loyalist monk Gesshō. Saigō's associations with these men were brief, and their impact on him was out of proportion to the amount of time he spent with them. Further, by the end of 1859, all four were dead, and Saigō was left to make what he could of their influences on him without the benefit of their guidance. One key to understanding Saigō's public life is to recognize that at times it was little more than a series of attempts to act out the ideas of others. This was never more true than during the years from 1854 until his first exile in 1859.

When Saigō arrived in Edo early in 1854, Perry had just completed his second visit, and the town was alive with speculation about the new United States-Japan treaty of friendship he had persuaded bakufu officials to sign. Nariakira had been deeply involved in bakufu politics for some time, but he had to be careful because his status as an outside daimyo (*tōzama*) technically excluded him. He needed a close confidant who could carry messages to other political leaders in Edo, and who knew his thinking well enough to be able to improvise if need be, but whose official status was low enough to make him inconspicuous, and who would be tractable enough not to improvise when it was not called for.

Saigō was the answer to all these needs, and so Nariakira appointed him to the post of gardener (*niwa kata yaku*) for the han residence.[28] Menial though this position was, it placed Saigō in the gardens where Nariakira went for relaxation, and made it possible for the two to meet at any time, informally and without attracting attention. It was an ideal solution to Nariakira's problem, because none of his political opponents was likely to pay attention to the comings and goings of a lowly gardener, and he is said to have boasted that he had laid his hands on a most valuable tool, which only he knew how to use.[29] It is not clear just when Saigō and Nariakira began working together. Saigō's appointment was in 1854, but his first audience with Nariakira was not until two years later, on 1856/4/12.[30]

In any event, once the two had met and established a working relationship, it was not long before Saigō was making regular visits to the residences of such political leaders as Matsudaira Shungaku of Fukui and Tokugawa Nariaki of Mito, and becoming well known to the men in their households. In conversations with these men, Saigō learned the vocabulary of the new brand of imperial loyalism articulated by thinkers in the Tokugawa collateral han of Mito, and he impressed many of them with his own character as well. In these years he built a reputation for himself as a man of passion and sincerity, and while his modesty would have made him uncomfortable with the idea, there is no doubt that in the eyes of others he had come to be regarded as a *jinbutsu* – a man to be reckoned with, and one who would accomplish things.

Not long after his arrival in Edo, Saigō met Fujita Tōko, and he was greatly impressed, not only with Fujita personally, but also with the ideas he expounded. He liked the emphasis the

Mito thinkers placed on loyalty and duty, and in view of his own opinions about the importance of tradition, we should not be surprised that he found the nostalgic values of Mito thought much to his taste. Of Fujita he wrote that talking with him was 'like bathing in pure water; my mind becomes clear and free of uncertainty.'[31] He met repeatedly with Fujita throughout the following year and evidently never tired of listening to him talk. Saigō may also have had a chance to meet Fujita's most influential pupil, Aizawa Seishisai, though there is nothing in the record to show that he did. He noted in one letter that Aizawa would soon be arriving in Edo,[32] and if he was coming and going at the Mito residence as regularly as he appears to have been, it is possible that he met this influential pupil of Fujita as well.

At any rate, he had become well known among those who were worried about Japan's future, and he had gotten into the habit of meeting regularly with some of them, men from Mito, Fukui, Higo, and other han, to discuss politics and current events.[33] Moreover, through his associations with such men, he had begun to discover the wide variety of diversions Edo had to offer, and he was quick to reassure his family in Kagoshima that he would not endanger his moral purity by making visits to the pleasure quarters.[34] In numerous ways, then, Saigō's horizons were broadening. He was becoming a man of the realm, if not exactly of the world, and a committed political activist; these must have been among the most exciting times of his entire life.

Not everything was good, however. In the autumn of 1855, Edo suffered one of the worst earthquakes in its history. On 1855/10/4, two days after the earthquake, Saigō wrote to a friend in Kagoshima that Fujita had been killed. Fujita's death, he lamented, was 'truly a terrible thing for the country.'[35] The Satsuma residence at Mita was utterly destroyed by this earthquake, but fortunately both Saigō and Nariakira escaped harm. The only lasting damage as far as Saigō was concerned was the sense of emptiness created by Fujita's death.

This loss came in the wake of an even more painful tragedy just over a year earlier, when Nariakira's only surviving heir had suddenly fallen ill and died on 1854/7/23. Not long before this, on 6/30, Nariakira himself had become seriously ill, but he had recovered. Judging from what Saigō says about the symptoms, both illnesses probably were dysentery or influenza, but Saigō was convinced that once again Narioki's concubine Yura was attempting to destroy Nariakira.[36] He declared that he could not write about these events without shedding tears. Death is a trivial thing, he asserted, and it would be enough for him if he could find a place to die nobly, if only that might help to bring an end to the troubles besetting the han.[37]

Suiting the deed to the word, Saigō joined with other young Satsuma samurai in a new plot to murder Yura, but Nariakira learned of it and put a stop to it. He then gave Saigō an angry lecture on the irresponsibility of being so concerned with petty local jealousies when the fate of the entire country was at stake.[38] For his own part, Nariakira may have wished Yura dead just as ardently as Saigō, but this purely personal desire was of less importance to him than the need to prevent the reopening of old wounds within the han.[39] Much like Narinobu before him, Nariakira was the *de jure* ruler of Satsuma. *De facto* power, however, remained with his father Narioki, just as it had remained with Shigehide. Nariakira had no intention of allowing his subordinates to provoke Narioki into a repetition of the measures Narinobu's subordinates had brought upon themselves in 1808. Like it or not, as long as Narioki lived, his political followers would control the han. Nariakira needed their support to complete his reforms, and so he could not afford to antagonize them.

No sooner had Saigō and his friends learned to live with this unpleasant reality than Nariakira gave them another bitter pill to swallow. Following the death of his last surviving heir, and in view of the political realities in Kagoshima, Nariakira announced that his successor would be Tadayoshi, the son of his half-brother Hisamitsu, in whose behalf Yura had been conniving all along. This was little short of complete victory for her, and it made the deaths of Nariakira's supporters in 1849–50 seem like wasted sacrifices, but Saigō and his friends had little choice other than to accept the will of their master.[40] Slowly but painfully, Saigō was learning the stern rules of politics under the steady guidance of Nariakira, and Edo in these years was a good place for him to gain first-hand experience.

With the arrival of the American representative Townsend Harris in 1856, bakufu officials had become preoccupied with two pressing controversies. One was the question of what to do about the United States-Japan treaty of commerce negotiated by Harris and ready for signature by 1858. The other was the problem of who should be named to succeed the shogun Iesada, who had never been more than feeble at best and was now expected not to live much longer. Because of his concern with international relations, Nariakira had a keen interest in both issues, and Saigō had become familiar with both through his role as Nariakira's messenger to the other men involved in the disputes.

For Nariakira, the opening of Japan to full interaction with the West (*kaikoku*) was the only course that could guarantee the country's survival, and so he favored the signing of the Harris treaty. Likewise, he wanted Japan to have a mature and capable leader for the difficult times ahead, and so he supported the shogunal candidacy of Hitotsubashi Yoshinobu, the son of the Mito hanshu Nariaki, and opposed the appointment of Tokugawa Yoshitomi of Kii, who had the best claim by blood but was only a child. Within the bakufu, both disputes had caused polarization. Abe Masahiro, the bakufu's senior councillor (*rōjū shusseki*), favored the treaty and the appointment of Yoshinobu, and counted Nariakira among his closest allies. Ii Naosuke, who became great councillor (*tairō*) in 1858, also wanted the treaty signed, but supported Yoshitomi as the next shogun.

Initially Saigō's part in these intrigues was only peripheral.[41] However, on 1857/4/3 Nariakira returned to Kagoshima, taking Saigō with him. Because he needed a reliable agent on the scene in Edo, he promoted Saigō to the post of deputy inspector (*kachi metsuke*) and sent him back there on 11/1, with orders to work under the supervision of another Yoshinobu supporter, Matsudaira Shungaku. It was at this point that Saigō began his brief association with Hashimoto Sanai, who had become Shungaku's most important agent in both the succession and the treaty issues.

Saigō and Hashimoto had met two years earlier, but had not gotten along well because of differences in temperament. As they became acquainted and exchanged ideas, they came to respect each other, and by 1858 they were on good terms and well suited to work together. It is indicative of how much Hashimoto impressed Saigō that, after the defeat of the rebel forces in 1877, one of the things found on Saigō's body was a letter from Hashimoto, which he evidently had carried with him for close to twenty years.[42]

Saigō had two agendas as 1858 began. One was to serve as Nariakira's proxy in the arrangements for the succession of Yoshinobu. The other was to help Hashimoto in Kyoto, where efforts were underway to win imperial approval for the Harris treaty, and to secure a court decree that would oblige the bakufu to appoint Yoshinobu.[43] His contact in Kyoto was the court noble Konoe Tadahiro, whose family had been associated with the Shimazu for many generations. In the Konoe household, Saigō became acquainted with the loyalist monk Gesshō, who was soon to play a key role in one of the major dramas of Saigō's life.

While Hashimoto maneuvered in Kyoto and Saigō hurried back and forth between there and Edo, however, supporters of Yoshitomi took advantage of the power vacuum created by the death of Abe Masahiro on 1857/6/17. In the spring of 1858, Ii Naosuke became *tairō* and without delay brought matters to a conclusion. The Harris treaty was signed on his order on 1858/6/19, and six days later Yoshitomi was named to succeed Iesada as shogun, taking the name Iemochi.⁴⁴ Saigō had anticipated this outcome, and had left Edo on 5/17 to report to Nariakira in Kagoshima, which he did on 6/7. Eleven days later he left Kagoshima again with new instructions, and reached Kyoto on 7/10.

Nariakira had decided to try to force the issue, and had sent Saigō ahead to make preparations for his return to Kyoto at the head of an army. With the backing of the court, he intended to use the threat of force to persuade the bakufu to carry out reforms, including the appointment of Yoshinobu in place of Iemochi as the new shogun. On his way back to Kagoshima the previous year, Nariakira had received an order from the court instructing him to be ready to return in force and guard the imperial palace in the event of a national political crisis, and he evidently intended to use this order as a pretext to lead his troops to Kyoto and confront the bakufu.⁴⁵

This story is not confirmed by primary evidence, and such a course of action seems rather rash for someone as sophisticated and careful as Nariakira. Four years later, however, under the pretext of carrying out Nariakira's last wishes, his half-brother Hisamitsu did lead an army to Kyoto, where the court appointed him to escort an envoy to Edo. Faced with a combination of the authority of the court and Hisamitsu's willingness to use force, the bakufu agreed to make reforms. Everything of substance in Hisamitsu's agenda between 1862 and 1865 originated with Nariakira, so there may be some basis for believing that Nariakira actually did intend to try bluffing the bakufu into submission, and passed on the strategy for doing so to Hisamitsu.⁴⁶

In any event, what is most interesting about this story is that when the rebel army left Kagoshima in 1877, its avowed purpose was to march on the capital and use the threat of force to bring about reforms in the government. In other words, as the leader of that army, Saigō aimed not to overthrow the Meiji state, but rather to persuade its leaders to adopt a different set of policies. As his temporal master had done in 1858, Saigō planned in 1877 to make his persuasion more effective by backing it with the threat of military force. Never remarkably original in his thought, Saigō repeatedly drew on the ideas of his mentors, and none of them influenced him more pervasively than Nariakira. It is vital to keep this in mind in any attempt to understand what motivated Saigō later in his life.

Whatever the outcome of Nariakira's scheme might have been, events took a different course. On 7/9, the day before Saigō reached Kyoto, Nariakira had developed a severe fever. After a week of delirium he died on 7/16, and the news reached Kyoto on 7/27. According to the biographical tradition, Saigō was devastated, and he resolved at once to return to Kagoshima and commit suicide at Nariakira's grave. He was persuaded not to by the monk Gesshō, who pointed out to him that if he were to die, there would be no one left who understood Nariakira's goals, and therefore no one capable of working for their realization.[47]

Nariakira's death may have been the most important turning point in Saigō's life. No other person had influenced his adult character or outlook more than Nariakira, and this impact was doubly profound because of what seems to have been the lack of an autonomous center in Saigō's personality. Despite several periods of impressive independent action in later years, Saigō appears never to have found an adequate replacement for the stabilizing influence Nariakira had provided. Because of what looks like a need to identify with external authority figures, or at least to find sanction for his choices outside of himself, and because of the extent of his dependence on Nariakira, it is possible that Saigō's life was fundamentally without emotional meaning after 1858.

Stunned as he surely was by the loss of his master, Saigō nevertheless had little time for grief. Ii Naosuke had begun a systematic purge of his political opponents, and his anger was further inflamed by the efforts of a group of court nobles and samurai to enlist the authority of Mito, the most important of the Tokugawa collateral families, against him. Before long, news reached Kyoto that Gesshō was among those Ii had ordered arrested, and Konoe Tadahiro asked Saigō to conduct the aged monk to a place of safety.[48] Unable to find reliable shelter in the vicinity of Kyoto, Saigō set out from Osaka with Gesshō and several samurai on 9/24 headed for Kagoshima, where he believed the long standing connection between the Shimazu and the Konoe families would guarantee Gesshō protection.⁴⁹

Unfortunately, bakufu agents had anticipated this move, and had gotten to Kagoshima ahead of Saigō, where they had thoroughly intimidated han officials. Eventually those officials decided that they would not surrender Gesshō to his pursuers, but also that they could not give him sanctuary in Kagoshima, so on 11/15 they ordered Saigō to conduct him to a temple in neighboring Hyūga province, where he would be kept in custody. Regardless of the han's true intentions, the significance of orders to cross into Hyūga under guard was not lost on Saigō. Referred to in Satsuma tradition as 'getting sent off to the east' (*higashime okuri*), such orders usually had meant an undignified death at the border station under the swords of one's escort, and by this time Saigō was probably in too morbid a frame of mind to consider any other interpretation of the han's decision.

On the night of 11/16 Saigō and Gesshō set out across Kago-shima Bay toward the Hyūga shore in a small boat, accompanied by Gesshō's personal servant and the Fukuoka loyalist samurai Hirano Kuniomi, both of whom had accompanied them ever since leaving Kyoto. The fact that there were no guards with them probably meant that the han had simply consigned them to whatever fate awaited them, but Saigō and Gesshō had already made their plans. When they were well offshore, they stood at the gunwale and exchanged farewell poems, and then together they plunged into the sea. Realizing what had happened, Hirano came about and pulled them from the water. By the time he could get them ashore, Gesshō was already dead. Saigō too had nearly succeeded in drowning himself, but eventually he revived.

When news of this development reached Kagoshima, the han decided to notify the bakufu that both men had drowned. Saigō would be sent to Ōshima, the main island in the Amami group, for an unspecified length of time, and to ally suspicion further, he would change his name to Kikuchi Gengō.⁵⁰ This decision probably sprang less from any desire on the part of han leaders to spare Saigō, than from the trouble that was sure to follow once the bakufu learned of the decision to spirit Gesshō away to Hyūga. It was a convenient way to avoid embarrassment, and at the same time to rid the han of a potentially troublesome individual. In short, as far as han leaders were concerned, Saigō was as good as dead once he had disappeared into the remote obscurity of Ōshima, from which there was no need ever to recall him.

Saigō spent several weeks at home recuperating, and then early in 1859 he set sail from Yamakawa, the southernmost port in Kyushu. On 1/12 the ship deposited him on the beach near the tiny fishing village of Tatsugō, on the island of Ōshima, where he was to spend the next three years of his life.

His feelings concerning his recent experiences are recorded in the last two letters he wrote before sailing from Yamakawa. On 1858/12/19 he wrote to Nagaoka Kenmotsu, a friend in Kumamoto:

> Perhaps you have heard already how I have become dead bones in the earth (*dōchū no shikotsu*), obliged to endure the unendurable. Though shamed before Heaven and Earth, I shall cling to life yet a little longer, for the sake of the Imperial Realm.[51]

On 1859/1/2 he replied to a letter from Ōkubo, in which his boyhood friend had asked for his advice as to what the other young samurai in Kagoshima ought to do next:

> ... I am dead bones in the earth, unfit for the fortunes of a samurai. Putting great deeds behind me, I shall escape to a far-off island, like a defeated general in flight. I would prefer not to become involved, yet I have been privy to the great plans of our departed Lord.... Somehow I shall bear the unbearable for the sake of Emperor and Court. Fool though I be, I will do my utmost until my journey comes to an end.[52]

Both Ōkubo's letter and Saigō's reply, as well as the letter to Nagaoka, were chiefly concerned with plans for some unspecified action in Kyoto that had been under discussion before Saigō left Kagoshima. He wrote both letters in response to a request from Ōkubo, who hoped to use his prestige among Satsuma samurai to keep them from acting rashly. In time those plans were to bear fruit, first in the murder of Ii Naosuke, and later in Satsuma's efforts to create an alliance of the court and the bakufu (*kōbu gattai*). In the latter strategy Saigō would play an important part.

In the meantime, Saigō was left to meditate on what had befallen him. Twice he had sought death, and twice he had met only frustration. In the first instance, Gesshō had talked him out of his desire to follow Nariakira to the grave. In the second, he had failed in his attempt to die with the same man who had persuaded him not to only four months earlier, while that man had gained the release Saigō sought. Unless we can dismiss the above remarks as cynical hyperbole, we must conclude that Saigō felt deeply humiliated to have survived. To be sure, he was capable of fine hyperbole, and even of caustic sarcasm, but cynicism would have been out of character for him. We may assume that he genuinely wanted to die, and was bitterly disappointed to have failed. There remains the question of why he found death so attractive.

The most obvious explanation for the suicide attempt is that Saigō hoped to realize the desire, postponed earlier, to follow Nariakira in death. However, Inoue Kiyoshi has suggested that Saigō's aim was to atone for failure.[53] He had promised Konoe Tadahiro that he would protect Gesshō, and he had proved unable to do that, even though it was through no fault of his own. The shame of which he speaks in his letters to Nagaoka and Ōkubo could have arisen from his failure to keep his promise to Tadahiro, for which his only remaining means of recompense would have been to die along with the man whose death he had failed to prevent. Such an interpretation would be consistent with Saigō's deeply rooted sense of duty and honor.

Inoue further suggests that, following Nariakira's death, Saigō's primary loyalty shifted from the man to his agenda.[54] Nariakira's chief goal had been to serve the court, and to regain for it the respect and authority he believed it had lost. Saigō's new commitment to Nariakira's agenda therefore obliged him to give his first loyalty to the court. This created a conflict with his prior sense of obligation to the Shimazu, who were, among other things, Nariakira's relatives, and thus placed him in the service of two masters, trapping him between mutually exclusive commitments in the pattern I suggested earlier.

If we follow Inoue's line of reasoning a bit further, we arrive at a possible motive for Saigō's involvement the Satsuma rebellion as well. When the Meiji government abolished the han in 1871 on the authority of the emperor, Saigō was forced to betray one loyalty in order to uphold the other: fulfilling his duty to the emperor made him a traitor to the Shimazu. This could have caused intolerable psychic dissonance, which he was unable to resolve until the uprising of the younger samurai in 1877 presented him with an opportunity to regain for Kagoshima some of the autonomy it had lost in 1871. This hypothesis is tempting, but it overlooks the question of whether Saigō was actually responsible for the 1877 rebellion at all, and we will have to return to that question later.

· 2 ·
Exile and Intellectual Growth,
1859–64

Altogether, Saigō spent five years in exile. From 1859/1 to 1862/ 2 he lived in the village of Tatsugō on the island of Ōshima. Then, from 1862/6 to 1864/2, he lived even farther south, first on Tokunoshima and then on tiny Okinoerabujima. Today these islands are served daily by air and sea, but they still give the visitor a sense of isolation. In Saigō's time they must have seemed terribly remote. Okinoerabu, just over the horizon from Okinawa, is so small that one can walk around its entire coastline in no more than a day, and even Ōshima, largest and most cosmopolitan of the Amami islands, seems primitive by comparison with Kagoshima.

There are works devoted entirely to Saigō's years in the islands,[1] but most biographers pass over the period with little more than a few stock anecdotes. However, as Inoue Kiyoshi argues, these years were crucial in Saigō's development, and they deserve more attention than they have received.[2] It was during this time of enforced idleness that Saigō's view of the world assumed its mature form, and so it is chiefly to the ideas he formulated while in exile that we must look for an understanding of his behavior in the last fifteen years of his life.

One reason for the importance of the years in exile is that they did not form an undifferentiated whole. The two periods were similar in that Saigō was isolated from events at home both times, but they were also different in important ways. For one thing, the first exile was not a punishment for wrongdoing, whereas the second one was. While he was on Ōshima Saigō was under no constraints and he received regular supplies from Kagoshima. He was free to move about on Tokunoshima as well, but during his first months on Okinoerabu he was kept in a cage, and even after he was released from that confinement his movement was still restricted. For another, the two periods had different emotional tones. During the first exile, Saigō's chief business was to come to terms with a run of exceptionally bad luck that had frustrated all of his hopes. In the second one, he had good cause to believe he had been unjustly condemned through the betrayal of men he thought were his friends, and he had to find a way to come to terms with that. Between the two exiles was an interlude of four months during which Saigō became involved in a string of events that led directly to the second exile. His experiences during that short time caused him to lose what was left of his innocence, and the bitterness that resulted probably never left him.

Saigō's health also suffered during his years in exile. In 1859 he was still a vigorous young man; by 1864 he had begun a slow process of deterioration that would continue for the rest of his life. He probably was not aware of any direct threats to his well-being while in exile aside from the *habu*, a venomous snake resembling a cobra, which is indigenous to all the Amami islands except Okinoerabu. He managed to avoid the habu, no doubt because he was forewarned and therefore cautious. However, there was nothing he could do about the swarms of mosquitoes, the islands' most ubiquitous inhabitants, and it was during his time in the islands, probably on Okinoerabu, that he contracted the filarial infection that in time would make him so corpulent with dropsy that he would be unable to ride a horse, or even to walk without difficulty.[3] Moreover, by the end of the 1860s, the obesity caused by the filaria had begun to produce gastro-intestinal and cardio-vascular complications. And it was also thanks to the filariasis, and the enlarged scrotum it caused, that Saigō later earned his reputation for great sexual prowess.[4]

The Ōshima years:
1859–62

Saigō's first impressions of Ōshima were not happy, as he made clear in a letter a month after his arrival: 'It has been thirty days since I arrived on this island, but there has not been a single clear day. We all hear how bad the rain is here, but this is really terrible.'[5] The islanders greeted Saigō politely, but they avoided him as though he were a deadly habu himself. In his eyes, they were scarcely more than subhuman brutes (*ketōjin*),[6] and he did not enjoy being among them. Not only was their company distasteful to him; their presence was a constant reminder of that more exciting world he had left so far behind. Nor was he quick to change his views. Half a year after his arrival, he wrote, 'As you know, I have been associated with men of high purpose for the past five or six years, and so now I find living with these brutes really difficult. I feel terrible, and I regret that I survived. There is nothing I can do now but await the judgement of Heaven.'[7] In time Saigō learned to accept the company of the islanders, and even to feel at home among them, though he continued to hint at the injustice of his fate by referring to himself as a despicable man (*hisei*), or simply as a hog (*tonsei*).[8]

In part the barrier was broken down by the children, who began coming to him to learn reading and writing. Toward the end of his second year he married a local woman, Aikana, and this also helped him to feel more comfortable. On the second day of the new year, 1861, his first son Kikujirō was born, and he reported the event to Ōkubo with a mixture of self-consciousness and satisfaction.[9] In the same letter he added, 'I myself have turned completely into an islander, and it saddens my heart.'[10] Inoue Kiyoshi points to this remark to suggest that if Saigō could speak of himself as an islander, he must have become reconciled to his fate,[11] but Inoue quotes only the first part; the second part gives the opposite impression, that Saigō was anything but reconciled. It seems he keenly regretted being so far away from events at home, and feared his opportunities were passing him by.

Regardless of where the balance of his feelings lay, Saigō could not remain idle indefinitely in the little seaside village of Tatsugō. And given the lessons in rural administration he had learned from Sakoda Taji'emon, he could not fail to notice the hardships of the islanders' daily lives. Whether he enjoyed living among these people or not, it was not in his nature to ignore their suffering, and he had spoken of it in the first letter he wrote from Ōshima:

> More than anything else it pains my heart to see the harsh way the people are governed. The administration of this island is unendurable. . . . it is the ultimate in suffering. I am astonished, for I had never dreamed it could be so bad.[12]

Before long he began to keep a record of what he observed, and

44

then he began sharing with his neighbors the supplies sent from Kagoshima for his upkeep, so that he ran short himself and had to ask for increased support.[13] Finally he could bear it no longer, and sometime during his second year he began to intervene in local administration.

The people of Ōshima had been living under the burden placed on them by Satsuma's sugar monopoly since the days of Shigehide, and Zusho's reforms had only intensified the pressure. There are numerous stories of how Saigō cajoled or bullied local officials into treating the islanders better,[14] and while few of them are reliable, the picture of Saigō they present is consistent with the impressions of him that emerge from the 1856 memorial on rural administration discussed in the previous chapter.

In all such stories, Saigō's great sympathy for the suffering of the islanders is surpassed only by the intensity of his indignation at the unjust behavior of the samurai officials, and the decay of moral integrity which that behavior reveals. Saigō does not ask that the burden of the islanders be lifted, or even lightened. After all, it is their function in society to hand over what they produce, and to keep only as much of it as they need to survive. In return, the samurai are obliged to behave with decency and virtue, and to earn the cooperation of the islanders through just administration rather than extorting it from them by intimidation and terror. These were ideas Saigō had learned initially in his early training, and they were developed further during his ten years of service among the peasants in the han. They continued to evolve while he was in exile, but they did not occupy all of his attention.

However involved he had become in the lives of the islanders, Saigō did not lose his interest in developments at home. From Ōkubo and other friends in Kagoshima he learned that the han's new leaders were planning to continue the work begun by Nariakira, and he was elated.[15] He learned with interest of the formation of a group of young samurai, and while he was grateful that they had included his name on their list of members, he cautioned them not to act rashly, or to waste their energy on undertakings that would yield no useful results.[16] With a change in han leadership, Saigō expected that he would soon be recalled from Ōshima, and when this did not happen, he concluded that someone must be conspiring to prevent it. Eventually he resigned himself to the idea that he might still have a long stay ahead of him in the islands.[17]

His friends in Kagoshima also kept him up to date on national developments. He was profoundly shocked to learn that Hashimoto Sanai had been executed in Ii Naosuke's 1859 purge, and at the news that Mito's dynamic hanshu Nariaki had died, he concluded that nothing could save the bakufu now, and its collapse into utter disarray was only a matter of time.[18] In fact, Saigō had long since come to believe that the bakufu would no longer be able to govern Japan without reform. In 1855 he had scoffed at a plan to convert Tokugawa vassals (*hatamoto*) into cavalry, dismissing them as too feeble to amount to anything.[19] A year later, he told his friend Ōyama Tsunayoshi that nothing short of a major bakufu reform could save Japan.[20]

In the midst of all this, however, there was also cause for celebration. Ii Naosuke had been murdered by a band of samurai from Mito and Satsuma in the spring of 1860, and in the following year his successor, Andō Nobumasa, had narrowly escaped death in another attack. After Ii's reign of terror, the bakufu had begun to pardon and reinstate the men he had purged, and Saigō was happy to hear this.[21] On reading the news of Ii's death, Saigō ran barefoot into the yard and hacked furiously at an old tree with his sword until his emotions were spent. He then returned calmly to his room and got drunk.[22] A year later he repeated this performance, telling Ōkubo, 'Yesterday, on the anniversary of the [Ii] assassination, I stayed drunk on *shōchū* all day long.'[23]

As 1861 came to a close, Saigō was busy building a new house for his growing family, to which a daughter had been added recently, and they held their housewarming celebration early in the new year. However, no sooner had they settled themselves than orders came for Saigō to return to Kagoshima. For some time, Ōkubo and others had been trying to persuade their superiors to bring Saigō home, and those efforts had finally succeeded. Bidding farewell to his family, Saigō left Tatsugō, and on 1862/2/12 he trod the soil of Kagoshima for the first time in over three years.

A small debacle in Kyoto:
1862/2–6

The situation Saigō found on his return to Kagoshima was dramatically different from the one he had left three years before. Ii Naosuke's attempt to reassert bakufu authority had come to an abrupt end with his murder. His successors, led by Andō Nobumasa, had understood the message in his death, and had embarked on a more conciliatory course, attempting to forge some sort of alliance between the bakufu and the court, along lines proposed by Ii not long before he was killed. When Andō was attacked it became clear that this policy was not especially popular either. A climate of indecision and hesitation ensued, and while the bakufu sought ways to regain the initiative, han leaders throughout the country found welcome relief from official scrutiny. In this atmosphere, Satsuma's rulers began preparing to take some initiative of their own.[24]

In accordance with Nariakira's wishes, his nephew Tadayoshi had become hanshu after his death, and Narioki, in retirement in Edo, had been appointed his guardian (*kōken*) by the bakufu. Narioki died in the fall of 1859, and Tadayoshi's father Hisamitsu took his place. Narioki had ordered the cancellation of most of the reform and development projects begun by Nariakira, but now Hisamitsu started them up again, and began building a base of support for himself in the han government.[25]

Just prior to his death, Nariakira had summoned Hisamitsu and had lectured him at length about the future he envisioned for Satsuma, instructing him to do everything he could to make that future a reality. Hisamitsu therefore considered himself charged to carry out Nariakira's agenda, and as soon as he became Tadayoshi's guardian he set his hands to the task. Within Kagoshima, Hisamitsu sought to complete the programs Nariakira had begun, in particular his military reforms and his efforts to establish Western style steel, weapons, and textile production. In national politics, he aimed to realize Nariakira's desire to restore the imperial house to full authority so that it could work with the bakufu in governing Japan.

Evidently Hisamitsu had no specific idea as to how Nariakira had intended to accomplish this latter task, but in any case he ended up committing his allegiance to the idea of a coalition of the court and the bakufu (*kōbu gattai*). It had been Ii Naosuke's

intention to create a coalition, and Andō Nobumasa had been
trying to carry out Ii's plans when the attack on him took him
out of service. Some sort of coalition was the first choice of most
bakufu leaders, but the idea was still in its formative stages, and
no one had yet envisioned its details. It is not clear whether
Hisamitsu understood what it might mean to form a coalition
government, or how Nariakira had thought it might be
accomplished. Judging from his behavior, however, he did believe
that Nariakira was committed to the kōbu gattai agenda, so his
own primary goal was to complete what he believed to be Nariakira's strategy.

As he built support in Kagoshima, Hisamitsu surrounded
himself with men who had been close to Nariakira, or who
shared his own understanding of Nariakira's agenda. He had to
be careful, however, because many of the most influential men
in Kagoshima had been associates of Zusho Hirosato, and had
grouped themselves around Narioki when the latter had returned
to power as Tadayoshi's guardian. The animosities that had
erupted in 1849–50 during the Kaei purge were still very much
alive among Satsuma's samurai, and Hisamitsu realized that only
the most careful maneuvering would allow him to pass safely
between the Scylla and Charybdis of the han's political realities
and see Nariakira's plans to completion. Potentially the most
serious threat to success was posed by the lower samurai. Hisamitsu understood reasonably well how to play the two factions
of senior vassals against each other to his own advantage; he had
no idea how to handle the young men of low rank, whose desire
to act decisively and without delay was much better developed
than their judgement about what to do.

In the meantime, these same young samurai had been eagerly
waiting for a chance to take dramatic action, but like the han's
senior leadership, they were of several minds. Many of them,
having accepted the leadership of Ōkubo Toshimichi, were content to wait until Hisamitsu's intentions were clear, and then
choose the course of action they thought best. Others, however,
were impatient. Led by Arima Shinshichi, an older man of considerable learning and charisma, they wanted to leave the han at
once and begin terrorizing bakufu representatives in Kyoto and
Edo. Unable to talk his zealous comrades out of their ambitions,
Ōkubo had gotten word of their intentions to Hisamitsu, and in
reply the hanshu Tadayoshi had written a letter to these young

men, urging them to be patient and to devote themselves to the service of the han.[26]

Since nearly all these men were of koshōgumi rank or lower, and had rarely even been noticed by their social superiors, much less addressed directly by the hanshu, Tadayoshi's personal appeal was enough to cool their ardor temporarily. Tadayoshi had addressed this letter to his 'sincere and faithful samurai' (*seichū no shi*), and these young men now adopted the phrase as their name, calling themselves 'The League of the Sincere and Faithful' (*Seichūgumi*). For a while they could be content merely to strut around and congratulate themselves on the prestige this new name gave them, but by the time Saigō returned to Kagoshima, two years had passed and they had done little more than strut and wait. They were eager to act, and their impatience was about to boil over.

Hisamitsu was afraid they would jeopardize the realization of Narikaira's goals by acting before he had finished putting together his base of support. For their own part, they had always associated Hisamitsu with his mother Yura. They did not know that he had had nothing to do with her schemes. Instead, far from viewing him as the man who might finally realize their beloved Nariakira's ambitions, they suspected him of conniving with Yura's cohort of old men to prevent the fulfillment of Nariakira's plans. Ōkubo and others had persuaded Hisamitsu to recall Saigō from exile by convincing him that only Saigō could control the Seichūgumi and keep them from derailing Hisamitsu's agenda.

Soon after his return, Saigō was summoned to a meeting with Ōkubo and two senior han vassals, Nakayama Shōnojō and Komatsu Tatewaki.[27] They explained to him that Hisamitsu intended to take a large body of troops to Kyoto, where he expected he could get a court decree calling for bakufu reform, precisely as Nariakira had meant to do in 1858. He would then proceed to Edo and present the decree to the bakufu, with his troops nearby to encourage compliance. Saigō's help was deemed indispensable, and not only because he could help guarantee the good behavior of the Seichūgumi. Equally important, he alone had the experience and the political connections in Kyoto and Edo, without which the plan could not be carried out. And he alone knew Nariakira's thinking well enough to evaluate the plan's details.[28]

But if Saigō had thought the plan a good idea in 1858, he

had a different opinion now, and his response was unequivocally negative. For one thing, there was no reason to assume that a plan devised for political conditions in 1858 would still work in 1862. For another, one did not simply present oneself at the imperial court and request a decree calling for bakufu reform, or for anything else. And even if the court were willing to cooperate, one did not provoke the bakufu so openly without a much better idea than Kagoshima's leaders had of what the response might be. To make matters worse, there was no consensus on appropriate han policy within Kagoshima. Both upper and lower samurai were polarized among themselves between those who supported Hisamitsu and those who did not, creating four distinct antagonistic groups. Moreover, upper and lower samurai distrusted each other, creating yet another polarization based on status. Saigō was astonished at how politically naive Hisamitsu and the others seemed to be, and he urged them to postpone their plans at least until the political climate in Kyoto and Edo could be tested with more care, and the animosities within the han could be soothed enough to produce some semblance of a single agenda.

In an audience with Hisamitsu Saigō repeated his reservations, and pleaded with him to reconsider. Hisamitsu, however, was determined to go ahead, and in the end he agreed only to postpone his departure from 2/25 until 3/15. Frustrated and angry, Saigō left Kagoshima and retired to a hot spring in the countryside.[29] However, Ōkubo sought him out and convinced him that whether he supported Hisamitsu or not, he was needed to help keep the Seichūgumi out of trouble. Saigō accordingly came back to Kagoshima, and subsequently left again on 3/13, two days ahead of Hisamitsu and his escort. He was to make his way to Shimonoseki, the Chōshū port city on the straits between western Honshu and northern Kyushu, and wait for Hisamitsu there. Along the way he would meet with his old friends in various Kyushu han and brief them on Satsuma's agenda.[30]

Accompanied by Murata Shinpachi, Saigō arrived at Shimonoseki on 3/22. He was met there by another Satsuma samurai, Moriyama Shinzō, and by Hirano Kuniomi, the Fukuoka samurai who had pulled him out of the sea after his suicide attempt in 1858. According to them, samurai from all over the country had heard of Hisamitsu's journey, and thinking it the first step in a general uprising against Edo, they were beginning to gather in and around Kyoto. Among them were a large number of Satsuma samurai, and it now seemed only a matter of time before they began striking out randomly at the bakufu. Horrified by what he heard, and hoping he could do something to calm these hotheads before they muddied the political waters irrevocably, Saigō sailed from Shimonoseki that night with Murata, Moriyama, and Hirano, and reached Osaka on 3/26.

As he feared, the city was crawling with hot-blooded young men. Hirano urged him to join the growing throng and become its leader, while for his own part Saigō decided that unless he were to meet with these men himself he would not be able to persuade them to abandon whatever course of action they might have planned. As he put it, they were all:

> ... warriors on the field of death. They had abandoned the lands of their birth and parted from their fathers, mothers, wives, and children. ... they were all counting on me, and I could hardly expect to help these warriors on their field of death unless I were to go out onto that field myself.[31]

Therefore he set out for Fushimi, just south of Kyoto, where the largest body of Satsuma samurai had gathered, under Arima Shinshichi's leadership, at an inn called the Teradaya.

Saigō's reference to a 'field of death' is intriguing. He may have felt personally responsible for the choices of these young men, if only because they all looked to him for leadership with such complete trust. It was natural for him to assume that only he could talk them out of their plans, and that he could do that only by going into their midst. Having staked their lives in the service of what they took to be a higher cause, they were not likely to listen to anyone who had not staked as much as they.

What is most intrigueing about Saigō's choice of words is that it would turn up again later in his life, first in 1864, when he went into Chōshū to negotiate a settlement to the bakufu's first punitive campaign against that han, and then again in 1873, when he proposed to settle the controversy with Korea by going there alone and risking his life. Moreover, though he left no evidence of his thoughts at the time, this same notion about a field of death, and his personal sense of responsibility to those already on it and looking to him for guidance, may offer the most plausible explanation of all for his decision to become involved in the 1877 rebellion.

At any rate, Saigō's surviving remarks about his reasons for going to Fushimi make it sufficiently clear that his intention was to try to defuse a potentially explosive situation by talking the samurai there into giving up their plans for terrorism.[32] However, thanks partly to unwarranted assumptions made by Hirano Kuni-omi, the men gathered at Fushimi believed Saigō was coming to lead them. Having convinced himself of this, Hirano had proceeded to share his conviction with anyone he met, including several samurai from Hisamitsu's escort, so it was Hirano's version of the situation that found its way back to Hisamitsu, who was already furious at Saigō for leaving Shimonoseki ahead of him and without authorization. Without waiting to learn more, Hisamitsu ordered that Saigō be arrested and sent back to Kagoshima, along with Moriyama Shinzō and Murata Shinpachi. There, on 6/6, Saigō was ordered into exile on Tokunoshima, and his ship left Yamakawa five days later. Ōkubo had met with Hisamitsu and tried to persuade him to give Saigō another chance, but he had given this up once it became clear that unless he let the matter drop, he might find himself following Saigō into exile.[33]

Having issued specific orders to all Satsuma samurai to refrain from terrorist acts, Hisamitsu saw Saigō's behavior as a deliberate provocation. Not long after Saigō had left Kyoto under arrest, Hisamitsu spent the rest of his anger on the men gathered at Fushimi. On the night of 4/23 he sent a group of samurai to the inn with orders for Arima and his followers to disperse. A fight broke out, in which Arima and several others were killed. More were arrested and sent back to Kagoshima, including Saigō's brother Tsugumichi and his cousin Ōyama Iwao. Because both the men with Arima and those sent by Hisamitsu to disperse them were members of the Seichūgumi, the battle at the Teradaya inn put an end to that group as a coherent force in Satsuma politics. Men who had drawn their swords against each other would not soon be able to call each other brothers in arms again.

The entire series of events left Saigō thoroughly disgusted and embittered. Hisamitsu had condemned him on the strength of reports from two of the men with whom he had grown up, and of whom he had expected support, not betrayal. Worse, Satsuma samurai had drawn their swords and hacked away at one another like the worst of enemies. Saigō summed up his feelings in unequivocal language:

> When I was on Ōshima, I waited daily for recall, and so I was bitter and irritable every day. Now it is clear I will never return from Tokunoshima, but that holds no bitterness for me, and

my heart is at ease. Perhaps I will return if a war breaks out. But if things remain stable, I will probably petition to stay in the islands. When one is branded a criminal by one's own kind without the least effort to learn the truth, and when one's friends are slaughtered, what can one count on? ... I want nothing more to do with this stupid loyalism![34]

Stung by the betrayal of friends, Saigō went into his second exile filled with disillusionment, and nothing would ever seem simple to him again. As he put it later, 'I realize now for the first time that in fact people cannot be trusted.'[35]

Moreover, he was now convinced that even more troubled times lay ahead for Japan. His experiences between 1854 and 1862 had led him to the conclusion that Japan was going to need more than just a few simple reforms to put things right. Some time after beginning his second exile he observed, 'The realm is terminally ill, and the symptoms cannot be healed no matter what remedy is applied. Make no mistake, some turmoil will break out within three to five years.'[36] As for his own future, he added, 'Until then I certainly will not be leaving this island.'[37]

One thing at least was clear: Hisamitsu had no intention of seeing him again. His influence among younger samurai was too great, and already his name had begun to acquire a kind of magic power that his superiors found difficult to understand but easy to fear. He was not sent back to Ōshima because that was too close to home, and also because one of his most intimate friends, Katsura Hisatake, was now the senior han official on that island. To put these two men together, it seemed, would be to invite trouble. Whether Saigō understood the power he was able to exert over others is not clear, but he did know of his reputation, and he spoke of it with some discomfort, saying, 'It is foolishness that people make so much of me in the world.'[38] However that might be, he was removed from the world now.

The end of the earth:
Tokunoshima and Okinoerabujima, 1862–64

Saigō arrived at Tokunoshima on 1862/7/5, but he was there for only two months before he was moved to Okinoerabu. There he was placed in a cage that had been built especially for him in the village of Wadomari. Today there is a replica of that cage where the original once stood. Made of heavy timbers and roofed with thatch, it is cubical in shape, and measures about six feet on a side. In one corner is a fire pit, and opposite that is another pit for use as a toilet. Sitting at the mouth of a river near the edge of the sea, the enclosure offers no shelter except from directly overhead, so that it differs from an animal pen only in being roofed. Given his size, Saigō probably could not even stand upright in it. Certainly he could not exercise, or protect his health in any other way. Built to specifications transmitted from Kagoshima, the cage was meant to be a death cell.[39]

Fortunately for Saigō, the man in charge of him at Wadomari, Tsuchimochi Masateru, fell immediately under the spell of his personality. Had Tsuchimochi not taken pity on him, Saigō almost certainly would have died from exposure in his cage. He was confined in it for only some two months before Tsuchimochi moved him into a larger building, but the toll it exacted can be surmised from the fact that he wrote no letters from the time he entered the cage until nearly half a year after he came out of it. That is, he seems to have spent considerably more time recovering from the effects of being in the cage than he actually spent in it. As noted earlier, he developed a number of serious problems with his health later in life, and many of these may have been merely the long-term effects of his confinement.

Able once again to exercise and to bathe, Saigō gradually regained his health, and began to settle into the routines that would occupy him for the rest of his time in Wadomari: reading, composing poetry, practicing calligraphy, teaching local children as on Ōshima, and conducting long discussions with Tsuchimochi and with his fellow exile Kawaguchi Seppō. His impact as a teacher was such that even today a special aura clings to civic leaders in Wadomari who can claim descent from the children he taught.[40]

Following his recovery, in the first letter he wrote after arriving on Okinoerabu, Saigō returned to a subject he had first mentioned in a letter written on Tokunoshima, concerning the possibility that he might request permission to remain in the islands. Now he elaborated, stating that even if he should be recalled to Kagoshima eventually, he probably would remain there only long enough to petition for leave to retire to private life. Then he would return to Ōshima and live out the rest of his days with his family there.[41] At this stage of his life, the meaning of such remarks is hard to assess, though the simplest approach is to take them at face value, because Saigō was not by nature a dissembler, nor very good at deceit. But if he meant them, it suggests that he genuinely had begun to lose interest in politics. If that is how he felt in 1863, when he made the latter remark, it becomes somewhat more difficult to account for the enthusiasm he brought to his work between 1864 and 1868, when he performed his most noteworthy deeds. Moreover it poses interesting questions about his later life, especially his motives after 1868, offering the basis for an alternative explanation of his behavior that, to my knowledge, has never been proposed by anyone writing in Japan.

That he had not lost all interest in politics is clear from the letters he wrote during the rest of his stay on Okinoerabu. Having heard about the suicidal expulsionist uprisings of groups of impatient samurai – the Tenchūgumi in the Kansai and Hirano Kuniomi at Ikuno – Saigō observed once again that civil war in Japan was imminent.[42] As news of the activities of the Western powers trickled down to him, he began to exhibit a more bellicose temperament, stating that it would be essential to '. . . cause the military prowess of our Divine Land (*shinkoku*) to radiate far and wide.'[43] And though he had foresworn loyalism after arriving at Tokunoshima, he now spoke of a willingness to return to action, remarking, 'I have begun to think now that I would like to play out the remainder of this farce (*kyōgen*) in combat.'[44] In fact, he did not have long to wait.

On 1864/2/21, his brother Tsugumichi and his friend Yoshii Tomozane arrived at Wadomari with his pardon and recall. A month later he was in Kyoto, and four months after that he had his first taste of the combat in which he had expressed interest, fighting against troops from Chōshū han in front of the Hamaguri Gate of the imperial palace. The events that led to that battle, known as the Kinmon incident, are complex and have been narrated in considerable detail elsewhere.[45] Of more immediate interest is the maturation of Saigō's world view during the two years he spent on Okinoerabu.

The theory of Heaven

During the course of his education, Saigō had been exposed to most of the philosophical systems that were available in nineteenth-century Japan, including the writings of Confucius, Mencius, Chu Hsi, and Wang Yang-ming, and the adaptations of them by Japanese thinkers. Of all the materials he encountered, none seems to have impressed him more than the *Genshi shiroku* of Satō Issai (1772–1859), a Mino han Confucian scholar who rose to prominence as head of the bakufu's official school, founded originally by Hayashi Razan. Saigō thought Satō's aphorisms important enough that he copied out over one hundred of them for his own reference, and later used them as the basis for the precepts he composed for the private schools founded in Kagoshima in 1874.[46]

Among the aphorisms Saigō copied from Satō are remarks such as this: 'In all one does, one must have a heart that follows Heaven; one need not think of revealing it to men.'[47] Elsewhere he wrote, 'One must accept that one's flesh is the property of Heaven, and in Heaven is the power of life and death.' And again, 'Take not men as your counterparts, but take Heaven.' As these examples suggest, the focal point for Saigō's thought was the concept of Heaven (*ten*), which he took to be the source of both political and ethical legitimacy, the arbiter of life and death, and both the model for and the measure of morality and virtue.

Saigō understood morality to be a private matter, not something to be debated openly or explained to others. His famous motto, 'revere Heaven and love people' (*keiten aijin*) embodies this concept of a personal relationship with Heaven, expressed not in words but in deeds. He once characterized his personal ethics as 'concealed virtue' (*intoku*).[48] One cannot understand Saigō without bearing in mind that while he tended to frame his ideas in brief formulas or aphorisms, relying on language at least to that extent, his interest was not in propositions or theories, but in the direct and real consequences of deeds. He evidently understood Wang Yang-ming well enough to have made that thinker's basic ideas his own. Saigō may not have believed that action and goodness are effectively the same, as Wang Yang-ming taught, but he evidently did believe that action is the only measure of one's true intentions, and that words are correspondingly cheap.[49]

It will be recalled that before he left for Ōshima in 1859, Saigō referred to himself as 'dead bones in the earth,' and as 'shamed before Heaven and Earth.' Not long after recovering from his suicide attempt, Saigō apparently came to the conclusion that he had survived only because Heaven willed it. He was now an instrument of Heaven, no longer in possession of his own life, and whatever fate befell him was but the unfolding of the destiny ordained for him.[50] Now, this view does not square well with the remarks he made after arriving at Tokunoshima. He did not believe he was there because of Heaven's will, but rather because of plain human duplicity, and he felt angry enough about that to repudiate the imperial loyalism he had inherited from Nariakira. However, this conflict of interpretation is more apparent than real.

By calling himself dead bones in the earth, Saigō evidently meant that he was dead to the world. Such a view would have put him outside of time, and outside the limits of the moral accountability to which living men are subject. To say that he had survived because of Heavenly intervention might be nothing more than a dodge, absolving him of the responsibility for failing to die with Gesshō. As Robert Jay Lifton has shown, survivor guilt is a powerful mechanism, and it exerts its distorting psychological effects regardless of whether one is guilty of any wrongdoing or not.[51]

According to Shigeno Yasutsugu, another Satsuma samurai exiled on Ōshima, Saigō did believe he had bungled his suicide attempt, and had lost face because he had tried to drown himself 'like a woman' instead of turning his sword on himself as an honorable samurai would have done.[52] Shigeno concluded that from this point on Saigō felt obligated to Gesshō to complete the fulfillment of a promise only half realized. Thus for the rest of his life he had a desire to hurry to his death. Ivan Morris goes further, contending that Saigō suffered from a 'death wish' psychosis.[53]

It is true that Saigō's rhetoric often turned on allusions to death and dying, as we have seen in his references to a 'field of death' in 1862. Perhaps he did have a morbid fascination with death, stemming from the shock of beholding Akayama Yukie's bloody undergarments in 1850. Or perhaps, like many another samurai in those days, he simply went further than necessary in conceptualizing death as the supreme expression of himself as a samurai. I think that survivor guilt or something like it may well have been an important factor in Saigō's behavior after 1858, but I also think that it would be too simple to dismiss his fascination with death as nothing more than the effect of a psychosis.[54] Surviving while Gesshō died evidently did confront Saigō with a source of profound shame, and perhaps he found that he could reduce the sting of that somewhat if he were to see it as not of his choosing and out of his control because of the intervention of Heaven.

In the end, while the question of Saigō's psychological motivation is tantalizing, there is simply not enough reliable evidence to permit more than interesting speculation. Saigō's selections from Satō Issai are the best clues we have concerning his view of Heaven as it bears on the private moral life of the individual. But Saigō did not dwell at length on private morality. By far the most important aspect of his thinking concerned public morality, as it is expressed in the behavior of samurai officials. We have seen this already in his 1856 memorial on rural administration. We find further evidence of it in a series of documents he wrote while in Wadomari, for the guidance of Tsuchimochi Masateru. Two of them are summaries of the duties of lower officials in the administrative structure of the islands. The third is a fragment of a discussion concerning grain storehouses for the provision of reserves against times of shortage.[55]

In Saigō's view, it is Heaven which places the emperor in power, and the emperor is therefore the embodiment of Heaven on earth, its direct physical manifestation. Because the emperor cannot govern the entire realm by himself, he establishes daimyo to rule portions of it in his behalf. In the same way, each daimyo appoints lesser officials to administer the smaller subdivisions of the lands under his charge. The lowly local official is thus not only the personification of the daimyo on the spot, but ultimately the local extension of the authority of Heaven embodied in the emperor. A failure of virtue on the part of the local official, thus, will diminish the virtue of the daimyo, and by extension that of the emperor as well. As enforcers of civil law and administrators of the social order, local officials have the power of life and death over the peasants, but they must never forget that their authority is not their own but comes from above.

It is worth pointing out in passing that there is room in Saigō's construal of Confucianism for both the Mandate of Heaven theory developed by Mencius, which provides a sanction for rebellion, and also for the Japanese view that the emperor rules absolutely by virtue of his descent from the Sun Goddess, and therefore cannot be overthrown. There is nothing to indicate whether Saigō was aware of the syncretic sleight of hand he executed here, but he probably did it unwittingly, because the formulaic style of thinking he found comfortable left him ill suited to notice subtleties. In any case, like his contemporaries elsewhere in Japan, if he hoped to sustain his belief in Confucian values, Saigō faced the necessity of finding a way to reconcile a Chinese style emperor, who could be overthrown under the right circumstances, with a Japanese style one who was inviolable by nature.

It is also worth noting that in his account of the delegation of authority from Heaven to the emperor and downward, he makes no mention of either shogun or bakufu. Those institutions, it would appear, were not self-evidently necessary parts of the civil order for Saigō, and so he would find no reason not to remove them if circumstances seemed to call for that. This is not to make of Saigō a restorationist before his time. It is only to recognize that, as nearly as one can tell, there was nothing in his understanding of the world that would make it inherently undesirable to remove the Tokugawa from power.

In any case, because of the way authority is delegated by Heaven, it is the conduct of the lowest official, the one closest to the peasant, that ultimately decides whether or not the emperor retains his right to rule. The local administrator, therefore, must take care to win the hearts of the people, by eliminating selfish desire and by identifying himself completely with his duties. An administrative post is not a possession, but a trust, and the measure of one's worthiness to occupy it is to be found nowhere else than in the happiness of the people.

At this lowest of the many levels of society, Saigō sees a division of responsibility according to which the peasant enacts the will of Heaven by laboring with his strength, while the official does so by laboring with his heart and mind (*kokoro*). Notice, once again, that Saigō takes no issue with the question of social equality between samurai and peasant. The social hierarchy that places one over the other is ordained by Heaven. The peasant toils and the samurai administers, and to have it otherwise would be to violate the natural order.

Yet if the official is on top, it is the peasant who provides the final measure of how smoothly the system is running, and of whether the official is truly virtuous. Failure to heed the will of Heaven invites retribution, in the form of natural disasters, crop failures, and peasant rebellions. Ultimately the only way to know the will of Heaven is to observe the peasant, because the latter embodies the expression of the former. If the people are content, then that means that Heaven is content. If the people are happy and tranquil, and if the laws are being obeyed, then the official knows he is governing in accordance with Heaven. Thus the official, who is the immediate embodiment of the authority vested in the emperor by Heaven, paradoxically finds the measure of his own worth not from above, in the power entrusted to him, but from below, in the joys and sorrows of those he governs. Moreover, the ability of the official to govern justly arises not from his social status or from his temporal power, but from the condition of his soul. As Saigō argued in 1856, the morality of the individual samurai is at the heart of the system. A man who honors and respects himself will behave honorably and respectably. A man of virtue will govern virtuously. And the best way to foster virtue is to inculcate respect and honor, not chiefly in those who are ruled, but in those who rule.

There is little difference, then, between the ideas articulated in these documents from 1863 and those in the one from 1856, and that should not be surprising, since most of these ideas are inherent in the Confucian education Saigō received as a child. The difference is that Saigō now has, in the concept of Heaven, a first principle or primary cause to bind his values together and give them a comprehensive rationale. This enables him to affirm the justice of the Tokugawa social order itself while at the same time it leaves him room to exercise his very human sympathy for the hard life of the peasant. And it also leaves him room to view the Tokugawa themselves, along with their institutions, as not necessarily indispensable to the social order they have created, and therefore as expendable if need be.

On his return to Kagoshima in 1864, Saigō expressed these ideas in more practical form in a memorial to the han on the administration of the sugar monopoly.[56] In the preface to this document, he argues that the system is so oppressive that foreign intruders would find it easy to turn the peasants against the han, whereas to alleviate some of its excesses not only would prevent that, but might also increase revenues. Most of the memorial is devoted to specific suggestions about improving the equity of the sugar exchange system, reducing the prices the islanders pay for tools, allowing greater flexibility in the assessment of quotas, and similar purely practical administrative changes.

The leading item, as we would expect by now, has to do with rectifying abuses in administration and reorganizing the bureaucratic structure so that officials in the islands are subject to tighter control and closer review by their superiors in Kagoshima. The first criterion for appointment should be good character, and justice should be encouraged by a specific and consistent set of rewards and punishments. As he argued in 1856, Saigō here asserts that the success or failure of institutions turns on the morale and the morality of the samurai who operate them. If corrupt men are in power, it will do no good to reform the institutions. This is an important point, for it was chiefly on these grounds that Saigō disapproved of the Meiji government. We will leave until later the question of whether that disapproval was strong enough to justify rebellion.

Saigō was now thirty-seven years old. His determination to establish righteousness through service to the imperial court was undiminished, and the sincerity of his beliefs was stronger than ever before, centered as it now was on the concept of Heaven. Thanks to his experiences since his emergence from Satsuma in 1854, he was less naive about politics, and aware now that it was the deeds of men, not their words, that revealed their true loyalties. Still smarting from the duplicity of former friends, Saigō had come to believe firmly in an absolute boundary between good and evil, drawn and sanctioned by Heaven, and discernible in the effects of administrative behavior on the lives of common people. The details of his political ideas would continue to evolve, but his intolerance for those who failed to meet his standards of integrity would only grow more unforgiving. Though most of his life was now behind him, both his best and his worst moments still lay ahead.

· 3 ·

The Rise to Leadership, *1864–65*

As in 1862, Saigō returned in 1864 to a world that was markedly different from the one he had left. In the two years since his ill-fated trip to Kyoto, new players had appeared on the stage, and had begun a drama whose entire plot would become clear only in retrospect, after most of the action was over. By the time Saigō became involved in the unfolding drama, it was already well underway, and his contribution will be easier to understand if we begin with a summary of what had happened while he was in exile.[1]

National politics:
1862–64

Hisamitsu's ambitious journey to Kyoto in 1862 had achieved all of its aims, in spite of Saigō's profound discomfort with it. The court had issued an order calling for bakufu reform, and had appointed Hisamitsu and his troops to escort its envoy to Edo. Reluctantly, the bakufu had accepted the decree, and had begun a wide-ranging liberalization of traditional policies. It also had reinstated the surviving victims of Ii Naosuke's purge. Two appointments were of particular importance. Tokugawa Yoshinobu, whom Nariakira and others had wanted to become the new shogun in 1858, was now named guardian for the shogun Iemochi. Matsudaira Shungaku, who had led the group supporting Yoshinobu, now became senior political advisor (*seiji sōsai*).[2]

For the next three years, attempting to build on the foundations laid in this 1862 trip to Edo, Hisamitsu pursued every opportunity to realize the aims of the kōbū gattai strategy, and thus to carry out the charge he believed Nariakira had given him. In a series of visits to Kyoto, he met repeatedly with a small group of men who seemed to share his aims. At the heart of this group were Tokugawa Yoshinobu and Matsudaira Shungaku, who after 1862 held the most powerful posts in the reorganized bakufu. Close to them and only slightly less powerful was Matsudaira Katamori, hanshu of the Tokugawa collateral han of Aizu. More or less of the same status as Hisamitsu himself were Yamauchi Yōdō, the former hanshu of Tosa, and Date Munenari, the hanshu of Uwajima.[3] Broadly speaking, they were attempting in their meetings to work out a formula by which bakufu and court could govern together, with advisory support from some sort of daimyo council. However, each of these five men had a different agenda, based on a slightly different understanding of Japan's current political realities and its future needs, so they were unable to reach agreement. In spite of repeated efforts, their discussions yielded nothing, and by the end of 1865 they had given up, in the face of mounting frustration and a growing sense of urgency concerning the intentions of the Western powers toward Japan, particularly France and Britain.

In fact, kōbu gattai had been bankrupt from the start, as its supporters would have realized if they had paused for a moment to reflect on the underlying significance of Hisamitsu's 1862 trip to Edo. With little more than token resistance, the bakufu had accepted a decree from the court, handed to it by a court-appointed envoy whose authority was backed up by an outside (*tōzama*) daimyo. This sequence of events amounted to a complete reversal of policies that had been at the foundation of bakufu control in Japan since 1600. If the bakufu could be cowed that easily into yielding its hitherto exclusive prerogatives to those it had barred completely from politics for over two centuries, it was already far too feeble to provide the basis for any sort of workable coalition government.[4] At any rate, by the middle of 1865, Satsuma's leaders had effectively given up on the bakufu. Though they still assumed that the Tokugawa would remain in power, they no longer believed the bakufu capable of providing leadership.[5] But if kōbu gattai was a lost cause, so was expulsionism, the other prominent agenda of the early 1860s.

From the beginning, the emperor Kōmei had refused to accept any sort of foreign presence in Japan, and restless samurai throughout the country had rallied to his support. Angry at the bakufu's failure to make the foreigners go away, these men began attacking anyone they thought to be in favor of further contact with the West. They soon had political leaders in Kyoto terrorized, and they kept the city in a state of constant tension. Chōshū, an outside han in western Honshu, emerged as the leading advocate of the xenophobia expressed in the *sonnō jōi* slogan ('revere the emperor, expel the barbarian'), and soon after Hisamitsu's trip to Edo, Chōshū forces escorted another court envoy to that city with an order for the shogun to come to Kyoto to discuss national affairs. Once again the bakufu agreed, and in the spring of 1863, Iemochi journeyed to Kyoto, where he yielded to pressure and promised that all foreigners would be driven from Japan beginning on 1963/5/10.[6]

The bakufu was now in an untenable position. It had given its word both to guarantee Western treaty rights in Japan and to expel all Westerners from Japan, and it was under redoubled pressure from the foreign powers because of repeated attacks on their persons and property. Two of these episodes were of particular import.

First, in 1862/8, as Hisamitsu and his escort made their way through the village of Namamugi, between Edo and Kamakura, four British civilians strayed into their path on horseback. In the confusion that resulted, Hisamitsu's guards attacked the group, killing one and wounding two others. The three surviviors escaped, and Hisamitsu went on his way, leaving the body of Charles Richardson lying in the road. Though clearly the result of an unfortunate combination of misunderstanding and hasty reaction, this incident was to have a number of important consequences. Then, in 1863/5, taking the shogun's promise of expulsion literally, Chōshū's coastal guns began firing on Western ships passing through the straits of Shimonoseki, setting in motion another chain of events that would have important consequences. The bakufu was unable to prevent such incidents. It could only watch helplessly as the situation slipped further out of its control.

Frustrated by steadily increasing hostility toward them among ordinary Japanese, and by their own inability to find out who was actually in charge of Japan's government, the foreign powers began to take matters into their own hands. In 1863/6 a squadron of Western ships battered the Chōshū guns into submission, and in 1863/7 Britain subjected Kagoshima to a naval bombardment in retaliation for the killing of Charles Richardson at Namamugi. Neither episode decided anything of consequence in the relationship between Japan and the West, but together they showed the

Japanese that forcible expulsion would not work because Western military power was too great. By the beginning of 1864, it was clear that the Western powers were in Japan to stay, and it was equally clear that the bakufu had been unable to prevent that.

In other words, by 1864 anyone who was paying attention had begun to realize that it was too late to save the bakufu, and past time to start searching for a viable alternative. At this point, however, no one could say yet what that alternative might be. People thinking along these lines may have assumed that one of the powerful han–probably either Satsuma or Chōshū–would take the bakufu's place, and carry on the diplomatic struggle as the emperor's new representative, without altering the traditional status quo a great deal. In particular, this was how the leaders of both Satsuma and Chōshū understood matters. For these two han, national politics had become a contest to see which of them would win the exclusive right to speak for the court. It was a contest colored by bitter and seemingly irreconcilable antagonism.

In the meantime, most people in the court had grown weary of living in the atmosphere of continual crisis produced by the terrorist activities of sonnō jōi advocates in Kyoto, whose presence also made the city an unhealthy place for kōbu gattai supporters. On 1863/8/18, troops from Satsuma and Aizu removed the Chōshū forces from their guard posts at the imperial palace and ejected them from Kyoto. Accompanied by a number of extremist court nobles, Chōshū's troops withdrew to the han, where they began to consider ways to regain their dominance of the court, and to humble Satsuma and Aizu. This would not be easy to do, however. The court objected to the high-handed way in which Chōshū samurai had taken over Kyoto and presumed to speak in the emperor's name. The bakufu was upset because Chōshū's attacks on Western shipping had put the sincerity of its diplomatic promises in question. Both the court and the bakufu were eager to make an example of Chōshū, partly to secure a bit more maneuvering room for themselves by lowering tensions, and partly in the hope of discouraging further spontaneous unilateral responses to the Western presence.

That fall a series of outbursts by samurai extremists put everyone even more on edge. In 1863/8 a group calling itself the League of Divine Retribution (*Tenchūgumi*) staged an uprising in Yamato, just south of Kyoto, and two months later Saigō's old acquaintance Hirano Kuniomi lost his life in another expulsionist demonstration at Ikuno, not far from Osaka. Both of these disturbances were quelled successfully by bakufu troops, but in 1864/3 another outburst closer to home presented the bakufu with a challenge of a more significant kind, when the loyalists in Mito han rose in arms. Securely entrenched in the mountains around Tsukuba, not very far away from Edo itself, they resisted bakufu efforts to pacify them, and it was feared that eventually they would escape from their encirclement and try to make their way to Chōshū. Once there, they could reinforce what the bakufu already regarded as its most intractable and potentially dangerous competitor for initiative in national politics.[7]

By the time Saigō got to Kyoto, tensions had built to a point where the right provocation might plunge the entire country into civil war, and he put it in just those terms himself, saying, 'There is nothing left now but to wait for civil chaos to break out.'[8] At that point, however, things settled into a brief stalemate and gave everyone a chance to catch their breath. In the ensuing lull, Saigō had a chance to evaluate the situation and formulate some ideas about it.[9]

The struggle for control of Kyoto:
1864/4–7

Saigō's circumstances had changed quickly. In less than a month, he had gone from ignominious confinement on Okinoerabu to an audience with Hisamitsu in Kyoto. Hisamitsu elevated Saigō's status, placed him in charge of Satsuma's military affairs in the Kansai (the area around Kyoto and Osaka) and then left for Kagoshima on 1864/4/18, taking Ōkubo with him.[10] Together with the senior vassal Komatsu Tatewaki, Saigō was now Satsuma's chief representative in Kyoto, and Hisamitsu told the two of them to confine their attention to guarding the imperial palace. From this point until the fall of the Tokugawa in 1868, Saigō and Ōkubo, in close contact with their superiors and with each other, emerged as the leading agents for the enactment of Satsuma policy, and carried on a steady correspondence through which it is possible to trace the development of Satsuma's objectives with some precision.[11]

Saigō's initial impressions of the national political situation were not optimistic. In a letter to his old friend Katsura Hisatake, he described what he had seen in Kyoto.[12] The court was demoralized, he said, and its leaders were so confused by what was going on that they could do nothing more than improvise from day to day. They had no coherent strategy, and were merely waiting to see what might happen next. The bakufu was no better off, and was making policies aimed only at improving its advantage in a situation that changed daily. Yoshinobu had become a political force in his own right, frequently operating independently of the bakufu and in conflict with its interests. He acted as if he wanted to become shogun himself, and took advantage of every opportunity to manipulate both court and bakufu for his own ends.

In short, while domestic chaos threatened to break out at any moment, and the Western powers moved toward their own imponderable but assuredly ominous goals, there seemed to be no political agency in the country with either a clear sense of the danger facing Japan, or the will to act on it. There was, in effect, no government. The only cause for optimism was the remote but tantalizing possibility of a reconciliation between Satsuma and Chōshū. Saigō said little about this last point, and so it is not clear what he had in mind here, but in any event, as he reported to Ōkubo a month later, Chōshū's hostility toward Satsuma over its participation in the expulsion of Chōshū forces from Kyoto on 8/18 was still too great.[13]

He did eventually have more to say about Chōshū, however, and there is an element of his thinking at this point that requires closer scrutiny. In his letter to Katsura, he mentioned the impending visit to Osaka of some senior Chōshū officials, including Kikkawa Kenmotsu, hanshu of the Chōshū collateral han of Iwakuni. Saigō proposed that he might go to Osaka and explore with Kikkawa the possibility of a reconciliation between Chōshū and Satsuma. With the right kind of open exchange of views, Saigō thought they might be able to reach some sort of an understanding, but it was more likely, he admitted, that the men from Chōshū would simply kill him. If that were to happen, it would then be clear to everyone that Chōshū and its agents were beneath contempt, and could be destroyed without compunction. One need feel no pity toward men for whom murder was an appropriate response to a sincere offer of peace.[14]

Given Saigō's enthusiastic and bellicose support during these months for the idea of a bakufu punitive campaign against

Saigō Takamori

Chōshū, we may wonder how sincere he really was in his talk of reconciliation, or how optimistic he felt about its chances for success.[15] From the perspective of Chōshū's leaders, when Satsuma troops jōined forces with the Tokugawa loyalist samurai of Aizu han to eject their troops from Kyoto on 8/18, they committed the double sin of cooperating with a bakufu supporter and of driving the most sincere of Japan's imperial loyalist samurai out of Kyoto, and if a Satsuma samurai were foolish enough to go alone into a Chōshū residence, the result was probably a foregone conclusion. Saigō certainly knew this, and so his proposal looks like nothing so much as deliberate provocation. Moreover, at this point Saigō still understood Japan to be a collection of locally autonomous domains in competition for national influence, and in his view anything that might weaken Chōshū's position would automatically strengthen Satsuma's. Thus, it seems unlikely that his desire to establish friendly relations between Satsuma and Chōshū was genuine at this time.

However, given his understanding of what the outcome was likely to be, it appears that he was genuinely willing to sacrifice himself in the service of what he saw to be a worthy cause. Whether the outcome were a reconciliation between Satsuma and Chōshū, or merely his own death, it would help to clarify the political stakes, thus making it easier for others to decide what to do next. His readiness to die, and the personal courage and sincerity behind it, are important. Even more important is the further development of Saigō's approach to conflict resolution that we see emerging here. In 1862, he had spoken of going onto a 'field of death' as the only way to convince desperate men of his sincerity, but the entire formula was not yet clear to him at that point. By the time he made this proposal in 1864, he had figured out that he could use a genuine willingness to die as proof of the authenticity of his stated intentions; one who is ready to lose everything for the sake of what he wants must be telling the truth.

This faith in the power of sincerity was a fundamental element of Saigō's personality, and one of the most persistent of the many motives for his behavior. That he understood its potential for influencing people is clear from the outcome of his mediation in the first bakufu campaign against Chōshū. The accuracy of his understanding was confirmed once again in 1868 when he managed to negotiate the bloodless surrender of Edo in much the same way. The really interesting question, to which we must

68

return later, is whether he intended to employ this proven technique one more time when he sought permission to go to Korea in 1873.

Whatever Saigō's true intent may have been, Hisamitsu rejected his proposal, and in the meantime Chōshū proceeded with plans that would change the situation dramatically. Earlier in 1864, Hisamitsu and his colleagues had agreed that senior Chōshū officials must come to Kyoto to discuss the han's recent conduct, and the bakufu had notified a number of other han to begin preparing for a possible military campaign against Chōshū. In reply to a summons from the court, however, Chōshū had requested that the hanshu be allowed to come to Kyoto to speak in his own defense, and that the young expulsionist nobles who had fled with Chōshū's troops on 8/18 be pardoned and reinstated.[16] This caused a deadlock, and then the tension increased further in 1864/6 when bakufu agents raided a gathering of Chōshū samurai at an inn called the Ikedaya in Kyoto.[17] In the meantime, both the bakufu and Chōshū had begun making overtures for Satsuma's support, each one seeking to increase its influence in the court by enlarging the number of its supporters. In reply, Saigō stated flatly that the men of Satsuma would act as Hisamitsu had instructed them to act, and would confine their attention to guarding the imperial palace.[18]

In the meantime, a number of Western powers were assembling a fleet to conduct a larger punitive mission against Chōshū, and Yoshinobu issued orders forbidding other han from coming to Chōshū's aid. Saigō condemned this action, not only because it was further evidence of Yoshinobu's self-seeking attitude, but also because it would provoke Chōshū further.[19] After the Ikedaya incident, Saigō observed that Chōshū was now in a completely untenable position, and must either capitulate to the bakufu and collapse or rise up in open rebellion against bakufu authority.[20] The arrival of large Chōshū military units in the vicinity of Kyoto during 1864/6–7 seemed to bear out his assessment of the situation, and to suggest that Chōshū's leaders had chosen the latter option.

In fact, he was not merely speculating about what was going on inside Chōshū. Earlier in the summer, he had ordered Kirino Toshiaki, a Satsuma gōshi and one of his close friends, to infiltrate extremist groups in Kyoto.[21] Since Kirino had a well-deserved reputation as a formidable swordsman and a committed expulsionist, he had little difficulty carrying out Saigō's orders. In a fairly short time, he had won the confidence of extremist samurai from Chōshū and other han, and had managed to gather a good deal of information about conditions in Chōshū. Of particular interest to Saigō was Kirino's discovery that some in Chōshū had begun discussing the armed overthrow of the bakufu (*tōbaku*). This was a novel idea for him, and when combined with other information, it would have an important effect on the development of his own views.[22]

In the meantime, Chōshū had positioned a large army around Kyoto and had refused to disband it until han representatives received permission to enter the city. Public opinion was divided concerning Chōshū, but most people in Kyoto, including Saigō, agreed that no discussion could begin until the army withdrew.[23] At the same time, Saigō made it clear that Satsuma had no direct quarrel with Chōshū. On the contrary, Satsuma troops were in Kyoto to protect the emperor, and would not move against Chōshū unless its army attacked the palace.[24] Despite his refusal to fight, Saigō suspected that Chōshū's desire was to regain the control of Kyoto it had lost in the 8/18 incident, and so he concluded that if the Chōshū army attacked, Satsuma must fight as though for its own survival.[25]

Though Saigō seems to have had some difficulty deciding where he stood, it was not long before he became convinced that a battle was inevitable,[26] and circumstances soon proved him right. On 7/19 the Chōshū army attacked Kyoto, and Saigō had his first taste of combat, commanding Satsuma troops in front of the Hamaguri Gate of the imperial palace, where the most bitter fighting took place. Saigō reported the battle to Ōkubo the next day, praising the Satsuma troops for their valor and condemning Chōshū, which he said had committed monstrous treason and must now face the punishment of Heaven.[27] It was almost a year later before he shared his feelings about the experience with anyone.

Then, writing to friends on Okinoerabu and Ōshima, Saigō reported that he had received a trifling bullet wound in his leg, and he added, 'As you know, I like a good fight, but now that I have experienced real combat, I know how truly terrible it is, and I have no desire to do it again.' On the other hand, it seemed a dream that he had gone so quickly from the shame of his imprisonment to the glory of defending the imperial palace. Only the fear of appearing immodest kept him from describing the battle in more detail.[28] In any event, he concluded, Chōshū's attempt to regain control of Kyoto had been thwarted, and the time had come now to put that han decisively in its place.

The awakening of a nationalist vision:
1864/7–9

However uncertain nobles in Kyoto had been about their choices prior to this attack, they were now decidedly of one mind, and on 7/23 they issued to Yoshinobu an order to punish Chōshū as an enemy of the court. Saigō had anticipated this development, and had sent men into Chōshū to gather information.[29] He told Ōkubo that he wanted to find a way to keep Chōshū's leaders in the castle town of Hagi from enlisting the support of Kikkawa Kenmotsu and others in control of subordinate domains. He believed that if Chōshū's forces were allowed to form a united front, they would be more difficult to subdue, and he wanted to move quickly, before they had time to recover from their defeat in Kyoto.[30] In the middle of 1864/8, he observed that if Satsuma handled itself well in the expedition against Chōshū, its own position was bound to improve, in the eyes of both the court and the bakufu. It seems, then, that he supported the bakufu's desire to humble Chōshū, not because it would help Edo, but because it would hurt Chōshū and help Satsuma.

On 8/8 he wrote his friend Koba Dennai, who had been in charge of him during his first exile on Oshima, that England, France, Holland, and the United States were about to launch a massive naval raid against Chōshū.[31] It was widely believed that when they had finished with Chōshū, they would proceed to the Kansai to continue negotiations for the opening of trading ports at Hyōgo and Osaka, which had been agreed to in the treaties of 1858 but had been put off by the bakufu because of the anti-foreign violence of the earlier 1860s. This was important to Saigō, but more urgent was his belief that the bakufu's expedition against Chōshū must be timed so as to come as soon as possible after the Western attack, because that would improve the chances of a complete capitulation in Hagi.[32]

Saigō's position in the autumn of 1864 was what it had been in 1863, when he had argued that each han must achieve local self-sufficiency (*kakkyō*) in order to meet the foreign threat.[33] Saigō could see that a Western attack on any given han would threaten the interests of all others, and that if the han were busy fighting each other, the country would be more vulnerable. What he had not yet realized was that no matter how secure individual han might be in the domestic context, it was the security of the whole nation that most urgently needed to be guaranteed. To see that would have required him to abandon the understanding of domestic politics with which he had grown up, and to begin thinking of Japan as a single entity whose interests transcended those of its various parts. His understanding of Japan's political choices was still determined by the han separatism that had been the first premise behind local government ever since the seventeenth century. That understanding was now dangerously out of date, and Saigō was about to have that fact brought home to him, in what as to be one of the most decisive encounters of his career.

As differences of opinion in the bakufu delayed the appointment of a commander for the Chōshū expedition, Saigō grew restless and decided that he might be able to expedite matters if he could appeal directly to someone with influence in Edo.[34] As it happened, one of the bakufu's chief naval advisors, Katsu Kaishū, was in Osaka. Saigō arranged a meeting with him, intending to persuade him to exert pressure in Edo and get the expedition underway. However, Saigō was in for a surprise; his meeting with Katsu dramatically and irrevocably altered his outlook.[35] As Saigō put it to Ōkubo later, 'I was surprised to find that Katsu is a man to reckon with. I had expected to intimidate him, but instead I wound up deferring to him with respect.'[36] As had been the case in his relationships with Fujita Tōko and Hashimoto Sanai, Saigō's encounter with Katsu was one of the few times in his life when he met someone whose personality and presence were even more powerful than his own.

Saigō began his conversation with Katsu by insisting that the bakufu must stop wasting time and get on with the reduction of Chōshū to submission. To his astonishment, Katsu showed no interest in that idea, and talked instead about the Western naval squadron that had attacked Shimonoseki on 8/5 and had forced Chōshū to sign a treaty of non-belligerence. To think in terms of working with the bakufu toward any set of goals, he said, was foolhardy. Officials in Edo spent as much time competing with each other as they did trying to govern the country. They were not likely to cooperate with political outsiders such as Satsuma when their own political interests were at stake.

On the contrary, the bakufu was preoccupied with merely trying to survive, and could no longer serve as the basis for a national government. It could not even keep its own subjects in line, much less cope with the foreign diplomatic challenge. It was completely out of its depth, but did not realize even that much. Thus it had agreed to a series of treaties that were disadvantageous to Japan and dishonorable to the emperor. It was time to create a council of powerful daimyo to advise the court and to represent Japan in negotiations with the West. Theorizing about the proper form of government for Japan might be an amusing pastime, but it was no substitute for effective administrative procedures, and it was abundantly clear that the bakufu was no longer capable of performing effectively. Only a daimyo council, representing a broader but more coherent set of national interests, could deal successfully with the West. As it had proven repeatedly, the bakufu would never support such a council voluntarily. But the Western powers were about to gather at Hyōgo, effectively moving the arena of decision away from Edo, and simultaneously offering a powerful sanction that could be used to force the bakufu to share its prerogatives. With skillful exploitation of opportunities only just beginning to take shape, leaders of such han as Satsuma and Chōshū could use the possibility of their own cooperation with the foreign powers to back Edo's policy makers into a corner.

Unable to resist either the precision of Katsu's logic or the force of his personality, Saigō went over to his position completely, and immediately began talking of trying to create the daimyo council about which Katsu had theorized, and of governing Japan by deliberation (*kyōwa seiji*) rather than by edict, as the Tokugawa had done since 1600. The foreign powers had left Yokohama for Hyōgo on 9/9, and since no less a figure than Matsudaira Shungaku of Fukui supported the idea of deliberative government, it was clearly time to gain the cooperation of Yoshinobu and establish an assembly of great han.[37]

Saigō remained as eager as before to complete the disposition of Chōshū, but he now had different reasons. For one thing, he now believed that Chōshū must be pacified so that Japan's leaders could concentrate on meeting the Western challenge at Hyōgo. For another, Chōshū must be brought into line without being seriously harmed, because its strength was essential in the confrontation with the West. A contest between Satsuma and Chōshū based on the assumptions that had guided Saigō's thinking until now could in fact prove fatal to both han, because the real threat to their interests was the West.

Saigō understood that the arrival of the foreign powers at Hyōgo would amount to an international incident. Now, however, he realized that their earlier attack on Chōshū was also an international incident, and not just a potentially advantageous development in a struggle between two han for control of the imperial court.[38] The Chōshū problem must be settled quickly and with a minimum of both national disorder and local damage. On 9/19, Saigō wrote to Ōkubo, 'I have begun to wonder whether there might be a way to have the people of Chōshū take care of the disposition of Chōshū.'[39]

With the articulation of this new objective, Saigō at last had attained the vision of which he had been incapable before. Nari-akira had taught him that he must let go of the petty local jealousies he had inherited from the long history of reform and factional competition in Kagoshima. Now Katsu had taught him that he must do the same with the equally irrelevant understanding he had of competition between han for national political advantage. Saigō had realized that Japan was much more than just the sum of all the han and their conflicting interests. It was a polity in whose cohesion all of its subdivisions had equal interest, and in whose survival they must all cooperate if each hoped to survive.

Whether Saigō understood all the implications of viewing Japan as a polity, either in 1864 or at any later time, remains open to question. What matters is that his meeting with Katsu altered his agenda, and gave him a conceptual framework within which he could think of destroying the existing government in order to replace it with one more capable of governing Japan. He was no nationalist, and he never became one in any important sense, but he finally had outgrown both localism and regionalism, and had become ready to think in terms of something much more like nationalism.

The Chōshū settlement:
1864/9–12

On 10/5 the Owari hanshu Tokugawa Yoshikatsu accepted command of the Chōshū punitive expedition. Saigō had already begun

74

exploring the possibilities for a negotiated settlement, telling Ōkubo that he thought Chōshū's collateral han would not be eager to share Hagi's fate and would abandon it when confronted with the threat of force.[40] Overtures to Kikkawa Kenmotsu in Iwakuni had yielded promising results, and while Saigō thought the bakufu's punitive army would have to be deployed in order to produce the results he wanted, he repeated his desire to find some way to let Chōshū put its own house in order, and avoid a military conflict.[41]

In the meantime, the bakufu had fallen into progressively more difficult circumstances, as Katsu had predicted it would. Because it had promised the Western nations to guarantee their treaty rights, it was unable to explain why it had not prevented Chōshū's attacks on their ships. And because it had promised the court to close the treaty ports, it could not explain why the foreigners not only were still in Japan, but were assembling at Hyōgo to demand the opening of more ports. Yoshinobu had been trying to gain some leeway with the court, but officials there were not interested in his problems and had ordered him to settle the Chōshū matter without further delay, and to hasten preparations for another visit to Kyoto by the shogun. Saigō expected that it would be another month before the shogun set out from Edo, and he observed that the bakufu was faced with 'a genuinely vexing set of circumstances.'[42]

Yoshikatsu arrived in Kyoto to assume command of the Chōshū punitive forces on 9/21 and met with Saigō, who had been appointed as one of his aides. On 10/22 a general strategy meeting convened in Osaka, but by then Saigō and Yoshikatsu had already agreed that they would try to negotiate a peaceful settlement with Chōshū.[43] Saigō's apologists credit him with convincing Yoshikatsu to try negotiation, whereas Conrad Totman asserts that the idea was Yoshikatsu's and Saigō played no significant part in its adoption.[44] Ultimately it makes no important difference whose idea it was to resolve the Chōshū problem with words rather than with weapons. More to the point is what the idea says about Saigō's perception of Japan's situation.

On 1864/9/1 the bakufu had ordered the complete reversal of the reforms carried out after Hisamitsu's trip to Edo in 1862. Combined with its response to the uprising in Mito and other bits of evidence, this move made it clear that a major retrenchment was underway, aimed at restoring the full scope of the bakufu's authority. Given the impact on national politics of Satsuma and other han since 1860, such a retrenchment, if it was to succeed, would have to include a sweeping assault on the initiative and autonomy of han governments. In this light, Saigō began to realize that if Chōshū were crushed, the only remaining threat of any consequence to bakufu power would be Satsuma, which probably would suffer Chōshū's fate if it had to face bakufu military might alone.[45] The bakufu might be feeble by comparison with its early days, but it could still field an army vastly larger than any single han could. Moreover, it was possible that the foreign powers would resort to force if they did not get what they wanted from the bakufu, and this made it doubly important to keep Chōshū's military capabilities intact.

Besides these concerns, Saigō had become convinced that with the right approach Chōshū could be persuaded to surrender and atone for its excesses, and that therefore it was not necessary to fight. Yet the bakufu clearly meant to make an example of Chōshū, and that did not sit well with Saigō at all. As he saw it, if one's opponent were willing to acknowledge his wrong and make amends, there could be no justification for attacking him. To attack anyway in such circumstances would be to destroy one's own claim to righteousness, and would place one even more in the wrong than one's opponent. Both as an official of the punitive army and as a private citizen, Saigō could not tolerate such duplicity in himself. It was no less important for the han. In driving Chōshū away from the palace on 1863/8/18 and again on 1864/7/19 Satsuma had established itself as a loyal and honorable servant of the court. To attack Chōshū when there was no need for it would be no better than what Chōshū had done when it had attacked the palace.[46]

On 10/25 Yoshikatsu left Osaka for his headquarters in Hiroshima, having set 11/18 as the date for a general attack on Chōshū. Saigō set out the next day, and met with Kikkawa Kenmotsu on 11/3. He had with him ten Chōshū samurai who had been captured during Chōshū's assault on Kyoto on 7/19, and he released then into Kikkawa's custody as a sign of his good faith. Leaders of Chōshū's main and collateral han had already met, and had agreed that Chōshū would capitulate, punishing those responsible for the assault on Kyoto and transferring into the care of some neutral han the five court nobles who had fled to Chōshū on 1863/8/18.[47] When Yoshikatsu reached Hiroshima on 11/16, the severed heads of those who had led the assault on Kyoto were waiting there for his inspection. After interrogating Kikkawa and satisfying himself about Chōshū's intentions, he ordered the postponement of the general attack. Saigō wrote that he had accomplished the impossible, and that he now understood what was so good about being a samurai.[48]

With Chōshū's agreement to submit a written apology and to move the five court nobles out of its territory, Saigō's only concern was to see that all the participants kept their promises. By then, however, Chōshū samurai outside the circles of decision making already had taken matters into their own hands. A number of small militia units (*shotai*), led by their creator Taka-sugi Shinsaku, had taken the five nobles and withdrawn into the mountains, giving notice that they had no intention of participating in the humiliation of the han. Unless they could be persuaded to surrender the five men, Saigō feared civil war might erupt in Chōshū and undo all he had accomplished. Having convinced his superiors to let him try persuasion, he hurried from Hiroshima to Kokura, in northern Kyushu. There he met with several men who had been in Chōshū, including two samurai from Fukuoka and the Tosa samurai Nakaoka Shintarō.[49] A faithful Chōshū supporter, Nakaoka had planned to murder Saigō as an act of both revenge and defiance, but after talking with him, he agreed to help persuade Takasugi and his followers to let the five nobles leave Chōshū.[50]

On 12/11 Saigō crossed from Kokura to Shimonoseki and met with Takasugi, Yamagata Aritomo, and other shotai leaders, and convinced them of the necessity of moving the five nobles out of Chōshū. He then returned to Hiroshima to inform Yoshi-katsu of their agreement. Soon after Saigō left Shimonoseki, Taka-sugi and the shotai rose in rebellion against Hagi. Many of the punitive army's commanders saw in this development the failure of the settlement, and wanted to go ahead with the military subjugation of Chōshū. Together, Saigō and Yoshikatsu talked them out of it, and on 12/27 Yoshikatsu ordered the withdrawal of the punitive forces.

According to records kept by the Fukui han field command at Kokura, it was the efforts of Saigō and Kikkawa that had made the peaceful resolution possible.[51] For his own part, Saigō had finally gotten the chance to test the scenario he had been talking about ever since 1862. In going to Shimonoseki, he had placed himself on the 'field of death' defined by Takasugi and Chōshū's other samurai leaders. That he had risked his own life is beyond question; no one else in Japan had better reasons for wanting Saigō dead than the samurai of Chōshū, for it was he more than any other who had humiliated them in their attempt to reclaim Kyoto by force the previous summer. It is equally clear that it was his own personal courage and his readiness to take the Chōshū men at their word that enabled him to win their trust. As Inoue Kiyoshi puts it, he had placed his own beating heart in their hands.[52] What else could they do but agree with him?

Saigō left Kokura early in the new year and arrived in Kagoshima on 1865/1/15. Since his departure from there for Ōshima at the beginning of 1859, he had spent barely a week in the city.[53] Now, yielding to pressure from his friends, and in token recognition of what society expected from a man of his stature, he married for the third and final time.[54] Late in 1864, he had been promoted again, this time to the post of chamberlain (*soba yaku*), which made him a personal advisor to the hanshu.[55] These improvements in his status, combined with the magnificent performance he had just given in Chōshū, must have caused him to question his senses, so completely did they exceed the normal expectations of one who had begun life as a lowly castle town samurai, and who until less than a year earlier had been locked up on a tiny island at the end of the earth, with no prospect of seeing his native land again. At last, perhaps, he had finally seen the realization of some of the great expectations he had come to embrace during his first period of service in Edo with Nariakira between 1854 and 1859, and some of the frustration and embitterment of his years in exile had been recompensed.

Saigō abandons the bakufu:
1865/1–5

If Saigō and Yoshikatsu were pleased with what they had achieved in Chōshū, bakufu leaders were not. Their aim had been to make a dramatic example of Chōshū as part of their effort to regain the authority they had been losing steadily ever since 1853. Though Yoshinobu tended less and less to identify his interests with those of the bakufu in Edo, he too was frustrated at the outcome of the punitive campaign, and he remarked that Yoshikatsu must have gotten drunk on Saigō's influence.[56] Consequently, plans for a second assault on Chōshū began taking shape almost at once.

On 1865/2/5 the bakufu ordered that the Chōshū hanshu Mōri Yoshichika and his son must be brought to Edo under guard, along with the five nobles whom Saigō had succeeded in moving to the ancient provincial capital of Dazaifu in Fukuoka han. There, they were being guarded by a body of men from Fukuoka, Kumamoto, Kurume, Saga, and Satsuma. Because of recent changes in the power structure in Fukuoka, tipping the balance of political influence there in favor of the bakufu, it might soon become impossible to guarantee the safety of the five nobles, and it had been chiefly on the strength of that guarantee that Saigō had persuaded the Chōshū samurai to hand the five men over. In short, he might soon become unable to keep his promises to Takasugi and the others in Chōshū, and his own integrity would come under question.

Saigō went up to Dazaifu and met with the commanders of the guard units on 2/25. He also conferred with the five nobles; this was his first meeting with Sanjō Sanetomi, by far the most outspoken and formidable of the five. Then, on 3/5, he left Fukuoka for Kyoto, having agreed in these conferences to do whatever he could to prevent the bakufu from gaining custody of the nobles.

What he found in Kyoto astonished him. Since their uprising early in 1864, the Mito loyalists not only had managed to hold their own, but had made their way overland as far as Echizen province, not far away from Kyoto and nearly halfway from Mito to Chōshū. Late in the year, however, they surrendered, and over the course of several weeks in early 1865, the bakufu executed nearly 400 of them. Some 450 were left, and they were to be exiled. Satsuma had been ordered to accommodate thirty-five of them in the Amami islands, and to provide a ship to transport them there. Ōkubo, who had taken Saigō's place in Kyoto, refused to have any part in the operation. In an uncharacteristically passionate outburst, he condemned the bakufu for murdering so many men without cause, and predicted its doom.[57]

Saigō, who was not so reticent about his feelings, waxed eloquent. He composed the formal notice of refusal, asserting that no victor ever treated his vanquished foe so cruelly, and that history could offer no precedent for the villainy of the bakufu.[58] He was especially angry that those of low status had not received pardons, or at least more lenient punishments. This was fully in

79

keeping with his view of social relations, predicated as they were for him on a clear hierarchy in which those closer to the top had not only more power and authority, but also more responsibility toward those beneath them. His concern for the proper treatment of defeated enemies, and for the samurai, especially those of low rank, is clearly articulated here for the first time, and it grew stronger as time went on.

The treatment of the Mito insurgents was one of the bakufu's most costly mistakes, because of its profoundly negative effect on popular feeling. But this was not Edo's only problem. Earlier in the year two senior bakufu officials had led a large force of troops to Kyoto with the intention of neutralizing court initiative through a combination of intimidation and bribery. These men demanded the dismissal of Yoshinobu and other bakufu officials in Kyoto, but the court simply ignored them. Instead, it decreed that the troops they had brought with them would take up guard stations along the coast between Osaka and Hyōgo, and the contingent's leaders would return to Edo and bring the shogun to Kyoto with all possible speed. A month later, the court instructed the bakufu to cancel its demand for custody of Chō-shū's leaders and the five nobles, and to rescind its orders for the reversal of the 1862 reforms.

However clear the message in these developments might be, the bakufu did not see it, and went ahead with plans for its second campaign against Chōshū.[59] Saigō remarked that Kagoshima would refuse to participate, insisting that Edo's disagreement with Chōshū was a purely private matter, in which there was no appropriate place for Satsuma or, by implication, for any other third party.[60] He left Kyoto on 4/22 and got back to Kagoshima early the next month. With him was Sakamoto Ryōma, a Tosa samurai who had been working with Katsu Kaishū for some time. Because he had left his han without permission, Sakamoto was considered an outlaw. And because Katsu had recently been dismissed from his bakufu position, he could no longer shelter his protege. So Saigō had agreed to take Sakamoto to Kagoshima with him.

His presence there at just this time was of vital importance. His close friend Nakaoka Shintarō, whom Saigō had met late in 1864, was still in Chōshū, and both men believed that Satsuma and Chōshū must work out a reconciliation of their differences and begin cooperating. With one of them in each han, it was now possible to start working toward this end. During 1865/5

Sakamoto and Nakaoka moved back and forth between Satsuma and Chōshū. They managed to convince Kido Takayoshi, a close associate of Takasugi Shinsaku, to talk with Saigō, and a meeting was set up at Shimonoseki, but then Saigō was summoned to Kyoto and had to go directly there without stopping to meet Kido. Because of delays such as this, and the many long-standing suspicions they did nothing to allay, it was almost another full year before the Satsuma-Chōshū alliance came into being.

While this was going on, Saigō continued to observe the unfolding of events on the national scene. On 1865/i5/5 he wrote that the shogun had left Edo with the aim of leading the second Chōshū campaign himself. His departure from Edo, in Saigō's view:

> ... means only that he will go to greet his nemesis in person. This campaign will not enhance bakufu power. Rather, disorder will increase in the country from now on, and I think the collapse of the Tokugawa is near at hand. ... The shogun's departure from Edo is an occasion for the country to rejōice.[61]

Just prior to this, Ōkubo had made a similar observation. Speaking of the shogun's arrival in Kyoto, Ōkubo said, 'I am looking forward to this eagerly, because it is sure to be an especially interesting performance.'[62]

Remarks such as these are difficult to misunderstand. Both Saigō and Ōkubo now looked forward with undisguised relish to what they felt certain would be the bakufu's humiliation in Chōshū. By the middle of 1865, in other words, both Saigō and Ōkubo had given up on the bakufu, and had begun looking toward the day when it would be no more.

· 4 ·

The Destruction of the Tokugawa Regime, *1865–8*

During the first half of 1865, as the remarks quoted above indicate, it became clear to Saigō and others in Satsuma that there was no longer any point in trying to envision a future for the bakufu. Its determination to conduct a second punitive campaign against Chōshū, combined with its unconscionable treatment of the Mito insurgents, had angered so many people that the only support it still enjoyed came from those who had a personal stake in its survival. Aside from its own members, that included only the French ambassador Leon Roches, who had begun searching for a way to rescue both the bakufu and the Tokugawa family from disaster so as to piece together a client government that would give preferential treatment to French interests in Japan.[1]

Britain, France's chief competitor for advantage in Japan, had realized the futility of supporting Edo, and had begun searching for ways to establish a beneficial relationship with those who seemed most likely to become the new rulers in whatever arrangement emerged from the collapse of the old order. The British ambassador, Sir Harry Parkes, had begun courting Satsuma's leaders, who had accepted his offers of help only with great caution. With no desire to become British proxies, they were willing to let Parkes help them establish contacts through which to purchase Western armaments, but they rebuffed his offers of direct material and financial assistance.[2]

In any case, Saigō and his comrades tended to view the diplomatic contest between Britain and France as a peripheral matter. They realized that unless they could find a way to guide Japan toward stable government, and lay new foundations for Japanese security and sovereignty, it would not matter very much which European power ended up with the greatest advantage. A number of interesting proposals for a new government emerged during the last years of Tokugawa rule, but those in a position to choose among them had little sense as to what alternatives made the most sense.[3] They could only speculate about what might work best, and until the bakufu's remaining political influence in Kyoto was neutralized and they had acquired the power to put their choices into action, even speculation was no more than a secondary concern. The time had now come for them to decide what to do about the bakufu, and to take whatever measures might be required to get it done.[4]

Saigō's trip to Kyoto in 1865/5 marked the beginning of a new pattern in Satsuma's leadership. He had spent most of 1864 in Kyoto, while Ōkubo had stayed in Kagoshima, and though they were directly responsible for carrying out han policies, their authority and their guidance came consistently from Hisamitsu in Kagoshima and from the han elder (*karō*) Komatsu Tatewaki in Kyoto. From early 1865 on, however, they both travelled between Kagoshima and Kyoto more frequently, but they were rarely in the same place at the same time. For the most part, when Saigō was in Kyoto, Ōkubo was in Kagoshima, and vice versa. In the months leading up to 1868, their control of Satsuma's political agenda became progressively more complete, and by the time the court announced the abolition of the bakufu in 1868/1, Hisamitsu and his advisors had receded into the background. Still in full possession of their titular authority, they had nevertheless lost most of their real power.

How this happened is not clear. A large part of it no doubt resulted from Ōkubo's impressive ability to spot opportunities when they arose and to capitalize on them without delay, and from Saigō's equally remarkable ability to mediate between disputing parties and bridge their differences with his considerable powers of persuasion. It is also likely that as these two continued to demonstrate the accuracy of their instincts and to deliver gratifying results, Hisamitsu and his subordinates came to trust them more, and to leave more of the details of the making and implementation of policy in their hands. In the end, what matters is that in Satsuma, as in Chōshū, by the time the final confrontation with Edo came to pass, it was the samurai, mostly of middle and lower rank, who were in charge.[5] Their traditional masters, though still in their traditional positions, had become little more than rubber stamps, with few meaningful prerogatives left other than to validate policies in the making of which they were sometimes not even consulted.

Saigō played a central role at several points in the drama that led to the birth of Meiji Japan, but one can argue that he had already done his most important work in facilitating the negotiated conclusion of the first bakufu campaign against Chōshū at the end of 1864. In saving Chōshū from destruction, he had given its leaders the extra time they needed to consolidate their strength and establish a new agenda for the han.[6] Perhaps more importantly, he had won the trust of a number of men who would soon be in positions of power in that han. The next step was for Satsuma and Chōshū to act on their growing recognition that the dangers they faced together were of more import than the long-standing animosities that divided them, and to work from the interests they had in common to establish a shared program of action that could guarantee their own survival and also could provide the basis for Japan's future survival.[7]

The Satsuma-Chōshū alliance:
1865–6

Once Saigō realized that the bakufu was determined to carry out a second attack on Chōshū, he went back to Kagoshima with Komatsu Tatewaki and Sakamoto Ryōma, intending to unify opinion in the han against the bakufu's plans. His resolve was hardened by his sense of outrage at the harsh treatment the bakufu had enacted against the Mito insurgents. Nakaoka Shintarō had then arrived in Kagoshima with another Satsuma samurai, Iwashita Masahira, whom he had met at Shimonoseki. These two urged Saigō to consider going up to Shimonoseki for a meeting with Kido Takayoshi, to which Kido already had agreed. Saigō concurred completely, and set out at once with that aim in mind. As noted above, however, before the meeting could take place, he received word of new developments in Kyoto, and went directly there instead of keeping his appointment with Kido, leaving no explanation for his failure to appear as promised.

Responding to imperial summons, the shogun had made another trip to Kyoto, eliciting the comments from Saigō and Ōkubo quoted at the end of the last chapter. He arrived on i5/22, and immediately asked the court to issue orders for a second

Chōshū campaign. The court refused, telling him to avoid any further violence, and to try instead to find a way to settle the dispute with Chōshū through consultation. The shogun accepted the order, having little alternative, but no one believed Edo could be made to give up its hostile intentions toward Chōshū as easily as that. Ōkubo had proposed that he should go to Kagoshima and try to persuade the han government to intervene formally on behalf of Chōshū, but Saigō disagreed.

For now, he argued, it was better simply to do nothing, and to let matters unfold. No one in Kagoshima had any hope of persuading bakufu leaders to rethink their plans at this point. Officials in Edo had lost touch with reality, and Saigō saw no point in trying to negotiate with what he called 'a pack of fools.'[8] Trying to talk sense to the bakufu would only cause frustration and anger, and so for now it was better to let them go ahead and try to have their way with Chōshū. It was to be expected that they would try to sow distrust between Satsuma and Chōshū, to forestall the possibility of concerted action. Saigō believed these circumstances presented the two han with a great opportunity, and he warned that failure to take advantage of it might lead to untold difficulties later on.

Ōkubo did return to Kagoshima on 7/8, but as Saigō wrote to him there from Kyoto, if the bakufu did try to go ahead with its second Chōshū campaign it would harm only itself. Officials in Edo had ordered Chōshū to send the hanshu of one of its collateral han to Osaka for cross-examination, but there had been no response. Anti-bakufu feeling was widespread and potent in Chōshū, Saigō reported, while in the Kansai people criticized Edo routinely and openly. A strike against Chōshū could succeed only if it were to be delivered swiftly and precisely, but alas, few of the bakufu's recent moves had been either swift or precise. Once again, Saigō called the bakufu leadership a pack of fools.[9]

Several days later Saigō reported that there appeared to be serious dissension growing within the bakufu, and wondered whether this might lead to even more serious trouble if the shogun were to remain in Osaka, where he had taken up residence after completing his formal business in Kyoto. Saigō concluded that the bakufu was falling apart, and eventually would collapse on its own.[10] There was no way to justify another campaign against Chōshū, Saigō asserted, and in any case, the bakufu would not be able to finish what it began.[11] Saigō's main concern was the welfare of the five nobles, who were still under guard in

Dazaifu. He feared that bakufu agents would manage to intimidate Fukuoka han officials and gain custody of the nobles, and
he insisted that Satsuma must be ready to intervene if that happened. Those five men must be protected at any cost; Saigō had
promised in Satsuma's name that they would be safe, so the good
faith (*shingi*) of the han was at stake.[12]

As Saigō was making these observations, during the summer
of 1865, Sakamoto and Nakaoka had continued in their efforts
to get Kido together with Saigō for discussions. On 6/24 the two
Tosa samurai arrived in Kyoto from Chōshū and told Saigō that
Chōshū leaders were still willing to talk, provided that Satsuma
could do something to demonstrate its own sincerity. As a symbolic gesture, Saigō proposed that Satsuma might employ its
connections with Thomas Glover, the English merchant in Nagasaki, to help Chōshū acquire the ships and firearms it needed
but had been unable to acquire on its own.[13] In return, Chōshū
might supply rice and other provisions for the maintenance of
Satsuma's troops in Kyoto, since that would save Satsuma the
trouble and expense of shipping those supplies all the way from
Kagoshima.[14] By the end of 1865, with the way smoothed
through these gestures of good faith, both sides were ready to
talk, and Sakamoto began urging Saigō to make the first move.

In the meanwhile, however, Saigō and Sakamoto had gone
back to Kagoshima on 9/24 to bring Hisamitsu up to date, and
to urge him to lead troops to Kyoto. Instead, Hisamitsu sent
Saigō and Komatsu back with the troops. They arrived in Kyoto
on 10/25 and immediately sent Kuroda Kiyotaka, another Satsuma samurai, to Chōshū to begin conversations with Kido.
Because other leaders in Chōshū were in favor of an agreement
with Satsuma, the habitually cautious Kido had to put his own
reservations aside and agree, but as with Saigō, it was Sakamoto
who finally managed to persuade him.[15] He arrived in Osaka on
1866/1/4. Saigō met him at Fushimi on 1/8, and escorted him to
the Satsuma residence in Kyoto, where Ōkubo, Komatsu, and
Saigō's old friend Katsura Hisatake entertained him lavishly. The
atmosphere was cordial, and there was a great deal of talk and
agreement about the crises facing Japan, but neither Kido nor
anyone from Satsuma wanted to be the first to broach the subject
of a formal alliance between the two han. After nearly two weeks,
Kido was out of patience, and was about to leave when Sakamoto
arrived, on 1/21.

Astonished that nothing had happened yet, Sakamoto got

Kido and Saigō talking substance the next day, and with his help they quickly worked out the terms of an agreement.[16] The resulting alliance between Satsuma and Chōshū was of decisive importance for the fate of the bakufu, though it is important to note that the two han had by no means joined forces to create a new government, but only to forget past hostilities and join forces for mutual survival. As Inoue Kiyoshi puts it, they had agreed to recognize a common foe in the bakufu.[17] As we have seen, Saigō had discovered this truth for himself during 1864; the new alliance now gave it formal expression. The main significance of this alliance was that it formally acknowledged the bankruptcy of the bakufu, and thus also, at least implicitly, the need to replace it with some other form of government. By the end of 1864, in other words, a few influential individuals had given up on the bakufu; by the beginning of 1866, the two most powerful outside domains in Japan had done so.

Saigō had already made his feelings about the bakufu abundantly clear, however, before 1866 began. On 12/6 he wrote to Minoda Denbei, one of Tadayoshi's advisors in Kagoshima, arguing that Satsuma should remove all of its personnel from Edo and close down its establishments there.[18] With the relaxation of the alternate attendance (*sankin kōtai*) system under the reforms resulting from Hisamitsu's visit to Edo in 1862, there was no further need to maintain residences in Edo, and even some of the Tokugawa family's own relatives (*shinpan*) already had withdrawn from the city. As Saigō saw it, the only Satsuma personnel still arguing in favor of remaining in Edo were either afraid of the bakufu, which was patently silly, or reluctant to move away from the sordid pleasures of Edo's brothel district, which was despicable. Already, in Saigō's view, the national unity once predicated on the bakufu had been lost, and Japan had fragmented into self-sufficient local units (*kakkyō*). Civil cohesion no longer existed, and civil war was bound to erupt eventually. When the crisis came, moreover, the outcome would be settled in Kyoto, not in Edo.

In another letter on the same day, Saigō spoke of the bakufu's ongoing failure to elicit any responsiveness from Chōshū. Most people were simply disgusted with Yoshinobu's efforts to gain control of national politics, and his only remaining supporters were the Tokugawa vassal domains of Aizu and Kuwana. Only a hero could save the day now, Saigō argued, and only an assembly of daimyo like that earlier proposed by Katsu could now hope to govern the realm (*tenka*) effectively.[19] On 12/12 Saigō reported with disgust that Shibata Tōgorō, a direct bakufu vassal (*hatamoto*) originally from the Satsuma collateral han of Miyakonojō, had tried to talk Satsuma officials in Kyoto into helping the bakufu.[20]

Meanwhile, the dissension Saigō had noticed earlier in the bakufu was resolving itself into a clear rift between officials in the bureaucracy in Edo (*bakkaku*) and those around Yoshinobu in Kyoto. Representatives from the Edo bakkaku already had tried to bribe Satsuma into siding with them against Yoshinobu's faction, offering the sum of 5,000 ryō as a reward for Satsuma's services during the Chōshū attack on Kyoto on 1864/7/19. Saigō responded to this overture with open disgust, and approved of the han's decision to reject the money. After all, Satsuma had not defended the imperial palace in the hope of material reward, but rather out of a sense of loyalty and duty. To accept the bribe would be to cheapen the han's integrity, to insult the hanshu Tadayoshi, and to invite ridicule from all other han.

In short, as far as Saigō was concerned, the Tokugawa world of bakufu and han (*bakuhan seidō*) was already in effect a thing of the past, its eventual destruction no more than a matter of time after the beginning of 1866. What would replace it was still a matter for open speculation, and there was still a great deal of hard struggle ahead, but in Saigō's mind it was now clear which options for the future no longer remained viable. Of course, there were a good many others who did not see things this way. Some still believed the bakufu could be saved. Some had given up on the bakufu but still hoped to keep the Tokugawa family in power. Some hoped for the creation of a genuine deliberative assembly of major daimyo, including the Tokugawa, to be sure, but ranking them as equals with all the others. And some feared that Satsuma and Chōshū would combine forces to destroy the Tokugawa bakufu and replace it with a new bakufu of their own.

The second Chōshū campaign:
1865–6

When the squadron of Western ships left Yokohama to conduct a second attack on Shimonoseki in 1864, it had been widely assumed that they would not stop with the punishment of

Chōshū, but would eventually turn up at Osaka to press their demands for the opening of Hyōgo. On 1865/9/16, nine steamships dropped anchor at Hyōgo, and those assumptions became a reality. Saigō and Sakamoto went down to Osaka to look at this flotilla, and then left there on 9/24 hoping to persuade Hisamitsu to lead troops back to Kyoto. This was an opportunity for which Saigō had been waiting ever since his meeting with Katsu.

This new move by the Western powers presented a challenge to the court itself, and the only way to meet that challenge safely and effectively was to assemble the daimyo council, proposed by Katsu and advocated by Saigō at every opportunity since their meeting, to hold 'deliberations on the affairs of the realm' (*tenka no kōron*).[21] Unfortunately, the court was still paralyzed by the same lack of vision and conviction Saigō had lamented in the spring of 1864. If the bakufu were to prevail on the demoralized court and get its approval for the opening of Hyōgo, 'nothing would be more shameful for the imperial realm' (*kōkoku*).[22] However, thanks to the skillful maneuvers of Yoshinobu, that is almost exactly what did happen.

On 9/20 there was a meeting at the court to discuss the opening of Hyōgo, and most bakufu representatives argued for approval, but Yoshinobu had an agenda of his own, and used his influence in the court to prevent the formation of a consensus.[23] Using the threat of resignation, as he had done before, he persuaded the court to issue orders on 9/21, not for the opening of Hyōgo, but for a second punitive campaign against Chōshū. The court insisted on calling a daimyo council to discuss the Hyōgo question, but on 10/1, before this deadlock could be broken, the shogun Iemochi packed up and left Osaka for Edo without warning. Yoshinobu, together with Matsudaira Katamori, the hanshu of Aizu, persuaded him to come back, and in the wake of this unexpected move, the court on 10/5 announced its approval for the bakufu's treaties with the West, but not for the opening of Hyōgo. A daimyo council would convene to decide that issue. The foreign powers hoisted anchor and left Hyōgo for Yokohama on 10/8, evidently satisfied by these developments.

No one emerged from these events in a better position than Yoshinobu, and for Saigō this meant that a collision between Satsuma and the bakufu was now the only way to preserve the interests of both the han and the country. As we have seen, he returned to Kyoto on 10/25, soon after Yoshinobu's success, and at once began making the preparations that led eventually to the Satsuma-Chōshū alliance. While this was happening, Yoshinobu was instructing the court concerning the need to humble Chōshū, and on 1866/1/23 the court accepted Yoshinobu's recommendations.[24] Within Satsuma, these events caused the balance of feeling to shift decisively toward a confrontation with Edo. On 3/4, Saigō left Osaka, accompanied by Sakamoto and his wife, and reached Kagoshima seven days later.

Saigō's first concern after returning to Kagoshima was to check on the well-being of the five nobles at Dazaifu. As he had feared, the bakufu had sent agents to Fukuoka to arrest the five men and bring them to Edo. To prevent this, Saigō sent Kuroda Kiyotsuna to Dazaifu with a contingent of troops and orders to defend the nobles at any cost. As it turned out, the bakufu agents did not give up until Kuroda's troops confronted them with drawn swords.[25]

During 1866/2, Saigō had expressed regret that Yoshinobu, supported staunchly by Aizu and Kuwana, had gained control of the court, and was flirting with the French ambassador Leon Roches, whose own efforts to ingratiate himself with Edo continued unabated. Edo was caught in a bind, with no idea how best to reconcile the conflicting demands of court, han, and foreigners, and Saigō took some relish in observing that for the bakufu, choosing a policy likely to satisfy everyone was 'about as risky as trying to stack eggs.'[26] In particular, Edo officials were at a loss as to how to get any response from Chōshū, and had been sending officials to Hiroshima, still the bakufu military headquarters as it had been during the first punitive expedition, with one set of demands after another. Saigō believed the outcome of this process might well determine the future shape of the country (*tenka no keisei*).[27] Moreover, if Chōshū and Edo were to go to war, the resulting disruption might well provoke widespread peasant uprisings, and that in turn would only hasten the collapse of the bakufu.[28] When Saigō left Osaka on 3/4 with Sakamoto and his wife, it was with the recognition that the situation was nearing a point of crisis, and it was urgent for Satsuma to prepare itself for whatever might come next.[29]

In the meantime, Saigō had heard from Iwashita Masahira about meetings the latter had had in Edo with Leon Roches and Sir Harry Parkes.[30] Iwashita had told both men that if the Western powers expected to realize the ambitions that lay behind their treaties with Japan, they had best forget about the bakufu, and begin relying on the court and the great daimyo. These latter had a reasonable chance of keeping their promises; Edo no longer had any such hope. Roches was not interested in anything Iwashita had to say, committed as he was to forging some sort of unilateral link with Edo. Parkes, on the other hand, was so impressed with Iwashita's arguments that he requested a meeting with Saigō and Satsuma's other leaders in Kagoshima, to which we will return presently.

On 1866/5/1, Saigō was appointed along with Komatsu Tate-waki, Katsura Hisatake, and a number of others to carry out reforms in Kagoshima. Some of these men, including Godai Tomoatsu, had just returned from Europe, where they had been negotiating with various commercial firms both to arrange for help in setting up new industrial facilities in Kagoshima and to initiate regular trading relationships.[31] On 5/10, Saigō wrote to Ōkubo that the reforms were proceeding well, adding that he felt confident that the affairs of the han and of the country were in capable hands with Ōkubo. He himself had meanwhile taken some time off to recuperate at a hot spring, he said.[32] The waters evidently did not have the desired effect, because Saigō had further problems with his health in the autumn. When he was promoted to chief inspector (*ometsuke*) he declined on account of illness. However, he was not so ill as to reject his appointment at about this same time to the han's council of elders (*karōza*), which was the highest and most powerful political body in the han after the daimyo himself.

Saigō's confidence in Ōkubo was well-placed, as the latter demonstrated between 3/11 and 10/15, while evading bakufu efforts to order Satsuma to mobilize troops for the second Chōshū campaign.[33] Saigō was ecstatic when he learned of Ōkubo's refusal to involve Satsuma in this new campaign. On 5/29 he wrote Ōkubo to tell him how his courage had galvanized popular feeling in Satsuma. Both Hisamitsu and Tadayoshi were pleased with Ōkubo's actions, while he himself could only dance with delight. Ōkubo's exemplary action, he asserted, would help to clarify what was at stake in the national political struggle; moreover, it was a 'beautiful thing for the domain.'[34] However, regardless of Satsuma's refusal to participate, bakufu forces began fighting along Chōshū's borders on 1866/6/7, in what was to evolve into an unmitigated disaster for Edo.[35]

Not long after this, as noted above, the relationship between Satsuma and England, which had begun unfortunately enough at

Namamugi in 1862, and had then evolved even more regrettably in the bombardment of Kagoshima the following summer, took a more constructive turn. After meticulously careful preparations on both sides, Sir Harry Parkes visited Kagoshima from 6/17 through 6/22.³⁶ On 6/18, Saigō and Parkes exchanged views aboard HMS *Princess Royal*, with Terajima Munenori, recently back from studies in England, acting as interpreter. In England, Terajima had become friends with prominent government and business leaders, including Laurence Oliphant. He had told Oliphant that most of Japan's trade goods were produced by individual han, not by the bakufu, and that it therefore made more sense for Western countries to deal directly with the han. As a result of these conversations, the British government had told Parkes to seek closer ties with Satsuma.

Asked about Terajima's claims by Parkes, Saigō agreed that they made sense, but only up to a point. In theory, practically any of the han, backed by the authority of the court, had the power to guarantee the observance of agreements between Japan and the West, whereas the bakufu had lost the ability to guarantee much of anything, because it no longer represented the popular will. However, the han, like the bakufu, were fundamentally incapable of representing any interests but their own, so it was not a good idea to negotiate directly with them. International agreements binding on the whole country could only be made with the country's sovereign government, which was in Kyoto. The best way to protect the interests of both Japan and the Western powers was to convene a daimyo council. For one thing, such a body would speak for the leaders in the court, standing between them and the foreigners with whom they had no desire for direct contact, and thereby winning their support away form Yoshinobu, who had more than once been able to influence them by threatening to resign and leave them to face the West alone. For another, it would eliminate the dangers of particularism inherent in direct negotiations with any single han.³⁷ Parkes made no comment on Saigō's statements, but by the time he left Kagoshima he seemed pleased with all he had seen and heard.

If things appeared to be getting better for Satsuma, they were getting drastically worse for the bakufu, whose forces had met with one defeat after another in Chōshū, and whose fortunes seemed to have hit bottom on 7/20 when the shogun died in Osaka castle. On the same day, the court received a memorial from Hisamitsu condemning the Chōshū campaign.³⁸ Hisamitsu called on the court to recognize the evidence accumulating everywhere, and to give serious thought to a change in government structure (*seitai henkaku*) so as to facilitate more effective handling of public affairs (*tenka no kōgi*).[39] Commenting on this memorial, Saigō wrote to Ōkubo that, since it was daily more obvious that neither France nor any han would be able to rescue the bakufu, perhaps the time had come to return the emperor to power.[40] Meanwhile, unable to prevail militarily, the bakufu had sent Katsu Kaishū to Hiroshima to try to negotiate a cease-fire with Chōshū. On 10/15, Saigō set out for Kyoto to meet with Ōkubo and discuss the new possibilities created by the death of Iemochi. Then, on 12/5, the bakufu named Yoshinobu the new shogun. Twenty days later, on the 25th, the emperor Kōmei died, and was succeeded on 1867/1/9 by the young Mutsuhito, whose reign was designated Meiji. These events altered the political situation dramatically.

Since 1853, Kōmei had been unflinching in his refusal to contemplate a foreign presence of any kind in Japan, and it had been in response to his firm position that Iemochi had been obliged to make his promise of expulsion in 1863. However, Kōmei had also been a stauch supporter of the institutional status quo, with the bakufu exercising delegated authority to govern the country. With Kōmei removed from the picture, there was no longer any significant force within the court to keep people from thinking about some alternative to the bakufu and its rule. With the convenient breaks in continuity provided by the deaths of Iemochi and Kōmei, and the appointment of Yoshinobu as shogun, then, it appeared that there might be no better time to call a daimyo council so as to try working out some new arrangement.

Yoshinobu's appointment as head of the bakufu had already given Edo an important jump on this process, but bakufu opponents had an equal advantage in the malleability of the new emperor, whose youth and lack of experience meant that he would pose no obstruction to their plans, and to whose authority they could appeal as a check on bakufu initiative.[41] Ōkubo was particularly intrigued by the new possibilities opening up. He had been in contact with Iwakura Tomomi, a young noble who had been purged from the court for his extremist views before Chōshū was driven out of Kyoto by Satsuma and Aizu on 1863/8/18, and had been confined to his lodgings north of the city ever since. Ōkubo and Iwakura had begun talking in detail about

the possibility of an imperial restoration.[42] Saigō was also beginning to see new possibilities. On 12/9 he went to Osaka and met
for the first time with Parkes' capable interpreter, Ernest Satow.

Saigō had learned from Godai Tomoatsu that Satow was at
Hyōgo and wanted to talk to someone in authority from Satsuma. As Saigō reported the conversation to Komatsu on 12/9,[43]
Satow was having trouble understanding why, if the bakufu was
actually the government of Japan, it could not control the
behavior of the domains under its authority, such as Satsuma and
Chōshū. How could it hope to govern the entire country if, as
it had shown, it could not even defeat a single domain? England
could hardly make treaties with a powerless government, Satow
stated, but it was impossible to tell where to turn, if not to Edo.
In fact, it was not clear that Japan had any government at all.
Saigō replied that Satsuma and Chōshū intended to combine their
resources in support of the court, and that within two or three
years the confusion would be resolved. Astonished, Satow
pointed out that Japan did not have two or three years to play
with, and that the issues of Chōshū and Hyōgo must be resolved
without delay. Moreover, England was worried about France's
efforts to join forces with Edo, and unless Satsuma took the lead
and moved quickly, Yoshinobu, backed by France, might well
finesse the entire game. If Satsuma moved promptly, on the other
hand, it probably could take advantage of the unresolved Chōshū
and Hyōgo issues to corner Yoshinobu and force substantial
concessions from him.

Satow's view of the situation, no doubt rendered more plausible by his impressive command of Japanese, erased whatever
doubts may have remained in Saigō's mind about the advisability
of convening a daimyo council. On 1867/1/22 he left Kyoto for
Kagoshima, determined to persuade Hisamitsu to take part in a
meeting of great han leaders in Kyoto.

The failure of deliberation:
1867/4–9

Saigō reached Kagoshima on 2/1, but before he could do anything, he was immobilized by illness, as he reported to Ōkubo
at the end of the month.[44] While he recuperated, he lobbied
influential members of the han government, so that when they

met to consider Hisamitsu's involvement in the daimyo council, they were already in agreement. Hisamitsu agreed to participate in a meeting of daimyo, so Saigō hurried to Shikoku, where he met with Yamauchi Yōdō in Kōchi and with Date Munenari in Uwajima. Both men agreed to join the council, and Saigō hurried back to Kagoshima, arriving on 2/27. A month later he left Kagoshima with Hisamitsu, accompanied by some 700 troops, and they reached Kyoto on 4/12. Munenari and Shungaku arrived soon after them, and Yōdō, the final member of this core group, got to the city on 5/1.[45]

This was the second time these four men – Hisamitsu, Shungaku, Munenari, and Yōdō – had gathered in Kyoto for deliberations, but their chances of achieving anything were not much better than they had been the first time. Yoshinobu still enjoyed considerable influence in the court, and these four were not united in their views. Hisamitsu was clear about one thing, at any rate. On 4/20 he was summoned to pay his respects to Yoshinobu at Nijō castle, but he politely refused, stating that he must make his bows at the court first.[46]

Discussions began on 4/21, before Yōdō's arrival, and continued for over a month. As before, the stumbling block proved to be the question of whether Hyōgo or Chōshū should be dealt with first. Hisamitsu and Shungaku argued that an appropriate settlement of the Chōshū question would enhance bakufu credibility within Japan, while Yoshinobu, supported chiefly by Yōdō, held that the international issue raised by the Hyōgo problem should take precedence over the purely domestic question of Chōshū. When they moved their discussions to the court, this deadlock persisted. On 5/24 the court finally decreed that Chōshū should be treated leniently and that Hyōgo should be opened for foreign trade.

This amounted to complete victory for Yoshinobu. Hisamitsu, Shungaku, and Munenari petitioned the court to stipulate that the bakufu must pardon and reinstate both the hanshu of Chōshū, Mōri Yoshichika, and his son, but before this matter could be discussed, Yōdō left Kyoto for home on 5/27, effectively dissolving the council.[47] Thus the meetings accomplished little, though Hisamitsu, with Shungaku's help, had managed to gain some concessions for Chōshū. With Yoshinobu the clear winner, the other members of the group had little reason to remain. Shungaku, Munenari, and Hisamitsu all left Kyoto by the middle of 1867/8. Hisamitsu had moved from Kyoto to Osaka, and after getting court approval for a proxy to represent him, he left for Kagoshima on 9/10.[48]

The great han council which Katsu had proposed and in which he and many others had placed such great hope thus had proved a mere straw in the wind. If the four core members had been more united in their thinking, or if they had had a less determined and resourceful adversary than Yoshinobu, they might have accomplished more. As it was, the times had changed too much, and it was far too late for any combination of constituents drawn from the traditional bakuhan order to address the problems now facing Japan.

While the daimyo council met, Satsuma's lower ranking leaders met also, and on four occasions Saigō conveyed their views to Hisamitsu in memorials.[49] In all four documents, Saigō insists that loyalty to the court and concern for the will of the people must be uppermost in Hisamitsu's considerations, but the first memorial is of particular interest because in it Saigō argues for the first time that 'a restoration (*isshin*) is of first priority.' The most trenchant statement of his views comes in the third document.

There, he argues that the way to put the minds of the people at ease is to restore power to the court, reduce the bakufu to the same status as other han, and decide the fate of the country on the basis of 'public affairs' (*tenka no kōgi*). The court must then negotiate new treaties with the foreign powers, within the framework of international law. Saigō urges Hisamitsu to do his utmost for the imperial realm, restore power to the emperor, and carry out a restoration.[50] In the fourth document, Saigō argues that it is vital to gain popular support by recognizing the will of the people and displaying sincerity which, as the manifestation of administrative integrity, is the essence of good government.[51] In other words, Saigō is here asking Hisamitsu to behave in the manner and by the criteria that took form in Saigō's mind during his years in exile. Thus, after working his way toward the idea by a number of different routes over the course of the preceding five years and more, Saigō had finally arrived at the belief that imperial restoration was the solution to Japan's problems. And in arguing for it, he had appealed for support to the beliefs he had put together while on Okinoerabu.

While the great daimyo group attempted to settle disputed matters through deliberation, other developments continued apace. On 6/16, Hisamitsu had an audience with two Chōshū samurai, Yamagata Aritomo and Shinagawa Yajirō, in which he explained Satsuma's position on the state of national affairs. They then met with Saigō, Ōkubo, Komatsu, and Ijichi Masaharu, to discuss details. On 6/17 they headed back to Hagi to brief Mōri Yoshichika, and to tell him that Satsuma, like Chōshū, was now ready to start preparing for what they all had begun to call *buryoku tōbaku*, the overthrow of the bakufu by armed force.

In the meantime, two different agendas emerged from Tosa. On 5/21 there was a meeting at Komatsu's residence where Itagaki Taisuke explained that while Yōdō was clearly pro-bakufu, most of Tosa's lower-ranking samurai were not, and wanted to join forces with Satsuma and Chōshū in planning the destruction of the bakufu. Then, on 6/14, three other Tosa samurai – Sakamoto, Nakaoka, and Gotō Shōjirō – arrived in Kyoto with a proposal for a Satsuma-Tosa alliance. During their sea voyage from Kyushu, Sakamoto had spoken to Gotō about an eight-point outline he had devised for government reform and Gotō, who was close to Yōdō, was much impressed.[52] After talking with these men, on 6/22 Saigō agreed to an alliance between Satsuma and Tosa in which the two han would cooperate. This pact was based on the assumption that something like Sakamoto's eight-point outline would serve as a starting point for the creation of a new government, but it made no mention of armed force. Gotō left Kyoto on 7/3 to meet with Yōdō and discuss with him the posibility of trying to persuade Yoshinobu to avert a military confrontation by surrendering his authority to the court voluntarily (*taisei hōkan*).

With the forging of the Satsuma-Tosa alliance, Saigō had once again gotten himself caught between mutually exclusive commitments. Strictly speaking, the Satsuma-Chōshū alliance was not an agreement to destroy either the bakufu or the Tokugawa, and the two han did not formally agree on those aims until 10/8, but by the middle of 1867/6 those were their aims, in fact, and they had already begun making preparations to carry them out. Now Saigō had committed Satsuma to a new pact with Tosa, whose effect would have been to sacrifice the bakufu deliberately in order to save the Tokugawa family and its power. On the face of things, Saigō was now deceiving either Chōshū or Tosa. According to the editors of the *Saigō Takamori zenshū*,[53] Saigō did not think Gotō and Yōdō would be able to persuade Yoshinobu to surrender his authority to the court, and so their plans posed no real threat, but since neither Saigō nor anyone else yet had any good ideas about the shape of the new government, he had decided that Sakamoto's eight-point outline would serve as a place to start, and so had agreed to the Tosa alliance as a way to give that outline some formal status. It is also possible that Saigō saw his show of support for Tosa's taisei hōkan strategy as a way to distract Yōdō and other bakufu supporters, and thereby to gain some time for Satsuma and Chōshū to complete their preparations for the coming confrontation.

I have argued that Saigō was attracted temperamentally to a formulaic or aphoristic style of thinking, and that therefore he sometimes found it difficult to grasp the subtleties of complex propositions. I think that difficulty was real enough that it should be part of any interpretation of Saigō, but it is hard to believe he was so profoundly obtuse as to be unaware of the apparent duplicity of his agreement with Gotō. Writing to Shinagawa and Yamagata in Chōshū on 7/7, Saigō described the alliance with Tosa as an 'expedient' (*watari ni fune*),[54] which suggests that he did understand what he had done. If that is the case, then this stands as the most conspicuous instance of willful deceit in a life that was otherwise remarkably free of double dealing. One wonders how Saigō may have felt about this flagrant inconsistency as time went on, but he has left us no clues about that.

About a month after Saigō signed the Satsuma-Tosa alliance, he had a second meeting with Ernest Satow in Osaka, which he reported in letters to Ōkubo on 7/27 and to Katsura Hisatake on 8/4.[55] Satow, he said, was still angry about Leon Roches' continuing machinations in Edo, and Saigō played on Satow's sense of righteous indignation in the hope that anger might prompt him to reveal more about Britain's intentions than discretion would allow. Satow warned Saigō that even if Satsuma and Chōshū did combine their forces, they would not be able to resist a bakufu army trained and supplied by France. Such an eventuality would cancel any hope the two han had of replacing the bakufu with a more effective government for Japan. Such a change of government was what Britain hoped for also, but its official position of neutrality would keep it from intervening in Japanese affairs unless asked to do so. If Satsuma and Chōshū so desired, Britain would provide all the help it could, but it was up to them to make the request.

As Saigō explained in his letters, this was exactly what he had hoped to achieve by provoking Satow's anger. He had had no intention of asking for British aid, but he had feared that if he simply said that, Satow might misunderstand his disclaimer as a covert request. By getting Satow to make an explicit offer of help, Saigō also could make his explicit refusal that much more unequivocal. In any case, he made his position quite clear. Japan, he said, would take care of its own domestic problems, and would transform its government to the best of its ability without foreign help. Satsuma and Chōshū meant to go it alone against Edo, and accept whatever consequences might follow, relying only on what support they could get from Tosa, Higo, Aki, Fukui, and a few other han. Satow pointed out that there might be some reason for optimism: France was likely to be at war with Prussia soon, and certainly would not give the bakufu resources it needed to fight its own battles closer to home. Saigō agreed that a war between France and Prussia undoubtedly would be a boon for Japan. But he also admitted that he felt profoundly ashamed at finding advantage for Japan in the tribulations of other peoples.[56]

Out of the failure of the daimyo council experiment, then, three strategies had taken shape by mid-summer, 1867. In the first (buryoku tōbaku) Satsuma and Chōshū, aided by Tosa, Higo, and Aki, envisioned the destruction of the bakufu and the removal of the Tokugawa from power. Success in this approach would clear the ground completely for the creation of a new Japanese government. In the second (taisei hōkan) a small group from Tosa envisioned a less drastic scenario, predicated likewise on the destruction of the bakufu, but assuming also that some way could be found to retain the Tokugawa family in power under a different institutional arrangement. The feasibility of this outcome was to be guaranteed by Yoshinobu, who would take the initiative and return to the court all powers and entitlements he enjoyed as shogun. This would cut the ground from under the bakufu, leading to its demise, but it would not endanger the prerogatives of the Tokugawa family. The third approach (kōgi seitai) likewise saw the removal of the bakufu as the first priority, and the preservation of the Tokugawa family as the second, but it was willing to go further in disempowering the Tokugawa, so as to make possible the creation of a more egalitarian deliberative form of government with its center of gravity no longer located in the Tokugawa family.

Leaders in Satsuma and Chōshū understood clearly that neither taisei hōkan nor kōgi seitai would go far enough to solve the problems of the Japanese polity they had joined forces to address. Thus, in the final months of 1867, there evolved a contest whose purpose was to decide which of these three agendas would prevail. The outcome may have been a foregone conclusion, as it certainly appears to be in hindsight, but Saigō and his colleagues faced a number of extremely resourceful opponents, and there were still many among the elite in their own han who disapproved of their plans, and resisted their implementation however they could.[57]

The destruction of the early modern order

One of the first things to happen as autumn began was the failure of the Satsuma-Tosa alliance. On 9/7, Gotō attended a meeting of Satsuma's leaders, and learned for the first time of the tobaku plans taking shape. He pleaded with Saigō to delay acting so that Yōdō would have time to try his taisei hōkan approach, but Saigō refused, saying that the time for talk was past. He promised that no one would interefere with taisei hōkan, but he formally repudiated the alliance with Tosa. In no case, he warned, would Satsuma and Chōshū alter their plans for the sake of Tosa's.[58]

This attitude created some problems with the tobaku alliance as well. Aki han had expressed interest in joining forces with Satsuma and Chōshū, but was reluctant to commit itself fully to the tōbaku agenda until Yōdō had had a chance to see whether taisei hōkan might work. Even after joining the tōbaku alliance formally inaugurated on 10/8, Aki continued to harbor doubts. Except for Satsuma and Chōshū, most of those involved in the events of late 1867 continued to vacillate until the ambiguities were summarily erased by the outbreak of fighting between imperial and Tokugawa armies at Toba and Fushimi. In the meantime, forces that had been in motion since as early as 1862 continued to focus and converge, and the pace of events accelerated steadily toward the denouement.

Early in 1867/10, Ōkubo met with Shinagawa and Iwakura to plan the logistical details of the coup d'etat they were calling the 'return to rule by the emperor as in the days of old' (ōsei fukko). Naturally their primary concern was with such practical matters as where to position troop units, and what to do in case things went contrary to expectations.[59] Writing to Kuroda Kiyotaka on 11/27, Saigō reviewed the essentials of their strategy.[60] Troops from Satsuma, Chōshū, and Aki would use Osaka as their base. Satsuma would occupy and secure Kyoto, while

Chōshū and Aki would deploy around the city to serve as relief if needed. If things went badly, Satsuma troops would disguise the emperor and slip him out of the palace to a place of safety in Aki. No doubt Saigō's prior experiences of combat in the streets of Kyoto qualified him to evaluate strategic problems and address them effectively.

Ōkubo, who had looked forward to the second Chōshū campaign as an 'interesting drama' in 1865,[61] was careful to see to it that the coup he now plotted would have ample dramatic elements of its own. Like most of his colleagues, he understood that their actions must include good theater, as well as good strategy and tactics; the history of previous transfers of power in Japanese politics made it clear that whether a turnover *was right* or not, it could not be guaranteed success unless it also *looked right*. Thus, he agreed with Shinagawa and Iwakura that they should have an ample supply of silk battle flags made up in advance, bearing the devices of the imperial army, to help make it clear to bystanders both who they were and what were the sources of their legitimacy.[62] These plans were worth the effort, evidently. When the imperial armies advanced through Toba and Fushimi to confront bakufu loyalists in battle, people along the way greeted them as liberators, cheering and dancing, running into their midst, and offering them food, liquor, and other gifts. According to Saigō, these same crowds greeted Satsuma's banners with cries of 'Satsuma, Great Radiant Deity' (*Satsuma daimyōjin sama*).[63]

Saigō was only slightly less conscious of appearances than Ōkubo, and often referred to the emperor as 'the jewel' (*tama*), expressing an attitude that was widespread among the bakufu's enemies. As they put it repeatedly in their diaries and letters, they must 'seize the jewel' (*tama o obau*).[64] It would not be enough, in other words, merely to control the imperial palace or the members of the court; they must control the physical person of the emperor himself. It would be risky, if not actually impossible, for them to issue decrees in the emperor's name, or to speak in his behalf, if he were himself at liberty to come forth and issue conflicting decrees, or to speak in his own behalf. As they understood keenly, one cannot manipulate the contents of symbols unless one has uncontested control of the physical objects in which they are embodied. Thus these men were all mindful of the need to secure the emperor, whom they understood to be the most important symbol of all.

With all preparations completed, on 10/8 Saigō, Ōkubo, and Komatsu submitted a petition to the court asking for a decree to topple the bakufu.[65] It justified the destruction of the bakufu as a step necessary to clarify the obligations (*taigi*) incumbent on the emperor's supporters, and to bring into play the true will of the emperor himself (*magokoro*). The crimes of the bakufu included violating court decrees, forgetting the duty of an imperial servant, failing to expel the foreigners, losing the confidence of the people, and generally bringing chaos upon the realm. That is, the bakufu was to blame both for domestic unrest (*naiyū*) and for external peril (*gaikan*). Yoshinobu had committed violations of his own, employing threats and guile to manipulate the court for his own selfish ends, and obstructing the sincere efforts of others to find solutions to Japan's problems. Tōbaku orders were issued as requested, to Satsuma on 10/13 and to Chōshū on 10/14, thus giving the two han imperial authority to make war on the bakufu and its supporters, specifically Aizu and Kuwana.[66] By the time these orders came out, however, Yoshinobu already had taken the initiative, changing the political stakes once again, and cutting the ground from under his opponents.

On 10/3 Gotō had delivered Yōdō's proposal for taisei hōkan, and on 10/13 – the same day Satsuma's tōbaku order was issued – Yoshinobu assembled all of the daimyo then in Kyoto at Nijō castle and informed them of his decision to return his authority to the emperor. His own petition to the court arrived there on 10/14 – the same day Chōshū's tōbaku order came down – and was accepted the next day. Thus, before Satsuma and Chōshū could act on their authority to destroy the bakufu, Yoshinobu effectively dissolved it by giving its prerogatives back to the court. Ten days later, on 10/25, Yoshinobu resigned his appointment as shogun.[67] The court deferred acceptance of this resignation pending deliberations by a council of all major daimyo in the country, including Yoshinobu. He had surrendered his political authority to the court, but he had retained his court rank and the other perquisites of his status as head of the Tokugawa family, including all hereditary lands and vassals belonging to them. Thus he was no longer shogun, but he was still far and away the most powerful daimyo in the country, and still well placed to take control of whatever new political arrangement might take shape.[68]

The struggle was far from over, then, in spite of the careful manipulation of all the right symbols by the leaders of Satsuma and Chōshū. These men had left Kyoto in a body on 10/19, before Yoshinobu had completed his preemptive maneuvers. After presenting Chōshū's tōbaku order to Mōri Yoshichika and his son, they went on to present Satsuma's to Tadayoshi and Hisamitsu, arriving at Kagoshima on 10/26, the day after Yoshinobu had unilaterally ended over two and a half centuries of Tokugawa rule.

It took some time for Saigō and Ōkubo to persuade everyone in Kagoshima that it was time to terminate Tokugawa rule. In particular, a number of monbatsu opposed the dismantling of the system under whose institutions they enjoyed their personal status as the han's elite. Both Hisamitsu and Tadayoshi, however, were in support of tōbaku, so it was only a matter of time before they simply ordered opponents of the agenda to be quiet and get out of the way. Tadayoshi left Kagoshima on 11/13 at the head of 3,000 troops, joined up with Chōshū forces at the Inland Sea port of Mitajiri, and arrived at Osaka on 11/20. Three days later the combined army took up positions in and around Kyoto.[69]

On 12/5 Saigō wrote to Minoda Denbei in Kagoshima that all was ready. Shungaku of Fukui and Yoshikatsu of Owari had arrived in response to the court summons for a daimyo gathering, and only Yōdō, late as usual, had not yet made his appearance. Loyalist samurai from Tosa were gathering in Kyoto, and both Shungaku and Yoshikatsu had declared themselves in support of ōsei fukko as a first step toward the realization of the kōgi seitai agenda. The only serious opposition appeared likely to come from Aizu and Kuwana, long Yoshinobu's staunchest supporters. With all in readiness, coup leaders had set 12/8 as the date for action. The only thing detracting from Saigō's sense of satisfaction was the murder on 11/15 of Sakamoto and Nakaoka at the same Teradaya inn where Satsuma's young samurai had killed each other on orders from Hisamitsu back in 1862. Saigō was outraged, and lamented the loss of these two exceptional men.[70]

As the deadline drew near, Iwakura apparently lost his nerve, and Saigō had to write him a strong note of encouragement, enjoining him to stand firm lest all their hopes be lost. Nothing was more important now, Saigō insisted, than to keep Yoshinobu from taking advantage of the confusion to escape the fate planned for him. He must be made to surrender everything – not just his office, but also his lands, titles, and other perquisites. Otherwise he might well come out of the transition in control of whatever emerged.[71] Iwakura vowed to do everything he could.

On 12/8 the court convened to address the question of what

to do about the Mōri and the five nobles, all of whom had been under official censure ever since they had fled the city after the 8/18 changeover in 1863. After considerable wrangling, all were pardoned and allowed to enter Kyoto again. While this was going on, troops from Satsuma, Chōshū, Owari, and other han quietly moved into positions around the palace, causing Aizu and Kuwana forces to pull back in angry confusion. With Yōdō's arrival on the same day, there was no further need for delay. On 12/9 the court announced that all the offices of the Tokugawa institutional order, from shogun on down, were forthwith abolished. In their place would be a new office of state, the *dajōkan*, staffed by three tiers of officials to be known as *sōsai*, *gijō*, and *sanyō*, and staffed by appointees from among the nobility, the daimyo, and the samurai, respectively.[72] Following these announcements, a meeting convened in the Kogosho, a ceremonial building within the palace compound, with all the major players and the young emperor present.[73]

The central question was the fate of Yoshinobu. Ōkubo and Iwakura insisted he must be stripped of his rank and his lands; Yōdō held that no decision concerning Yoshinobu could be made unless he were present himself. A deadlock resulted, and late that night Iwakura called for a recess to give everyone a chance to cool off. He then notified Yōdō that he would bring a short sword with him when they reconvened, and would use it without hesitation against Yōdō unless he ceased obstructing the meeting.[74] According to the biographical tradition, it was Saigō who gave Iwakura this idea. Outside supervising the guards, Saigō did not learn of the deadlock until the recess. He told Ōkubo to advise Iwakura not to waste time with words, but to adopt the last resort, or, as some biographers would have it, he said, 'All you need to resolve this problem is one short sword.'[75] Whatever the case, the rest of the meeting went smoothly, with no further resistance from Yōdō.

The group then promptly decided to notify Yoshinobu that his resignation as shogun had been accepted, and that he must also surrender his lands and titles. Shungaku and Yoshikatsu were delegated to report these decisions to Yoshinobu, but on 12/10 he asked for permission to delay his reply so that he could quiet the growing anger of his supporters. Two days later he left Kyoto and withdrew to Osaka, taking the men of Aizu and Kuwana with him.[76]

This withdrawal brought on another stalemate, during which

Gotō, Shungaku, and Yoshikatsu attempted to modify the decision reached in the Kogosho meeting so that Yoshinobu could be permitted to join the new government if he capitulated. According to Saigō, if things unfolded that way, Yoshinobu probably would be appointed to the post of gijō, and if that were to happen, he still had enough influential supporters in the court to be in a good position to gain control of the government. Even the five nobles, who had finally returned to Kyoto from Dazaifu on 12/28, would not be able to offset Yoshinobu's influence, and Saigō was very worried.[77] He did not know it yet, but Yoshinobu had already resolved these uncertainties with his own decisions.

On 12/26 Shungaku and Yoshikatsu met with Yoshinobu in Osaka, and he told them he had decided to go back to Kyoto with his troops to discuss the new government's demands on him. Two days later he rejected the Kogosho decision, refusing to surrender his hereditary landholdings.[78] Shungaku and Yoshikatsu reported these developments to Kyoto on 12/30, but by then a series of events in Edo had altered the political atmosphere, offering Yoshinobu a provocation he could not ignore, and turning the course of events irrevocably toward a military solution.

The same day Yoshinobu's reply was reported in Kyoto, Saigō had a visit from two Akita han samurai who had just arrived from Edo. The next day, 1868/1/1, Saigō wrote to Kagoshima that on 12/25 troops from Shōnai han on guard duty in Edo had surrounded Satsuma's residence in Mita and burned it to the ground. There had been an unexplained fire in Edo castle, and Shōnai had blamed Satsuma for it. In fact, it was not Satsuma, but Saigō himself, who lay behind these events. In the autumn of 1867, he had sent two Satsuma samurai – Imuta Naohira and Masumitsu Kyūnosuke – to Edo, evidently on his own initiative.[79] Their mission was to recruit vagrants, masterless samurai (rōnin), and others in Edo and roam the city doing whatever they could think of to provoke bakufu supporters and create a volatile atmosphere. For Shōnai samurai, already pushed to the limit, the fire in the castle was too much, and so they had struck at Satsuma. By the time news of these events found its way back to Osaka and Kyoto, Yoshinobu was already in a belligerent mood, having decided he would condemn Satsuma in a memorial to the court. When the troops of Aizu and Kuwana, gathered around Yoshinobu at Osaka, learned of the recent excitement in Edo, it was all the provocation they needed.[80]

They set out from Osaka toward Kyoto, but in the vicinity

of Toba and Fushimi they ran into troops from Satsuma, Chōshū, and Aki, who refused to let them pass. On 1/3 Saigō wrote to the Satsuma forces at Fushimi that Yoshinobu's army must not he allowed to proceed without written permission from the court.[81] He suggested to Ōkubo that the plans they had made to move the emperor might need to be altered, so that it did not look like he was being taken against his will.[82] Then he went down to Fushimi, where fighting had already begun. From there he reported that the imperial troops were performing magnificently, and he urged that the silk battle flags be brought out to improve morale. The court, he urged, should name a commander to lead a punitive army against Edo.[83]

By 1/5 Yoshinobu's army was in full retreat and the imperial forces had entered Osaka. The next day Yoshinobu escaped from the city and headed back for Edo by sea. Saigō reported to Katsura Hisatake in Kagoshima that, while they had taken Osaka, they had not captured Yoshinobu.[84] Though outnumbered five to one, he told another correspondent, the imperial army had scored one victory after another.[85] The western half of Japan had become the emperor's territory, but Saigō expected stronger resistance in the northeast, where Aizu han might provide the nucleus for a more concerted defense of Tokugawa rights. He suggested that a reduction of taxes by half ought to bring the support of the people over to the imperial cause.[86] In fact, Aizu did exactly as Saigō had expected, and the hardest fighting of the Meiji civil war (*boshin sensō*) was in the heart of the Tōhoku region, in and around Aizu, which occupied roughly the same territory as present-day Yamagata Prefecture.

At this point, with things going so well, Saigō wrote to his old friend Kawaguchi Seppō, who had passed the hours with him on Okinoerabu, and had coached him in both his calligraphy and his Chinese poetry. After summarizing recent events, he then added that Tadayoshi had reproached him severely for risking his life at the front during the Toba-Fushimi fighting. In response to that, he had the following to say:

> So, I've joined the company of the elderly, and I'm no good for fighting any more, only for looking after. What a disappointment. I've decided that once the fighting has quieted down, I'll ask for leave and go into retirement. I'm no longer fit for public service. I'm just too timid, and there's no help for it.[87]

Saigō wrote this letter on 1/16, and it was discovered only

106

recently. Certainly it is not difficult to understand Tadayoshi's concern for Saigō's welfare; Saigō himself had expressed the same concern for Ōkubo, writing him on 1/7 to cut short a tour of the battlefields around Osaka and return to Kyoto.[88] Saigō's response to Tadayoshi's concern, on the other hand, is intriguing. Perhaps it is nothing but another example of the hyperbole in which he occasionally indulged himself. Or perhaps it offers a vital clue to his behavior in the years that lay ahead.

He had passed his fortieth birthday during 1867/12, and perhaps he was becoming more conscious of his own mortality. He had already been seriously ill several times, and his bouts of illness were becoming more frequent. Moreover, with the emperor restored to power and his enemies nearly all put down, Saigō may have begun thinking that he had outlived his usefulness to the realm, and that it would be inappropriate for him to remain in public office when there was no longer any reason for him to do so. There is little doubt that after 1868 Saigō gradually became more and more troubled about the policies of the new government and the behavior of his former friends, though one can find no single obvious reason for his unease. Inoue Kiyoshi argues that Saigō's doubts about the Meiji government began to grow only after the heavy-handed destruction of the Tokugawa partisans known as the Shōgitai in their stronghold at Ueno.[89] This letter to Kawaguchi suggests that he has already feeling ambivalent about the future within days after the imperial army's first victories outside of Kyoto.

At any rate, there was still work to be done. On 1/23 Saigō wrote to Ōkubo proposing that since Aizu was bound to become a focal point for organized resistance on behalf of Yoshinobu, a quick move against that han would help to shorten what otherwise might be a long war.[90] Sendai han, Aizu's neighbor, was ready to join a combined force, and Saigō thought the bulk of the imperial army should be transferred to Sendai by ship to help pacify Aizu. Ōkubo and others did not agree with Saigō about this, but they all agreed on the need for haste in cornering Yoshinobu before he could rally new support for the Tokugawa. By the time he reached Edo on 1/13, Yoshinobu probably had already decided that his only remaining option was surrender, but no one on the imperial side yet knew that. On 2/2 Saigō argued adamantly that there must be no quarter given, and that nothing less than Yoshinobu's suicide would be acceptable.[91] For his own part, Yoshinobu had withdrawn to Kan'eiji, the Tokugawa family temple in Ueno, and was beginning to indicate his desire to capitulate.

Orders for an armed pursuit were issued in Kyoto on 2/3, and the army set out toward Edo at once, encountering only token resistance along the way. By 1868/3 it had reached Shizuoka, and preparations were underway for the final assault on Edo.[92] However, influential voices had begun calling for leniency, and if Saigō could have disregarded most of them, he could not ignore that of Katsu Kaishū, who wanted to get the matter settled quickly. Katsu sent a messenger to Saigō, proposing that Edo might be surrendered peacefully in exchange for Yoshinobu's life. Saigō had been eager to attack the city, but now he decided to try Katsu's proposal first. He hurried to Kyoto, where he persuaded his colleagues to accept Katsu's overture, and then returned to Edo, where he met with Katsu on 3/13–14.[93] The army entered Edo on 4/4, and the next day Saigō wrote to Ōkubo that all resistance appeared to have collapsed.[94] Yoshinobu left Edo on 4/11, and while he would occasionally advise the government in years to come, his hour in the spotlight was over.

Saigō reported to Ōkubo on i4/27 that the pacification of Edo was going smoothly, but that hospital facilities for the army's wounded were inadequate, and too many were dying. He asked formal permission for Parkes' staff physician, William Willis, to begin treating the injured, first in Kyoto, and then later in Edo also.[95] Saigō's concern here was not only with proper medical care for wounded soldiers, but also with appropriate treatment for the samurai who had been injured while fighting the emperor's battles.

Once again what was at stake for him was the question of virtue implied by the reciprocal nature of relations between people of high and low status. However lowly the imperial army's troopers might be, they had risked their lives in the noblest of causes, and that made them noble in their own right. To treat them with less than the utmost care and solicitude would have brought dishonor on their superiors. This view is fully consistent with the arguments we have seen Saigō making about the proper treatment of the peasants, which suggests, among other things, that his main concern now was not so much with the samurai as such, but rather with the danger that higher-ranking people responsible for their welfare might dishonor themselves through inappropriate behavior.

If Saigō's concern for the fate of the samurai class is sufficient to explain his behavior after 1868, then it would seem that the first evidence of that concern appears in these arrangements he made for the care of those injured in the Meiji civil war. However, his views about the samurai are not sufficient to explain his behavior, however necessary they may be as a part of any interpretation of what he did between 1868 and 1877. On balance, his often repeated wish to retire from public life seems no less important than whatever sense of obligation he may have felt toward the samurai, and his feelings about the behavior of his former colleagues are probably just as important as the other two factors. The tendency has been to explain Saigō's choices after 1868 entirely by reference to one single factor or another, but the available evidence simply does not lend itself to single-factor explanations.

· 5 ·

Reform and Reaction in Kagoshima, *1868–71*

The decade from the palace coup of 1868 to the death of Ōkubo in 1878 is one of the most dramatic periods in Japanese history, encompassing more change in ten years than the country had experienced in the previous ten decades.[1] Most of those who write about Saigō concentrate on this period, partly because he began it in triumph and ended it in utter ignominy, chiefly because the most controversial events of his life occurred during this decade. Thus the period demands careful scrutiny, and it might be protested that I have not given it as much space as it deserves. However, the big controversies in Saigō's life cannot be understood when analyzed out of context, but only when taken as parts in a larger whole. The previous four chapters have provided the context within which we can now examine the last ten years of Saigō's life and assess their significance.

In this chapter and the next, I will examine four topics. The first is the series of reforms carried out in Kagoshima between 1868 and 1870, when the old factional tensions of the bakumatsu period and the passions associated with them boiled over again in a confrontation between samurai of high status and low, and former members of the lower status groups finally had their chance to strike back at those above them. The second is the career of the national caretaker government (*rusu seifu*) between 1871 and 1873, during which many of the reforms that defined the Meiji transformation were carried out under the leadership of Saigō and Sanjō Sanetomi while Ōkubo, Iwakura, Kido, and others toured the West in search of new ideas. The third is the emergence, development, and resolution of the controversy over Korea, which was less a debate about the relative urgency of domestic and overseas agendas than it was simply a power struggle within the Meiji leadership. And the fourth is the hardening of political separatism in Kagoshima, especially after about 1876, where those who had conducted the reforms between 1868 and 1870 attempted to create an independent state beyond the reach of the Meiji government, and where the fear of absorption into the new order finally led to rebellion in 1877.[2]

We must remember that all of these episodes except the first were phases in the evolution of *national* politics, and are important primarily as stages in the struggle to define and then to implement centralized and unified government for Japan. We must also remember that while Saigō was involved in all four, and helped to give each one its particular historical flavor, he also had issues of his own to deal with, and in the end they were more important for him than these questions of national politics.

Unfinished business:
1868–69

The most urgent business following the surrender of Edo castle was to pacify Tokugawa partisans still in the city. Earlier in the year some of them had organized themselves into a group calling itself the Shōgitai, and had established a base at Ueno, not far from the Kan'eiji temple where Yoshinobu had withdrawn after his return from Osaka. Soon after he left Edo in 1868/4, bands of Shōgitai members began seeking out government troops in the streets and starting brawls, much as Saigō's irregular provocateurs had done in the final months of 1867. On 5/15, government forces attacked the Shōgitai stronghold, located on the heights at Ueno in the area where the bronze statue of Saigō stands today, and scattered them after a fierce battle that lasted all day and took a heavy toll on both sides. Satsuma troops under Saigō's command bore the brunt of the fighting, and Saigō thought they had been placed intentionally where they would be certain to take heavy losses. After the surrender of Edo castle, overall military command in the Kantō region had been given to Ōmura Masujirō, a resourceful tactician from Chōshū, and it appears that Saigō did not like taking orders from this man whom he regarded as his inferior. Apparently, Saigō also suspected Ōmura of deliberately sacrificing Satsuma's troops in order to spare those of Chōshū.

Soon after this engagement, on 5/29, Saigō left Edo for Kago-

111

shima, intending to recruit troops for the campaign against Tokugawa supporters in the Tōhoku region. Matsudaira Katamori had returned home to Aizu after the debacle at Toba-Fushimi and had put together an alliance of pro-Tokugawa han in northeastern Honshu, exactly as Saigō had predicted on more than one occasion. Imperial forces had begun a campaign against them soon after the surrender of Edo. Saigō meant to lead reinforcements to join the fighting against Katamori's Tōhoku league, but by 6/14, when he arrived in Kagoshima, his health had failed again, so he retired to a hot spring to recuperate. He was delayed in Kagoshima until 8/6, and by the time he and his troops reached the front in Echigo Province the fighting there was well underway.[3] Having arrived late already, Saigō now acted as if he had no enthusiasm for the venture. Instead of combining forces with other imperial units, he set up his own headquarters and refused to cooperate with the main command. In order to coordinate movements, subordinate commanders such as Kuroda Kiyotaka, Yoshii Tomozane, and Yamagata Aritomo had to hurry back and forth between the two command positions.

As the Tōhoku han began to surrender one by one, government commanders exacted terms that were not excessively harsh even if they were not especially generous either. When the forces of Shōnai han surrendered, Saigō intervened personally and ordered Kuroda to supervise terms that were exceptionally lenient, in light of the destruction visited on Satsuma's Mita establishment less than a year earlier by men from this same han.[4] This action may not have pleased Saigō's fellow commanders in the imperial army, and may even have aroused their suspicions about Saigō's loyalties, but it won for him the eternal gratitude of the people of Shōnai, who still honor his memory today.[5] Moreover such leniency was consistent with the views he had expressed about the proper treatment of vanquished foes, after the bakufu summarily murdered nearly half of the Mito rebels in 1865.

Saigō left Shōnai on 9/29 and returned to Kyoto, where he helped to organize the withdrawal of Satsuma's troops from the city.[6] He left there on 10/23 at the head of the army. Early the following month these troops made their triumphal entry into Kagoshima, full of pride and enthusiasm for the promise of the new world they had helped to bring into being. Nearly all of lower rank, these samurai now demanded and then personally carried out a series of reforms that amounted to a full-scale assault on the privileged position of the han's traditional elite, the monbatsu. In these reforms, to which we will return in a moment, the full legacy of bitterness and resentment created during the Bunka and Kaei purges of 1808–09 and 1849–50 came back with unquenched fury and reestablished the lines of factional polarization Nariakira had tried so hard to erase.

Most of Saigō's biographers have called attention to his rather peculiar behavior between the spring and the autumn of 1868, and many have speculated that the idea of turning against the new government was already taking shape in his mind. There is nothing to suggest that he was any less committed to the imperial cause than hitherto, but something clearly was amiss. When the last battles of the civil war were fought between government troops and the followers of Enomoto Takeaki at Hakodate in 1869, Saigō again raised troops and went to join the fighting. This time, the campaign was not only well underway before he set out for the front; it was all over by the time he arrived. Once again, as in the case of his performance in Echigo, a suspicious observer might have been tempted to conclude that Saigō had been tardy on purpose, and that what looked like nothing more than an odd lack of enthusiasm was actually evidence of some hostile intent toward the new government. However, before we conclude that Saigō was balking deliberately, or beginning even at this early date to harbor rebellious ambitions toward the Meiji government, there are several other factors we ought to consider.

Foremost among these, we should recall that his health was not good at any time during the last ten years of his life, and that his erratic behavior on a number of occasions might have been nothing more than a temporary loss of control caused by serious illness. On 1869/7/8, he wrote to Katsura Hisatake from a hot spring near Kagoshima that for some time he had been suffering from severe fever, accompanied by abdominal pain, a skin rash, and incessant diarrhea, including blood in his stools.[7] Even if not completely incapacitated by illness, he may also have been suffering from fairly serious depression, resulting from the accumulated effects of numerous small and otherwise inconsequential experiences. For example, it was not a happy man who wrote to Kawaguchi Seppō from Kyoto after the Toba-Fushimi battle.[8] Likewise, the hardship visited on Satsuma's troops in the Ueno Shōgitai battle may have upset him a great deal, whether it resulted from deliberate malice on Ōmura's part or not.

The only explicit statement of what was on Saigō's mind as 1868 passed into 1869 appears in a letter he wrote to his friend

Toku Fujinaga on Ōshima, on 1869/3/20. He began by summarizing his activities during 1868, from the surrender of Edo to his return to Kagoshima at the end of the year. Then he continued:

> At that time I asked for leave, thinking I would retire. I did get permission for temporary leave, but then I was informed that I must serve in the han government. There was nothing I could do about that . . . so now I'll remain in service for at least another year or two. I had wanted to come to the island this spring, but now it seems that will be impossible.[9]

We should take Saigō's repeated remarks about retirement at face value. They might represent some sort of elaborate subterfuge intended to lull the suspicions of potential adversaries, but that seems to strain logic. For one thing, he did not make such remarks often, and there is no suggestive pattern to their occurrence, though they became more frequent and explicit after 1868. For another, he had been making them since the early 1860s with no apparent variation in tone.

At any rate, there was no reason for him to be anything less than candid with his old friend Toku, who was among a small company of intimates with whom Saigō tended always to be more frank, more open, and more thorough in his letters. This company also included Koba Dennai, the senior han official on Ōshima during his first exile, Tsuchimochi Masateru, his overseer on Okinoerabu, Kawaguchi Seppō, his fellow exile there, and especially Katsura Hisatake, whom he had known for many years, and who had looked after his family on Ōshima after he left there in 1862.[10] Katsura also figured indirectly in Saigō's past as the younger brother of Akayama Yukie, the samurai whose suicide Saigō's father had witnessed, and whose blood-stained undergarment he had brought home to his son.[11]

There is a different tone in Saigō's letters to these men, and it is only here that he speaks freely about his private feelings. His letters to others, including those to Ōkubo, are no less thorough in their attention to detail, but there is a formality about them that puts them in a different class. They give us, as it were, the public Saigō; those to his intimates, most of whom he came to know during his periods of exile, present the private Saigō. His remarks about retirement appear only in letters to members of this group of intimates, almost as if he felt he could trust them with his most secret thoughts and most cherished hopes.

There are other indications that Saigō had lost interest in politics after 1868. By the time he returned to Kagoshima late that year at the head of the army, his personal popularity throughout the han was such that he could have taken complete control of the reforms if he had wished. Instead, he left the city and took up residence at Hinatayama hot spring, which is at least a full day from Kagoshima on foot. There, he shaved his head and spent all his time soaking in the mineral waters, hunting rabbits and other small game, and going for long walks in the countryside. Early in 1869, Ijichi Masaharu wrote to Ōkubo that Saigō had been at Hinatayama for forty-five days tending to his health, and adding, 'I hear he goes about with four or five of his dogs and several of his young followers.'[12]

Even if he was not tired of politics, and did not believe he had finished his work for the emperor, Saigō had still other reasons for wanting to withdraw from the world, in this case arising from the desire literally to hide his face in shame. On 1868/8/2, his brother Kichijirō was wounded at the Echigo front. Four days after Saigō's belated arrival there, he died of complications. Saigō already felt deeply indebted to Kichijirō, who had carried the entire burden of looking after the Saigō family in Kagoshima ever since 1852. Instead of taking over the family after his father's death, as was the custom, Saigō had simply assumed the legal responsibilities of family head, and had allowed Kichijirō to take over all of the practical problems of housing, feeding, and clothing a family that by then included three generations. Now Saigō would never be able to repay all those debts. In his letter to Toku he lamented:

> My younger brother Kichijirō was killed in Echigo. It was a terrible loss for me. Fortunately, my other two brothers returned unharmed. And yet, just when it was I who should have been the first to die, I let my younger brother go ahead of me. I can do nothing about it now but weep.[13]

Once again, Saigō had survived while someone close to him had died, and this may have revived old doubts and frustrations that had lingered ever since the deaths of Nariakira and Gesshō.

In short, taking both the remarks about retirement and the evidence of his daily routines together, Saigō's behavior after 1868 seems to give every indication that he wanted nothing more to do with public life, and waited with ill-contained impatience for the day when he could leave it all behind and go into permanent retirement with his family on Ōshima. In light of the controversies surrounding him during the last decade of his life, and the passion with which so many biographers have taken sides in those controversies, it is difficult to say just how much evidence it would take to establish these hypotheses about Saigō as the most plausible. I think, in the end, they make their own best case, because all other theories about Saigō's motives during the final ten years of his life, however elegant they are structurally, are more complicated than this one, and require more artful manipulation of the evidence.

In other words, it is quite possible that at this point in his life, with Nariakira's unfulfilled ambitions all realized, Saigō had no more interest in politics or in public life. He had discharged his obligations to his lord, and he had done exemplary service to the imperial court. It was time now to let others tackle the problems of building the new government, and there was no place for him in that process, provided that the requirements of sincerity and righteousness were not violated, and that the will of Heaven was not betrayed. Yet if Saigō thought he could slip out through the backstage door and spend the rest of his life doing the things he enjoyed most – raising his children, hunting, fishing, and soaking in the waters of his favorite hot springs – he was mistaken, and was soon to learn that for himself.

Reform in Kagoshima:
1868–70

By the beginning of 1869 nearly all Tokugawa partisan resistance had been put down, and the leaders of the ōsei fukko coup could turn their attention to finishing what they had begun. On 1868/3/14 the government had issued the five-article Charter Oath, and later that month the emperor made a trip to Osaka. There he inspected warships, reviewed troops, and performed other symbolic acts that would make him both more visible and more memorable to the public. Thus began the reconstitution of the emperor's person as the focal point for a new concept of the Japanese polity, one that would enable the leaders of the Meiji Restoration movement to consolidate and secure their power.[14] On 7/17 this process continued; Edo was renamed Tokyo, and on 10/3 the emperor moved into the shogun's castle, transferring the seat of government away from Kyoto, where it had been for a millenium, and relocating it in Japan's new political center.[15]

While these symbolic displays were going on, Ōkubo and others in the government pondered more fundamental problems: they had no secure sources of revenue, and no military forces of their own. Thus, whatever legitimacy the emperor's presence might confer on them, they had no real power to back up their claims, and whatever measures they might adopt at the center would have little meaning unless they also made changes in local and regional institutions. More than one of them had proposed that all the other daimyo should do as Yoshinobu had done, and return their lands and people to the throne, but this presented a greater risk than most of them were willing to take just yet.[16]

The first step in this direction came on 1869/1/23, when the hanshu of Satsuma, Chōshū, Tosa, and Saga (Higo) submitted a petition in which they voluntarily restored control of their lands and subjects to the emperor (*hanseki hōkan*).[17] The court accepted this petition on 6/17. Eight days later, all other han were ordered to conduct surveys of their lands, resources, and populations. At the same time, former hanshū, renamed 'governors' (*chiji*) and left in control for the time being, were granted stipends equivalent to one tenth of whatever the assessed productivity of their han had been. All samurai, hitherto distinguished by elaborate status gradations, were lumped together into the class of 'samurai families' (*shizoku*). Earlier, the government already had ordered all han to carry out administrative reforms aimed at standardizing local government.[18] It was this series of events that provided the justification for the reforms Satsuma's returning armies carried out.

As we saw at the outset, reform had been practically incessant in Satsuma since the late eighteenth century. Control of the process had changed hands, and each change of control had led to another change in the content and aims of the reforms. The only continuity in all of this change had been the dominance of all high-level administrative positions by the han's senior vassals, the monbatsu, and both the Bunka and the Kaei purges had been in essence little more than monbatsu reactions against what they saw as challenges to their power and its continuity. When the lower samurai seized control after their return from the Tōhoku campaign, their first priority was to bring that particular continuity to an end, and to dispossess the monbatsu.

117

Saigō evidently had wanted no part in this program, and had withdrawn from Kagoshima as soon as he got home. While he relaxed in the soothing waters of the hot springs at Hinatayama, Satsuma's lower samurai began their assault on the traditional status quo. Their leaders – Kawamura Sumiyoshi, Nozu Shizuo, and Ijūin Kanehiro – submitted a petition to Hisamitsu demanding the abolition of the monbatsu and the selection of officials without regard to status or wealth, entirely on the basis of talent. Believing that Saigō might be able to moderate these demands, Hisamitsu pleaded with him to become involved, but he refused. Only when Tadayoshi personally came to Hinatayama on 2/23 and asked for help did Saigō relent and agree to take part in the reforms. Two days later he accepted appointment as 'consultant' (*sansei*) to the han government.[19] It was this sequence of events that had frustrated his plans to return to Ōshima, as described in his letter to Toku Fujinaga. He continued as sansei until 1870/1/13, and then after a period of inactivity he was promoted to a higher position (*dai sanji*) on 7/23, where he remained until he left Kagoshima to join the central government at the end of the year.[20]

Hisamitsu had also appealed to Ōkubo for help, and on 2/13 he had arrived in Kagoshima from Tokyo,[21] but he was there primarily to deliver a summons, not to answer one. On 1/29, the court had issued invitations for Hisamitsu, Saigō, and Mōri Yoshichika to join the government, and Ōkubo had come to deliver those notices. Hisamitsu was reluctant to go, but agreed to do so when Ōkubo offered to stay behind and help direct the reforms in Kagoshima. Hisamitsu left for Kyoto on 2/26, but was back in Kagoshima within a month, displaying an aversion to involvement in the new government that would only grow stronger with time. Meanwhile Ōkubo met with Kawamura, Nozu, and Ijūin soon after arriving in Kagoshima, and tried to persuade them that if what they really wanted was to employ talented people without regard to status, then they ought to consider a number of capable monbatsu as well. Needless to say, these three were not impressed with Ōkubo's idea, making it clear that they were more interested in purging monbatsu than in appointing talented administrators.[22] Ōkubo tried with little success to direct the reforms in more constructive directions, and finally left Satsuma on 3/11.[23]

Thus neither Saigō nor Ōkubo appears to have played more than a peripheral role in the reforms of 1869–70. In fact, despite the determination of the lower samurai to turn the tables on their traditional superiors, it was chiefly those of high rank who undid the system of privilege based on status. On 2/28 Tadayoshi announced the return of his hereditary rights to the emperor and dismissed all monbatsu from their posts. He then supported the introduction of a new government structure that formally separated the Shimazu family's household administration from that of the han.[24] Komatsu Tatewaki had returned his sub-fief to Tadayoshi even before the latter had submitted his hanseki hōkan petition to the court. After the court accepted the hanseki hōkan initiative, all monbatsu holdings were returned to the han government, and the status of monbatsu was abolished. Though they continued to enjoy higher incomes, the monbatsu were now collapsed into the shizoku class along with their lower-ranking fellow samurai.[25] Thus it was not so much the lower samurai as it was Tadayoshi himself, and a number of his highest ranking vassals, along with the central government in Tokyo, who ended the monbatsu's centuries of privilege in Satsuma.

In the new arrangement, the men with the primary executive authority were Saigō's old friend Katsura Hisatake and his childhood playmate Ijichi Masaharu. It has been customary to view Saigō as the central figure in this series of reforms, but the evidence points elsewhere, to a group including not only Katsura and Ijichi, but also Kawamura, Nozu, Ijūin, and others. Saigō's appointment as sansei placed him at the same level as Katsura and Ijichi, but he appears to have played only a marginal role in the reforms, advising when needed but leaving the initiative to others. His inclusion in the executive group was largely tactical: the majority of lower samurai in the han would be unlikely to challenge the authority of any government in which Saigō held high office.

With the abolition of the monbatsu, there was no longer any institutional basis for status discrimination in Kagoshima. However, it takes more than a few changes in the legal system to erase habits of mind that have been in force for centuries. The gōshi had been elevated to the same level as the castle town samurai with the creation of the shizoku class, but the contempt of the castle town samurai for their rural fellows continued unabated, as did the resentment of the gōshi toward their erstwhile superiors. Recruited into the imperial guard without reference to their former rank several years later, Satsuma's samurai were still unable rise above old animosities and get along, and

119

they finally had to be separated. Evidently feeling personally responsible for these problems, Saigō took an active part in the conversion of former gōshi guard units into a new metropolitan police force for Tokyo, under the command of Kawaji Toshiyoshi.[26]

It is interesting to note that when Saigō left the government again in 1873 and returned to Kagoshima, those in the imperial guard who followed him home were nearly all former castle town samurai. The gōshi, now entrenched in the police force, stayed in Tokyo. When the castle town samurai finally rebelled four years later, it was in large part because they believed Kagoshima had been secretly infiltrated by agents from the Tokyo police, all of them former Satsuma gōshi, who had come home to murder Saigō. Numerous former gōshi did join the ranks of the rebel army, but equally large numbers of them showed no interest in what they apparently viewed as a quarrel between the central government and former castle town samurai from Kagoshima, who made up the nucleus of the rebel force. In other words, the status barrier between castle town samurai and gōshi continued to separate them a full decade after it had been formally abolished. Equally noteworthy, for all the passion the samurai brought to their assault on the monbatsu, it was those of middle status, not higher or lower, who clung to the old animosities the longest. That is, it was chiefly the lower-ranking castle town samurai – the former koshōgumi – whose smoldering resentments eventually flared out of control in the Satsuma rebellion.

The reforms of 1869–70 covered all areas of han administration,[27] but their most important elements involved the reorganization of the military.[28] Reform of military organization was not new in Satsuma. Nariakira had begun the training of han troops in Western drill and weapons, and there were further reforms after the English bombardment in 1863, and again in 1866. The reforms in the autumn of 1869 had their own particular significance, in that they not only altered military organization, but also fused civil and military administration together down to the lowest levels.

All samurai in the han between the ages of eighteen and thirty-five were mustered into standing (*jōbitai*) or reserve (*yōbitai*) units. Ninety men formed a company (*shotai*), and six companies comprised a battalion (*daitai*), of which there were initially three in Kagoshima and an additional twelve in the rural administrative districts (*gō*).[29] Totals changed later, but as of the beginning of 1870 Kagoshima could count some 15,000 men on active duty in these units. Battalion commanders were appointed by the government, but the senior officers in all units from the company on down were elected by their troops. In the city, the senior officers were men like Kirino Toshiaki, Shinohara Kunimoto, Nozu Shizuo, Kawamura Sumiyoshi, and Kabayama Sukenori. Some of these men soon left Kagoshima and went on to distinguished careers in the national army and navy – men such as Kawamura and Kabayama – but most of them stayed in Kagoshima, and died in the rebellion.

The most striking element in this reorganization of the military was that it absorbed the civil administration; in 1869/6 the local administrative structure was collapsed into the military hierarchy. Just as in the past, the senior official in each district was a steward (*jitō*), but these posts were now all filled by lower samurai appointed from Kagoshima. Under the traditional system, a jitō appointed from the monbatsu had held authority over local officials of gōshi status. Now, beneath the jitō was an assistant (*fukuyaku*), exercising command over local officials who doubled as company commanders (*shotaichō*) or as platoon and squad leaders (*buntaichō, hantaichō*). The nominal complement for a district was one company, but there were variations, ranging from as little as one platoon to as much as five companies.[30]

It is important to note the overwhelmingly military character of this new system. Rural administration in Satsuma had always had a nominally military cast because the gōshi who ran it were samurai, however low their status. Yet in practice most gōshi were samurai in name only, and were in effect civil bureaucrats, more or less at home among the peasants they supervised. Under the new system after 1869, rural officials were no longer quasi-military civilians; they were regular officers on active duty, with the added responsibility for civil administration. By 1870, every post in the civil government, down to the lowliest rural official, was filled by a military appointee. In other words, Kagoshima had become a military state in a condition of permanent mobiliz-ation. As such it was bound to be seen as a potential threat by the central government, which as yet had no military of its own, and which created the imperial guard in 1871 partly in the hope of shifting the loyalties of some of Satsuma's samurai from the han to the court. These reforms during 1869–70, then, ended up offering the new Meiji government the first in a series of provocations that eventually led to the 1877 rebellion. And that is not their only significance.

After Saigō left the government in 1873 and returned home, a new system of private schools (*shigakkō*) was set up in Kagoshima, and many have seen the establishment of these schools as the first step in the creation of a private army. Most who subscribe to this view assume that the shigakkō system was created by Saigō to serve his aims.[31] According to this view, it was at Saigō's initiative that by 1876 all significant administrative positions in Kagoshima were occupied by shigakkō officials, and the senior officers in the system were men such as Kirino Toshiaki, Shinohara Kunimoto, Murata Shinpachi, and others with long-standing ties to Saigō. In the eyes of Saigō's detractors, this was 'Saigō's kingdom' (*Saigō ōkoku*),[32] the last major hotbed of resistance to the Meiji government, and he had created it with the aim of destroying that government after his personal ambitions for Japan were frustrated in 1873.

Even a casual examination of the reforms of 1869 will show that the only thing really new in the creation of the shigakkō system after 1873 was the use of the term 'shigakkō' to describe it. All levels of the civil administration were already militarized by the end of 1869, and most of the men in command after 1873 had already been at their posts since 1869. The so-called 'militarization' of Kagoshima after Saigō's return in 1873, then, was actually a process that had run its course in 1869–70, and in which Saigō had played only a marginal role, at best. The men who eventually provoked the rebellion had been in control of Satsuma since 1870, and there is no evidence to suggest that Saigō was ever one of them. His importance was chiefly symbolic, and it was as a symbol that he had his greatest value to the leaders of the rebellion.

What is not clear – and never can be without the discovery of decisive new evidence – is exactly how Saigō felt about being used as a symbol to legitimize the militarizing reforms carried out by his lifelong friends.[33] One of the few clear statements of concern he did make about the reforms appears in a letter to Ōkubo from 1870/5/7. There he complained that most of those responsible for conducting the reforms were not doing their share, and had let most of the administrative burden fall on Ijichi Masaharu.[34] For a man harboring deep and abiding discontent toward the national government, and perhaps even plotting its destruction, this seems an odd thing to worry about. To be sure,

Saigō did have his doubts about some of the policies taking shape in Tokyo, and those doubts did grow over the years.[35] But when we return to Kagoshima for discussion of the events leading to the outbreak of the 1877 rebellion, we must keep the reforms of 1869–70 in mind.

Equally important, we need to remember that of all those in Kagoshima most clearly accountable for the sequence of events that finally led to the rebellion, the one who appears to bear the greatest responsibility had not yet gained prominence when these reforms took place. Ōyama Tsunayoshi, the first governor (*kenrei*) of Kagoshima, did not begin his rise to power until about the time Saigō left to join the national government. It appears that Kirino, Shinohara, Murata, and a handful of others were already beginning to think about rebellion when Saigō went up to Tokyo in 1871. However, until Ōyama Tsunayoshi came to power and gave their ambitions the governor's blessing, other officials in the local government had kept these men in check. Among those other officials, we must note, was Saigō. If this reading of the evidence is accurate, then it was Saigō's departure from Kagoshima in 1871, not his return in 1873, that marked the beginning of the process that led finally to rebellion.

In the meantime, as reform proceeded in Kagoshima, political leaders in Tokyo had reached a number of conclusions about what they must do next, and getting Saigō into the national government was near the top of their list of priorities. It was not just in Kagoshima that his widespread popularity gave him great symbolic value.[36] Several attempts had already been made to bring Saigō to Tokyo, but he had successfully sidestepped them all. On 1870/12/18 Iwakura Tomomi arrived in Kagoshima as an official messenger from the emperor himself, accompanied by Ōkubo, Yamagata Aritomo, and Kawamura Sumiyoshi, to summon Saigō to Tokyo. As when Tadayoshi had appealed to him personally at Hinatayama the previous year, Saigō could not ignore a direct request from the emperor, so he agreed to return to Tokyo with these men.

However, he warned Ōkubo that he had ideas of his own about what would be appropriate for the Meiji government, and Ōkubo assured him that if he would only agree to participate, he would have plenty of opportunities to put his ideas into practice. On 1871/1/3 Saigō left Kagoshima with Ōkubo. They went first to Yamaguchi to collect Kido Takayoshi, and then proceeded to Tosa, where Itagaki Taisuke joined them. The four of them reached Tokyo on 1871/2/2. It was one of the few times in their lives when they were all together, and it was the only time when they all shared more or less the same ideas about what they were doing. Yet if their political will was unified for the moment, it was not fated to stay that way for long.[37]

The final shape of Saigō's world view

What were these ideas about which Saigō thought he had to warn Ōkubo? As in the weeks before and after the end of his second exile, Saigō periodically put his ideas down in writing during the final decade of his life, and while he never said enough to produce a complete picture, there is enough material to fill in most of the outlines that had already taken shape by the end of his time on Okinoerabu. During Iwakura's visit to Kagoshima in 1870, Saigō handed him a memorial setting out his views on the government and its agenda.[38] The following autumn, Saigō penned three more memorials. One concerned the disposition of samurai stipends (*rokudaka shōbun*), one set out a specific agenda for the government, and one offered further details concerning rural administration.[39] In 1873, Saigō submitted a formal summary of the deliberations concerning Korea, which implicitly reveals some interesting things about his view of foreign policy,[40] and in 1875 he wrote a petition to the Kagoshima government on behalf of some local police officials who were concerned about prostitution and the social problems it posed.[41]

Unlike his letters, which are concerned chiefly with specific matters, Saigō's memorials and other writings gave him a chance to step back and generalize. Most such generalizations, coming as they do from an aphoristic thinker, take the form of dogmatic pronouncements based on Confucian precepts. Even at his most thoughtful, Saigō is not so much making arguments as he is simply making strings of precepts. Yet if we take these memorials together, they give us an agreeably complete picture of the thinking that motivated Saigō during the last ten years of his life. The picture will seem even more complete if we first review the outlines of his world view as expressed in the memorial of 1856, and the documents he composed in 1864, when his second exile ended.

According to the system of ideas Saigō brought back with him from the islands, it will be recalled, everything in human affairs is subject to the will of Heaven. Loyalty, filiality, benevolence, sincerity, courage, modesty, selflessness – these and similar values are at the heart of Saigō's system, and what they all have in common is that they can only be manifested in action. Thus, however good one's intentions, the only way to evaluate their moral worth is to observe the consequences of putting them into action. Peasant discontent, natural calamities, and the frustration of one's aims represent explicit messages warning that one has strayed from the true Way of Heaven.

Moreover, in the realm of laws and institutions, it is the patterns of the past, the dictates of tradition, that provide the best framework for effectiveness. Yet even if laws and institutions are essential, no matter how appropriate they may be, they are of little value if the men who administer them are corrupt or weak. The well-being of the realm is measured in terms of public morality, through the maintenance of proper social relations between individuals. Such relations are predicated on reciprocity between the loyal and obedient subject and the righteous and benevolent ruler. The subject toils with his body, while the ruler toils with his heart and mind, and together they produce a perfect complementarity expressing the natural order as Heaven wills it.

For Saigō, the key link in this chain is the integrity of the samurai official, and it is to this that he devoted most of his attention in his early memorials and other statements. It should come as no surprise to find that the memorials he wrote during the first half of the 1870s take this system as their first premise, and seek to realize its imperatives in their specific proposals.

Addressing Iwakura in 1870, Saigō asserted that the government must establish clear and consistent guidelines for internal review of individual performance, so that worthy officials could be rewarded and unworthy ones removed. No individual must be allowed to abuse the system for personal profit, and above all else the military must never be allowed to gain control of civil government.[42] Saigō returned to this concern for the integrity of officials repeatedly, and called for a full body of laws to regulate the behavior of both individuals and institutions.[43]

Saigō already had plenty of examples from which to infer the necessity of such controls. The behavior of the bakufu, and before that of the Satsuma government, had shown him the dangers of abuse inherent in the character of both institutions and administrators. Moreover, certain of his colleagues in the Meiji government provided him with models closer to hand. In particular he had doubts about Ōkuma Shigenobu and Inoue Kaoru, whom he suspected of using their authority in the Ministry of Finance (*ōkurashō*) to make lucrative private deals with some of Japan's emerging commercial giants, like the Mitsui group.[44]

Saigō believed that the institutional and cultural patterns of the West could provide some useful examples for Japan to follow, but he was worried about indiscriminate borrowing. Some innovations he believed were appropriate, while others were not. This was especially true of foreign religions. Buddhism had been a part of Japanese life for so long that it would not be easy to remove, but Saigō believed it must be removed. As a foreign creed, it was just as pernicious as Christianity. Both were inimical to the maintenance of proper hierarchical relations, as between lord and vassal, or father and son. Japan must seek out its own religious traditions, purge them of foreign accretions, and reaffirm them as the basis of its government. There could be no shame in being overwhelmed by the West so long as Japan adhered faithfully to is native traditions.[45]

Foreign models might be useful for the improvement of some Japanese institutions, but the model for the Meiji government itself must be the ancient court bureaucracy. The aim of the *ōsei fukko* coup, after all, had been to return Japan to the pure and wholesome condition it had been in during the rule of its first earthly sovereign, Jimmu. That style, in Saigō's view, was the union of religious and civil practice (*saisei itchi*), and so the guidelines for it must come from the Shintō tradition. In particular, court rituals must be cleansed of all but purely Shintō practices. Appropriate rituals would be determined by the Bureau of Religious Affairs (*jingikan*), and their implementation would be entrusted to official religious teachers (*senkyōshi*) and to local shrine priests (*kannushi*).[46]

If all of this seems rather idealized or abstract, it is offset by Saigō's views on rural administration, where his extensive personal experience permitted him to be very concrete. He believed that Western agriculture, unlike Western religion, was superior to that of Japan, and that therefore the Japanese must learn from the West. This would include the improvement of husbandry through the study of specialized texts, the adoption of more effective technology, the appointment of exceptionally efficient or effective farmers to government posts, and the creation of a national agricultural college to train new officials and to conduct research. Whenever appropriate, Western experts would be employed as advisors and teachers. And Saigō proposed the creation of a farmer's bank to control rural monetary policy and credit and to support development.[47]

The daily lives of the peasants must be carefully regulated to guarantee optimum productivity, and here Saigō brought together his abstract views on government structure and his concrete ones on agriculture. Since peasants already marked the repetitions in their yearly routines by natural cycles and the religious rituals associated with them, it should be a simple matter for the sen-kyōshi and the kannushi to indoctrinate communities about local deities, their relationships to annual agrarian cycles, and the connections between those and the religious foundations of government. Saigō in particular wanted to see local festivals revived. The people should be encouraged to worship their local gods (*kami*) on fixed occasions, to practice the traditional dances embodying religious and folkloric traditions (*kagura*), to maintain and use portable shrines (*mikoshi*), and to indulge in uninhibited eating and drinking at festival times. All of this would enhance local solidarity, promote greater productivity, and reduce discontent.[48]

Saigō also made specific proposals for the national budget and the distribution of resources to promote national development, including suggestions for taxation, fiscal policy, the maintenance of indigent samurai, and the regulation of tariffs and trade.[49] The most critical issues for him were foreign relations and the development of the military. Japan would need a strong military to survive, but strength must be built gradually, within the limits of the national budget. The same should apply to trade and industrial development. Haste might well prove disastrous. For example, if the military grew too fast, it would outstrip national resources and exhaust the economy, in the end creating a situation no less dangerous than the one it was supposed to guard against. Thus priorities and timetables must be established and followed in the allocation of funds.[50] One of Saigō's favorite examples of frivolous spending was the railroad. He saw it as an impressive example of Western achievement, and undoubtedly definitive of the Western ethos, but of no practical value for Japan at all. Efforts to make Japan look more like the West by building long rail lines would profit no one, and might well endanger national financial integrity.[51]

In phrases that are reminiscent of the nostalgic reform legislation of the late Tokugawa period, Saigō insisted that people at all levels of society must eliminate ostentation and luxury and learn to live simply and modestly.[52] This was especially true of officials, for how could ordinary people learn frugality and propriety if their rulers continually modelled the opposite? Saigō knew that many of his colleagues liked to spend their leisure time in the company of hostesses at teahouses (*chaya asobi*), and he was disgusted that they should have no qualms about setting such examples. In particular he disapproved of the behavior of Sanjō Sanetomi, who had come out of the ōsei fukko coup as one of the highest officials in the government. On 1872/4/6 Saigō wrote to the metropolitan police chief, Kawaji Toshiyoshi, and asked him to investigate Sanjō's recent activities.[53] What he meant to do is unclear, but it is interesting that in his view of politics, the behavior of officials during their private hours was very much the business of their colleagues, who evidently had not only the right but the duty to pry and snoop.

In part Saigō's views on the behavior of public officials arose from his convictions about the supreme importance of personal integrity. In part, though, they came from his beliefs about prostitution, which he thought of as a kind of rot eating at the core of society; it occupied a place in his mind similar to that occupied by illegal drugs in the minds of many today. The first indication of this came early in his public career, as we have seen.[54] He believed that prostitution weakens the social fabric, tempting those who have money to squander it, and those who have none to steal it. Prostitution not only corrupts; it encourages criminal behavior even in otherwise good people. Worst of all, prostitutes poison the character of the men who patronize them, once again endangering that personal integrity that is so important for Saigō.[55] We should not be hasty to conclude that a man who married three times and fathered nearly half a dozen children was categorically opposed to sex, but it is clear that he adhered to a strict sexual morality. If he was not actually what we would call a prude, at least he viewed sex as a private matter, and expected others to do the same. Judging from his views on prostitution, he also believed that sex should be confined to the conjugal bed. Most likely he saw it in the same light as liquor, food, money, power, and material comfort: there was nothing inherently bad about any of them, but they all posed temptations that could lead to excess and therefore to personal corruption.[56]

Some of the documents summarized above go into greater detail about certain aspects of Saigō's beliefs, but those details do not alter the overall effect of the picture outlined here. Likewise they are not at variance with the picture that emerges from Saigō's earlier memorials and other writings. He says nothing between 1870 and 1875 that we would not have expected him to say on the basis of his utterances between 1856 and 1864, nor does he fail to say those things we would have thought him most likely to say. The Saigō of the 1870s, then, is quite smoothly consistent with the Saigō of the 1850s and the 1860s. Barring clear evidence of some sort of psychological disorder – of which there is none – such consistency is, after all, what one would expect, not only in Saigō, but in anyone else.

Some of the concerns we see in his statements from the 1870s are more pressing than they were earlier, and perhaps some of his discontents bite more deeply than they did. On the whole, though, there is a surprising degree of continuity and coherence in his belief system over the years. Inconsistencies arise in his behavior, not in his thought, and it is not difficult to show that the irregularities in what he did arose primarily from his hapless attempts to act out a singularly simple, inflexible, and unforgiving system of values and beliefs in a world that was too fluid and too complex for him. It is to that world, and to his fate in it, that we turn now.

· 6 ·
Hard Times and Trouble in Tokyo,
1871–73

Saigō was in the national government for less than three years, from the time he arrived in Tokyo in 1871/2 until he left for home in 1873/10. It was a difficult and busy period, for Saigō and for Japan, and much of what makes the 1870s a time of such dramatic change took place during Saigō's term of service in Tokyo. The most conspicuous events were the abolition of the han and their replacement by prefectures (*haihan chiken*) on 1871/1/14, the departure of the Iwakura embassy for the West on 1871/11/12, and the break-up of the government over the Korea question in 1873/10. During this same period, however, a series of changes announced by the government eliminated most of the social distinctions between classes, created national military, banking, and education systems, and in other ways converted what was left of Tokugawa society into the beginnings of what we now think of as modern Japan.

Because the Korea controversy was the first major internal crisis of the Meiji government, and because the Satsuma rebellion was the last major domestic armed threat the government faced, both have received special attention, not only from Saigō scholars, but also from modern Japanese historians in general. Two other issues are prominent in the scholarship of the period. One is foreign relations, especially problems involving China, Korea, and Russia. The other is the disposition of the samurai, from the creation of the shizoku class in 1869 to the abolition of stipends and the right to wear swords in 1876.

Except for a few well-documented episodes, Saigō's part in all this activity is difficult to evaluate. As we have seen, he was active in the creation of the Tokyo metropolitan police, and he took part in the discussions that eventually produced the national banking system.[1] His role in the adoption of universal conscription and the creation of the commoner army is also well-known.[2] As we would expect from his beliefs about virtuous administration, he worried about corruption in government leaders, and made some enemies because he refused to be discreet about unethical links between government figures and private commercial enterprises.[3] And as his surviving memorials and other writings suggest, he was very much concerned with the promotion of agriculture, not only at the national level while he was in Tokyo, but even more so at the local level after he went back to Kagoshima in the autumn of 1873.

Saigō probably was not the single-minded champion of the samurai that many have made him out to be, but he was concerned about the fate of that class, especially its lower ranking members. He created some additional problems for himself through some of his efforts to provide for the maintenance of Kagoshima samurai, and it was his sense of obligation to them in particular that eventually led to his death. Finally, two other problems appear to have been of special concern for Saigō during these years. One was his health, which was already bad when he went up to Tokyo in 1871, and which continued to worsen while he was there.[4] The other was his relationship with Hisamitsu, which had never been good, and which grew steadily more troubled as time went on. Indeed, it may have been that nothing worried him more than Hisamitsu's anger.

Napping on a powder keg:
1871–3

It appears that Ōkubo was no less afraid of Hisamitsu than Saigō, but no one knew better than Saigō the consequences of angering him. When Saigō went back into exile in 1862, he suspected that Hisamitsu wanted him dead, but that he had chosen harsh exile rather than simple execution deliberately in order to cause Saigō as much suffering as possible. During the final years of the Tokugawa regime, Saigō performed well and followed Hisamitsu's own agenda closely enough that the two were able to work together, even if not to become friendly. Following the dismantling of traditional social classes and relationships by the reforms in Kagoshima during 1869–71, Hisamitsu began a slow burn, coming more and more to hold Saigō and Ōkubo personally and

131

solely responsible for everything he found distasteful about the new government.

From the perspective of Tokyo, it was clear that until secure national institutions were in place, the government would have to rely on the strength and support of Satsuma and Chōshū, so efforts began early to get Hisamitsu and Mōri Yoshichika to join the government. Neither man was eager to cooperate, and both of them repeatedly claimed illness as a pretext to avoid going to Tokyo. Yoshichika died early in 1871, proving the truth of his claims. With Hisamitsu the resistance came from nothing more than foul temper. As we have seen, he did make a brief trip to Tokyo in 1869, at which time he and Yoshichika both set out their views on the political situation in memorials to the court.[5] Hisamitsu finally gave in to incessant pressure and went back to Tokyo in the spring of 1873. He was appointed an advisor to the government, but instead of joining in its work, he bombarded it with criticisms, demanding a return to pre–1868 social and political usages, and asking repeatedly to be relieved of his duties.[6]

Early in 1874 Etō Shinpei led the disgruntled samurai of Saga in rebellion, and Hisamitsu left Tokyo again, having persuaded the government of the need to meet with Saigō and persuade him to keep Kagoshima samurai from rising in sympathy with Etō.[7] He returned to the capital on 4/21 and eight days later was appointed Minister of the Left (*sadaijin*).[8] This did not lessen his discontent, however, and on 5/23 he submitted a long memorial in which he again criticized the abandonment of traditional ways.[9] As a result of his continuing refusal to cooperate with his colleagues, or even to support them, he was finally relieved as sadaijin on 1875/10/27. He left Tokyo and had nothing further to do with the central government.[10] He spent the rest of his life in Kagoshima, and died on 1887/12/6, apparently still angry and unmollified.[11]

Judging from the tone of references to him in their writings after 1868, both Saigō and Ōkubo lived in perpetual terror of Hisamitsu's wrath. This did not keep them from pursuing their aims, certainly, and Ōkubo in particular seems to have had no trouble doing what he wanted to and enjoying remarkable success. Hisamitsu, in other words, was not able to constrain his former vassals in any important way, and in terms of any results it produced, his rage was purely impotent. But all who had worked close to him between 1859 and 1868 had vivid memories of how frightening he could be when angry, and those memories cast long shadows for Saigō and Ōkubo.

Hisamitsu's reluctance to take part in the government is not difficult to explain, and bears close resemblance to Saigō's. Like Saigō, Hisamitsu saw himself as Nariakira's agent, and all he wanted to do was carry out the plans Nariakira had left unrealized at his death. As the father of Satsuma's legitimate ruler, Hisamitsu had great authority, but he had no official status or power at any time, other than what he had acquired through honorary court rank. After 1866, because Tadayoshi was in sympathy with the aims of Saigō, Ōkubo, and others in the han, Hisamitsu was obliged to hold his peace and ride with the current. He was not opposed to the destruction of the bakufu as such, but his own final objective during the 1860s had always been to reassert the authority of the Tokugawa family through appropriate structural reform, whether that meant simply changing the bakufu or replacing it altogether. Thus it was the dismantling of the Tokugawa order after 1868 that he found abhorrent, together with the disenfranchisement of the monbatsu in Kagoshima after 1869. As I have shown, the initiative in that latter process actually came from Tadayoshi and the han's senior vassals themselves, though it undoubtedly was rendered more urgent and unavoidable by the demands of lower samurai, who probably would have carried it out more harshly in any case if those above them had not taken the decisive steps first. Neither Saigō nor Ōkubo could have prevented any of it, but Hisamitsu had asked them both to try, so he blamed it all on them, condemning them as disloyal vassals and hoping for nothing more ardently than to see them removed from power and publicly humiliated.

In the spring of 1872 the emperor made a tour of western Japan. Like his other travels during the early Meiji period, its purpose was to exhibit him to his subjects. This particular trip, however, was also meant as a grand conciliatory gesture toward discontented groups in Satsuma and Chōshū, and Saigō went along as a representative of the Tokyo government.[12] The emperor was in Kagoshima from 6/22 through 7/1, but Hisamitsu avoided meeting him, and not a single encounter took place between him and Saigō.[13] On 6/26 Hisamitsu called at the emperor's lodgings and got into a shouting match with one of his attendants, Tokudaiji Sanenori, when the latter refused to accept Hisamitsu's demand for the immediate dismissal of Saigō.[14] Two days later Hisamitsu gave Tokudaiji a fourteen-point memorial for the emperor. It called for the reversal of all that the new government had achieved so far, and the reestablishment of the social, political, and legal patterns characteristic of the Tokugawa world.[15]

Hisamitsu wanted the emperor kept in a passive role, and he wanted to see new laws to regulate intellectual orthodoxy, martial values, lewd conduct, relations between men and women, individual dress and behavior, and a host of other things that had been of more concern to bakufu lawmakers than to those of the Meiji government. In closing, Hisamitsu said:

> Under the current system of government, the country grows weaker every day. The imperial line, unbroken since time immemorial, has fallen prey to the evil abuses of republican government (*kyōwa seiji*), and we will end in subjection to the Western barbarians. It is happening right before our eyes, and I cry out in sorrow and grief. I wait upon your enlightened judgement of the crimes perpetrated by the insane and the disrespectful.[16]

If Kagoshima after 1868 became a hotbed of anti-government feeling, or the base for some sort of feudal resurgence, this and Hisamitsu's other utterances during the 1870s make it clear that such feelings were not the exclusive property of the lower samurai. It would have been natural for those samurai and others like them in Kagoshima to assume that, whether he said so or not, Hisamitsu would be likely to approve of an attempt to overthrow the Meiji government and replace it with one more suited to his taste. Thus when the rebellion finally began in 1877, the leaders of the rebel army made a special trip to Hisamitsu's residence to pay their respects to him before marching out of Kagoshima. And yet Hisamitsu condemned the Satsuma rebellion as harshly and completely as he had the government against which it was aimed. Moreover, it was clear to him where the fault for the uprising lay: after the outbreak of hostilities early in 1877, he called for an immediate cease-fire, and for the prosecution of both Saigō and Ōkubo as criminals against the state.[17]

Saigō's thoughts about Hisamitsu are not clear; his feelings are impossible to misunderstand, and it is clear that they were strong enough to provide a motive for some of his behavior. In 1871/11, hoping to improve relations, Saigō went back to Kagoshima to apologize to Hisamitsu for not paying his respects during the emperor's visit, but he found that the rupture between them was beyond repair.[18] On 1872/8/12 he wrote to Ōkubo that Hisamitsu's anger left him feeling as though someone were shooting at him with a cannon.[19] He added that Hisamitsu was unsparingly critical of both himself and Ōkubo, and had refused to have anything to do with the government as long as they were part of it. Inoue Kiyoshi has speculated that Saigō was so demoralized by Hisamitsu's criticisms that he considered homesteading in Hokkaidō, hoping to get as far away from Hisamitsu as possible.[20]

Still, however much he feared Hisamitsu, Saigō had no great esteem for him either, and made no effort to hide that from his intimates. Early in 1872, Hisamitsu had sent men to Tokyo to lobby for his own appointment as governor of Kagoshima. On 1/4 Saigō wrote to Katsura and wondered how a man who claimed to be too ill to travel to Tokyo could possibly be fit to serve in Kagoshima.[21] Eight days later he wrote to Katsura again, telling him that even Tadayoshi thought Hisamitsu's bid for influence was silly, and referring to it as a 'parade of pigs' (*tonsotsu*).[22] This problem with Hisamitsu seems to have been complicated by Saigō's view of his own position, with Kagoshima and its samurai on one side and Tokyo and the emperor on the other. He did not want his reputation in Kagoshima to be damaged by criticism from Hisamitsu's supporters, and twice he urged Katsura to be very careful with the letters in which he criticized Hisamitsu, lest they be quoted out of context in an effort to discredit him.[23]

On 1871/7/10 Saigō wrote to Katsura about a promise he had made to the samurai of Kagoshima.[24] Gradually he was realizing that if he fulfilled his obligations to the Tokyo government, he would have to betray the trust of the samurai. He told Katsura that if he should fail to protect their interests, his only remaining honorable option would be to die. As he indicated in another letter on 7/20, he was determined to push Meiji government reforms through to success, so as to finish the revolution begun in 1868 and bring Japan to a position of equality with the West. Yet to do that would oblige him to violate his lifelong obligations not only to the samurai, but also to the Shimazu, and this troubled him profoundly.[25]

Thus he found himself in an impossible position, forced to choose between the emperor and the Shimazu, but lacking any sort of ethical standard that would enable him to make an unequivocal choice. There was nothing he could do about Hisamitsu, and there was likewise nothing he could do about the steadily diverging requirements of loyalty to the Shimazu and loyalty to the emperor. On top of all that, tensions within the samurai class were growing rapidly, not only because they had begun to sense that their days were numbered, but also because they still clung to traditional attitudes about status and hierarchy, and were unable to form a united front within their own ranks.

In 1872/7, during the emperor's tour of western Japan, Saigō had been obliged to leave the entourage and hurry back to Tokyo to solve a problem in the imperial guard (*go-shinpei*), where status inequalities and inter-han animosities had exacerbated one another to produce a potentially disastrous situation. The imperial guard was composed of samurai from Satsuma, Chōshū, and Tosa, but nearly half of them were from Satsuma, while the commander was a Chōshū man, Yamagata Aritomo, and the Satsuma samurai resented being subject to his orders. Even within their own ranks, the Satsuma samurai were split into factions consisting of former castle town samurai and former gōshi. To make matters worse, Yamagata had retained a businessman named Yamashiroya to provide supplies for the guard, and this man had misappropriated large sums of the money entrusted to him, bringing on accusations from Satsuma troops that all Chōshū samurai were corrupt.[26] Saigō was able to calm everyone's tempers and avert disaster, in part by replacing Yamagata as commander of the guard. But as he wrote to Ōkubo soon afterward, all of the discontent brewing throughout the country among the samurai left him feeling as if he were 'napping on a powder keg' (*haretsudan chū ni hirune itashi ori mōshi sōrō*).[27]

All of these troubles contributed to Saigō's growing sense that conditions in Japan were generally unsatisfactory. When the Iwakura mission set out for the West, all members of the government had signed an agreement that the caretaker government would enact no major changes during the mission's absence without prior consultation.[28] In fact, this agreement was honored for the most part in the breach, as the caretaker government created the banking and education systems and introduced military conscription, among a host of other major changes, all while Iwakura and his fellows were abroad. In any event, Saigō did not like being bound by this agreement and what it implied for him. Just before the Iwakura group left, Saigō told Katsura that he felt like nothing more than a watchman, set by Ōkubo and Iwakura to protect their political turf until they came back.[29]

Not long before this, he had told Katsura about a meeting

he had had with Katsu Kaishū, their first since the surrender of Edo in 1868. The two men agreed how remarkable it was that neither of them had been murdered by Tokugawa partisans during those hectic days, and then they slipped into nostalgia, as Saigō explained:

> ... [Katsu] says that when he looks back on those days now, he thinks it would have been better if he had died then. I agreed wholeheartedly that I sometimes feel that way myself. I have nothing more than these few words to go by, but I know just how he feels in his heart.[30]

Clearly Saigō was not feeling good about the way Japan was changing, and he did not stop with nostalgia for the past. He looked hopefully toward the future as well:

> Surely when I am reborn I will enjoy a beautiful wife and fine food, and I will lounge in a palace of jade. I think thus of nothing but the life to come, and I have no other desires.[31]

What we see here is a man who would have been delighted to be anywhere other than where he was. Effective though he might be in the right circumstances, Saigō simply did not have the imagination, the flexibility, or the emotional toughness to be a successful politician, especially not in a world changing as rapidly as that of early Meiji Japan. Thus it is not surprising to see him reaching wistfully toward both the past and the future – anything to escape the dreadful and relentless uncertainty of the present.

Saigō recognized that Japan must have a strong military establishment loyal only to the sovereign and the state, and he agreed with Yamagata that the best way to provide such a force was through conscription and universal military service. But the adoption of that approach would betray the samurai, who had assumed Saigō would protect their traditional prerogatives. The samurai objected to conscription not only because it threatened their survival, but also because it insulted their dignity. Kirino Toshiaki dismissed Yamagata's proposal to enlist peasants as a foolish effort to make warriors out of dirt farmers.[32] For the samurai of Satsuma, it was bad enough that the idea of conscription had originated with Chōshū men; it was the ultimate of betrayal when Saigō supported it.

In the same way, Saigō knew that Japan must have a strong centralized government in order to survive in the international environment, but to create such a government would require the destruction of traditional daimyo prerogatives, particularly those of the Shimazu. He could agree that such a centralized state should not and must not continue to support the samurai as han governments had done, but he could not get from that awareness to an acceptance that the samurai were therefore obsolete. In his desperate scramble to find a way to reconcile all these conflicting demands, he only managed to drive himself into a different corner, this time dangerously closer to the heart of his own ethical system than ever before.

Saigō had no quarrel with government plans to regulate, to reduce, and finally to eliminate samurai stipends, because he agreed that it was necessary. In Kagoshima, samurai searching for a way to replace their former stipends eventually hit upon the old han sugar monopoly in the Amami islands.[33] The lives of the islanders had not changed after 1868; sugar production had continued under the same harsh conditions as before. Now the Kagoshima government converted the monopoly into a private commercial operation called the Ōshima Mercantile (*Ōshima shōsha*), and began using its profits to pay samurai stipends. On 1871/12/11 Saigō wrote to Katsura and expressed his approval for these changes.[34] His only concern was that if the Ministry of Finance found out about the new arrangement, it might try either to tax it or simply to take it over, and he warned Katsura to maintain a low profile and to keep the details secret.

Unfortunately, the creation of the Ōshima Mercantile made life for the islanders even more difficult than it had been under the rule of the han. When exiled to Ōshima in 1859, Saigō had condemned the han's uncaring exploitation of the inhabitants; now he supported a plan that would continue that same exploitation for the sake of the samurai. By 1873 the islanders could take no more. Recalling Saigō's benevolence and generosity while he was among them, and probably unaware of his support for this new form of exploitation, they delegated his former overseer from Okinoerabu, Tsuchimochi Masateru, to travel to Tokyo and seek his help. On 1873/6/19 Saigō reported Tsuchimochi's visit to Matsukata Masayoshi, a former Satsuma samurai and now a tax official in the Ministry of Finance.[35] He asked that Matsukata employ government pressure on Kagoshima to improve the exchange rate of sugar for rice, and thus to alleviate the excessive hardship of the islanders. He warned Matsukata that failure to ease the islanders' burdens could well lead to trouble there.

In other words, having approved the exploitation of the islanders for the sake of the samurai, and having warned Katsura to keep everything secret from the government, Saigō himself now revealed everything to the government in an effort to reduce the suffering of the very same islanders he had agreed to exploit. He could not ignore Tsuchimochi. Not only was he heavily indebted to the man – for his very life if nothing else – he had also written for this same man two moralizing treatises on the requirements for just administration, requirements his own support of the Ōshima Mercantile had flagrantly violated.

This whole sequence of events must have taxed Saigō's emotional endurance to the limit, to say nothing of his mental resourcefulness. The abolition of the han had been a betrayal of the Shimazu. On top of that, the adoption of conscription was a betrayal of the samurai. Hoping to set these problems right, Saigō supported the conversion of the sugar monopoly, which only led him straight into the betrayal not only of the peasants, but of his own belief system about how they should be treated by their superiors. To rectify those two transgressions, he had no choice but to go back to his betrayals of the Shimazu and the samurai.

Saigō was now under intolerable pressure, and desparate for a way to escape from his overlapping dilemmas. Small wonder that he likened the feeling to napping on a powder keg. Hisamitsu rained opprobrium on him from above, while from all around him came the grumblings of samurai, and all of these voices accused him of deceit, duplicity, and dishonor, the very things he tried so hard to avoid in himself and abhorred most of all in others. If he could find no way to reconcile these conflicting demands, then his prediction to Katsura would have proven correct, and his only remaining option would be to sacrifice himself. Weighing all these things together, Inoue Kiyoshi concludes that it was as a way out of this maze that Saigō turned his eyes toward Korea for the first time in the middle of 1872.[36]

I have found nothing either to confirm or to refute Inoue's assertion, but as I hope to show, it does not account entirely for Saigō's interest in Korea. In fact, Saigō's interest was not confined to Korea alone. Rather, that country for him was just one piece in the larger puzzle of Japan's foreign relations, and the image at the center of that puzzle was not Korea, or China, or any of the Western powers that had been so prominent in Japan's bakumatsu struggles. It was Russia, made fearsome by the awareness already widespread in Saigō's time of how easily that massive country could overwhelm and absorb Japan.

Saigō was convinced that the Russians intended to extend their military control into both Hokkaido and Korea, and then to use those areas to stage an irresistible assault on Japan itself.[37] He had set Kirino Toshiaki to searching for feasible ways to establish a Japanese garrison in Hokkaido, so as to check Russian ambitions there. When his interest in Korea began to grow, it was probably this same sense of the Russian threat more than anything else that guided his thinking. Unlike later government leaders, Saigō never used the image of a dagger pointed at Japan's heart to characterize Korea, but if he had done so, there would have been no doubt in his mind about whose hand held that dagger poised to strike. The entire sequence of events from the Sino-Japanese war of 1894–95, through the Triple Intervention of 1895 and the Anglo-Japanese alliance of 1902, to the Russo-Japanese war of 1904–05, would have made perfectly good sense to him.

Nor was Russia the only external problem demanding attention. On 1871/11/7, fifty-four seamen from Okinawa were slaughtered by natives on Taiwan after their ship went adrift there. Strident calls had been issued for the punishment of the Taiwanese, but the problem was complicated by the ambiguity of traditional relations that criss-crossed among Japan, Okinawa, Taiwan, and China. Okinawa had been under Shimazu rule since the beginning of the Tokugawa period, so naturally an attack on them was tantamount to an attack on Satsuma. Like others, Saigō was angry about the murder of the fifty-four fishermen, and eager for retribution.

Given the urgency of his concerns about both Russia and Taiwan, Saigō had no special reason to be interested in Korea until circumstances brought it to center stage for him. To see how that came about, we need to back up and examine some of the other events that produced the context in which Korea gained the attention not only of Saigō but of most other people in Japan as well.

As if I were flying:
1871–73

The first order of business after Saigō got to Tokyo in 1871 was the creation of a military unit loyal to the emperor alone. Plans for the abolition of the han had already been discussed, but everyone realized that the government would be unable to defend itself if such a major step should encounter resistance. Saigō left Tokyo on 2/15 to raise troops in Kagoshima, and returned just over two months later, accompanied by Tadayoshi and four battalions of Kagoshima's newly organized army. Three battalions from Chōshū and two from Tosa were added to create the emperor's personal guard. With this force in place, and Saigō's promise to lead it without hesitation even against Kagoshima if need be, the abolition of the han was announced on 1871/7/14.[38]

As it turned out, only Hisamitsu and a few others raised any objection at all. The daimyo had already been given guaranteed annual incomes based on the assessed productivity of their han as of 1869. The social reforms that had followed hanseki hōkan in 1869–70 had made them all members of the nobility (*kazoku*), a clear improvement in status. With haihan chiken, the central government assumed all of their outstanding debts, which freed them of worries altogether. The majority of them had every reason to welcome the change, unless, like Hisamitsu, they saw it simply as a threat to the social order that defined their personal identities. Most of them had been passive bystanders throughout the nineteenth century. By 1871 they had little left to lose through the abolition of their hereditary domains, and much to gain under the new government.

The social class most obviously at risk in these changes was that of the samurai. With the creation of the shizoku they had already lost the elaborate and finely graded distinctions by which they had been keeping track of their identities for two and a half centuries. Now they had lost the hanshu on whose support they had depended for generations, and many of them already understood perfectly well that the central government could not afford to go on paying them their stipends for very long. Except for unusual individuals, such as Godai Tomoatsu in Satsuma or Iwasaki Yatarō in Tosa, most samurai remained contemptuous of commerce, business, and farming, and were not about to dirty their hands or to compromise their own pride by trying to support themselves in such occupations. It was with these things in mind that Saigō had memorialized the government on the disposition of stipends, and had supported the appropriation and conversion of the sugar monopoly.[39]

Prior to the haihan chiken announcement, the government had been completely reshuffled. An order of 4/23 created military garrisons (*chindai*) in Tōhoku and Kyushu. Then, on 6/25, Saigō and Kido were named councillors (*sangi*).[40] Everyone else was reassigned in the ensuing weeks: Ōkubo ended up heading the finance ministry. All now agreed that the next steps were to begin promoting rapid domestic development and to seek revision of the unequal treaties with the West. In keeping with the Meiji Charter Oath these men had issued as soon as they had come to power in 1868, they also meant to inspect the West in detail, hoping to discover the secrets of its strength. To these ends, a group of over fifty people was assembled under the leadership of Iwakura Tomomi, with Ōkubo and Kido sharing secondary command. This group embarked at Shinagawa on 1871/11/12 and set out across the Pacific for a journey of nearly two years. In the caretaker government they left behind, Sanjō Sanetomi acted as head of state, with Saigō acting as his second, and replacing Ōkubo in charge of the finance ministry.[41]

As the previous section has shown, the ensuing two years were difficult ones for Saigō. He never found a solution to the problem of Hisamitsu's anger, but eventually he began to suspect that perhaps the best solution to the problem of samurai discontent might be to send them abroad on some sort of military campaign. Such an adventure would play well in the public eye, unifying patriotic spirit at home. And it would give the samurai something to do, thus taking their minds away from their grievances. More than that, if it succeeded it also would offer clear proof that the military value of the samurai made them indispensable to the government.

By the middle of 1872 the tensions among the samurai had grown to the breaking point. If Inoue Kiyoshi and other biographers are correct, it was at this point that Saigō began to think of Korea as a place for them to let off some of their steam. Hitherto he had tended to regard talk of overseas military adventures, in Korea or anywhere else, as premature and frivolous, and had gone on record as flatly opposed to the idea of any sort of action against Korea.[42] At a time when Japan needed all its resources for development at home, it was irresponsible to think of pouring wealth into adventures abroad. This line of reasoning, adopted by Ōkubo in 1873, was likewise the one that seemed most natural to Saigō until around the middle of 1872.

Interest in Korea had a long history in Japan. Successive governments had maintained some form of relations with the peninsula intermittently for centuries. And there were precedents for military action as well, not only in Hideyoshi's invasions, and in the glorious campaigns of the Shimazu armies, but also in the legendary invasion by the empress Jingū Kōgō at the dawn of Japan's recorded history.[43] During the bakumatsu period, the merits of a Japanese occupation of Korea were discussed by many thinkers, including Katsu Kaishū, Kido Takayoshi, Yoshida Shōin, Hashimoto Sanai, and even Nariakira, as a way to keep the Russian menace at bay.[44] Note that even this incomplete list includes three men who influenced Saigō's thinking tremendously.

Concern about Korea revived soon after the 1868 coup, when the Korean government refused to recognize the new Japanese government because the documents announcing its formation contained language which Korean officials found insulting.[45] Among the first to call for retaliatory action was Kido, and the first formal discussion of that possibility took place on the eve of the Iwakura group's departure. On 1871/11/9, there was a meeting to discuss Kido's demand for action; present were Kido, Iwakura, Sanjō, Ōkuma Shigenobu, and Itagaki Taisuke. Nothing was decided, and the matter was deferred for future review, but apparently no one questioned either the need for some kind of exemplary step, or Japan's right to take it.[46] It should be noted that Saigō was not involved in any of these early discussions, and did not become involved until the late summer of 1873, when he joined discussions between Itagaki and then foreign minister Soejima Taneomi. They decided to send men into Korea, China, and Manchuria to collect information. Among those sent were Beppu Shinsuke and Ikegami Shirō, who subsequently commanded elements of the Satsuma rebel army.[47]

The men who later created the Shigakkō system in Kagoshima began to gather around Saigō at about the same time he began to develop an active interest in Korea. These included Kirino Toshiaki, Shinohara Kunimoto, Beppu Shinsuke, and Ikegami Shirō. Kirino was originally a gōshi, while the others were koshō-gumi from the castle town. It is noteworthy that these four men had already figured prominently in the reforms of 1869-71, and had emerged from that process in command of military units under the new organization described in the last chapter. They had then followed Saigō to Tokyo and had taken posts in the imperial guard and other elements of the emerging Meiji military establishment. Others of prominence in the Shigakkō system, particularly Ōyama Tsunayoshi and Murata Shinpachi, had been intimate with Saigō since the 1850s.

According to Inoue Kiyoshi, the first reference to Korea in a Meiji period document is an entry in Kido's diary for 1868/12/14, where he mentions discussing the matter with Iwakura.[48] Inoue speculates that there might have been three possible motives for Japanese involvement with Korea. First, it would divert domestic attention abroad, giving the government leeway to consolidate its position at home. Second, it would enable Japan to draw on Korean monetary resources to pay its foreign debts. And third, it would put Japan in a dominant position on the peninsula before Russia could get there.[49] Interest in Korea then, for others as well as for Saigō, actually had little to do with Korea itself, but much to do with Japan's foreign relations with other countries, especially Russia.

In the summer of 1873, Soejima Taneomi had gone to China to discuss treaty relations and the Taiwan problem, and had found while there a surprising level of American and British support for the idea of Japanese military action in both Taiwan and Korea.[50] On 1873/7/21 Saigō wrote to his brother Tsugumichi concerning preparations for armed action against Taiwan.[51] Judging from details such as these, Japan's leaders were getting ready to tackle the problem posed by Taiwan and its relationship to China. In the spring of that year, however, Korea had taken a number of hostile measures against Japanese traders, and Itagaki and others now began to demand that Japan send troops to Korea to protect its citizens there. In a council meeting on 6/12, Itagaki argued for sending troops, while Saigō wanted to send an emissary first to discuss the situation with Korean officials.[52] Soejima returned from China on 7/26. As foreign minister he was the logical choice to go to Korea, but Saigō wanted that mission for himself, and managed to persuade both Soejima and Itagaki to let him have it. On 8/17 a full council session agreed to name Saigō as special emissary to Korea, but after a meeting with the emperor at Hakone the next day, Sanjō stated that no formal announcement of Saigō's appointment would be made until after the Iwakura group returned.[53]

The first mention of Korea in Saigō's writings appears in a letter to Itagaki dated 1873/7/29, barely two weeks before the council session in which it was decided to send Saigō to the peninsula. Saigō wrote to Itagaki not because they agreed about Korea, but because Itagaki was easily the most outspoken advocate of immediate military action. To win his support could mean to carry the council, and even as nearsighted a politician as Saigō could figure out that much. Most of what Saigō said about Korea in later statements appeared for the first time in this letter.

> Many thanks for coming such a long way to see me the other day.[54]
>
> Now that Soejima has returned, we should have a decision on the Korea matter soon, I imagine. If there is nothing further to discuss, would you let me know when we will be summoned to court, so that I will have a chance to suppress my illness and attend?
>
> If we have reached a decision at last, then must we really be so determined to start by sending troops? If we do send them, make no mistake that the Koreans will demand that we withdraw them, and if we refuse to do that, it will surely lead to armed conflict.
>
> Such an outcome would be contrary to our original aims, and I wonder whether we are really at the point where we have to provoke a fight. Would it not be better to send an emissary? I can foresee that if we did, the Koreans would surely resort to violence, and our right to strike them would then be clearly established.
>
> If we send troops first, it will be as it was in Sakhalin. The Russians have already sent defensive troops in there, and we fight with them from time to time. We probably ought to deploy defensive troops before Korea does, but if we do that it would set up all sorts of obstacles for us in the future.
>
> If we send an official emissary over there, I imagine the Koreans still would kill him, and I beg you to send me. I cannot be a fine diplomat like Soejima, but if it is only a matter of dying, that much I think I can manage. Therefore I hope you will send me. Please excuse me for being blunt, but I give you this in writing in the hope of your full agreement.
>
> Respectfully.
>
> 7/29[55]

This was the first of eight letters Saigō wrote to Itagaki, the last of which is dated 9/3. With only minor variations, all eight of them make essentially the same argument, in essentially the same terms.

On the evening prior to the council meeting which appointed him, Saigō had a private meeting with Sanjō,[56] who was worried that Saigō and Itagaki meant simpy to go and provoke a war with Korea. Saigō assured Sanjō that armed force was only a last resort, in case negotiations failed. Then, writing about this meeting to Itagaki, Saigō said that if the Koreans refused to be reasonable, then Japan would be justified in using force, and that in turn would offer a way to release potentially rebellious energy outside the country.[57] In other words, having assured Sanjō that his mission to Korea probably would not lead to war, Saigō then assured Itagaki that it probably would do just that.

Following the decision to send him to Korea, Saigō went to Itagaki's residence to thank him personally for his help, but found him away from home. On 8/19, therefore, he wrote:

> My illness has left me altogether. From Sanjō's residence to yours it was as though I flew, my feet without weight. There are no further obstacles in my way, and this is the happiest moment of my life.[58]

A few days later Itagaki called on Saigō. What they talked about is unknown, but it seems Itagaki cautioned Saigō not to be too eager to rush off to his death. On 8/23, Saigō wrote Itagaki again to tell him not to worry: he certainly did not covet long life, but he was also in no hurry to die. After all, the emperor had taken a special interest in his health, placing him under the care of his personal physicians, and it would be ungracious, at the very least, for Saigō to make light of the sovereign's concern by throwing away his life casually.[59]

All now seemed to be as Saigō wished it, but his contentment was not destined to last very long. Ōkubo had returned to Japan on 5/23 and had withdrawn to the countryside to see how the Korea problem would evolve. Kido returned on 7/23, and Iwakura finally got back on 9/13. Saigō went about his preparations for departure, while those in the opposing camp attempted to assemble a united front. Ōkubo was reluctant to become directly involved in the dispute, but under pressure from Iwakura he finally accepted appointment as sangi on 10/12. Other appointments had been made earlier. When the first council meeting convened on 10/14, those present were Saigō, Itagaki, Gotō Shōjirō, Etō Shinpei, and Soejima Taneomi, all in favor of Saigō's appointment as a special emissary to Korea, and Iwakura, Sanjō, Ōkubo, Ōkuma Shigenobu, and Ōki Takatō, all opposed, not just to Saigō's plans, but to any action involving Korea. Kido was supposed to have attended this meeting, but was too ill to do so.[60]

Nothing was settled on 10/14. In reply to Saigō's presentation, which was not recorded but which apparently was a repetition of the arguments he had been making to Itagaki all along, Iwakura protested that both the confrontation with Russia in Sakhalin and the one with China over Taiwan were more urgent than the problem of Korea, but Saigō was not moved by this approach. He was not present the next day, when Ōkubo made his case.

Ōkubo's arguments on the 15th were much more elaborate. He began by insisting that the government must consolidate its domestic position first, as it would be disastrous if a rebellion were to break out while the army was out of the country. To underscore this claim, he pointed out that the steps necessary to raise money for Japan's already heavy foreign debts might well increase popular discontent to the flash point. Moreover, a foreign war would create a volatile domestic climate in its own way, heightening patriotic fervor on one hand while generating resentment at additional taxes on the other. Waging war would create an unfavorable balance of trade, he went on, and the only real winner in an exhausting conflict between Japan and Korea would be Russia. Especially worrisome was Japan's debt to Britain, and failure to pay that off soon could place Japan in a position similar to that of India. In the end, nothing was more important than getting the foreign treaties revised and war in Korea would only delay that process.[61]

Ōkubo's arguments were cogent and persuasive, and the irony is that Saigō would have argued much the same points a year earlier. He did not see things that way now, however, and for whatever reason, both Iwakura and Sanjō agreed that they must abide by the 8/17 council decision, and announce Saigō's appointment as special emissary to Korea. To Ōkubo this felt like betrayal, and he resigned his appointment on 10/17, but he continued to work behind the scenes, where by his own political temperament he would have preferred to operate in any case. On 10/18, Sanjō suffered a nervous collapse, and Iwakura was named to take his place. Iwakura met with the emperor, and on 10/23 announced that confirmation of Saigō's appointment would be postponed indefinitely. Saigō then settled the issue by submitting his resignation, on account of illness, on the same day.[62]

In a covering letter, Saigō stated that there was no point in trying to persuade him to reconsider his resignation, as he had no intention of returning to government service.[63] He left Tokyo the same day, and on 10/28 he left Yokohama by ship, arriving back at Kagoshima two weeks later. At the time of his resignation, he held three positions: member of the Council of State (*sangiin*), commander of the imperial guard (*Konoe tōtoku*), and general of the army (*rikugun taishō*). The court relieved him of the first two posts, but retained him in the third. Thus, at the time of the rebellion he was still a senior officer in the national army, and therefore technically guilty of treason regardless of what his true intentions may have been.[64]

Saigō spelled out his final position on the Korean question in a memorial submitted on 10/17, the day of Ōkubo's resignation. It gives a fair synopsis of the arguments characteristic of all of his surviving statements on the matter:

We have sent a number of missions to Korea since the Restoration, and we have done our best, but it has all come to nothing. Recently the Koreans have driven Japanese citizens living there into difficult circumstances, interfering with the flow of commerce between our peoples. As a result, some in the government have proposed that we should send a battalion of troops over there to protect our citizens. But it would not be good at all to send troops. If doing so should lead to war, it would be contrary to our true intentions, and so the proper thing to do at this point is to send an official emissary.

We must do all that is humanly possible until Korea breaks off negotiations and makes its true intentions clear by resorting to war. Otherwise our own sincerity will be in peril. If we assume that Korea wants war, and send our emissary only after getting ready to fight, we will compromise our own propriety. We must try to realize our original aim, to establish a firm friendship with Korea.

If the Koreans resort to violence after all of that, then we can denounce their wrongs, and we can call them to account for their misdeeds. If we denounce them for their wrongs before we have sought a genuine solution through our own efforts, then the charge of failure to comprehend accusations of wrongdoing would apply to both parties. The outrage of the attacker would not be genuinely righteous, and the one attacked would not submit.

What matters most is to be absolutely clear as to the right and wrong of the problem. That is the way we framed it, and that is the way we adopted it. It was agreed internally that I would be sent as the emissary. And that is how matters have developed up to now.[65]

It is difficult to find anything in this document suggesting that Saigō wanted the chance to provoke Korea into a war with Japan. On the contrary, it reads very much as if what he wanted was to find a way to overcome mutual distrust and suspicion so that Japan and Korea could work toward mutually beneficial relations founded on good will. In any case, this was to be his final word on the issue of sending him to Korea, but it was not the last thing he had to say about relations between that country and Japan.

Early in 1876, Korea signed a treaty of friendship with Japan, negotiated with considerable reliance on threats and bluster by Kuroda Kiyotaka and Inoue Kaoru. A Japanese vessel conducting a survey had exchanged fire with coastal batteries on the Korean island of Kang Hwa, and this incident had given Japan exactly the pretext it needed to present Korea with the choice of signing a treaty or going to war. It was gunboat diplomacy in the grand manner, and if Saigō had hoped at any point for Japanese dominance on the peninsula, he should have welcomed the signing of this treaty as a great triumph. Instead, he condemned it out of hand.

On 1876/10/8, he wrote to Shinohara Kunimoto, commenting on the Kang Hwa settlement.[66] How regrettable, he said, that Japan had resorted to armed force in dealing with a country with which it had been in normal and peaceful contact for so long. It would have been better if Japan had attempted negotiation first, instead of firing on the island without even trying to discover the truth about the situation. In the end, there could be no excuse for a nation as powerful as Japan to intimidate one as weak as Korea, when a civil and forthright exchange of views would have served equally well. The whole episode was a source of shame for Japan, declared Saigō, in the eyes of the world and in the eyes of Heaven.

One wonders whether Saigō noticed the irony in this. Two years earlier, he had left the government because his colleagues, fearing he wanted to provoke a war, had refused to give him the chance to negotiate first. Now those same colleagues had resorted to military provocation themselves in order to secure a treaty, when negotiations might have served just as well, and it was left for Saigō to condemn them for doing almost exactly what they had feared he wanted to do. We need to see what sense we can make of this irony, and of the evidence available for an interpretation of the blurry historical reality behind it.

Unravelling the *seikanron* dispute

Because the evidence is so frustratingly spotty, and because the conflict of interpretations is so enduring in Japan, the Korea dispute itself has become one of the Gordian Knots of modern Japanese historiography.[67] Major new interpretations of the episode seem to appear in Japan only once or twice in a generation. Other less original readings of the evidence appear more frequently, but tend to be little more than affirmations or rejections of whatever the most ambitious new interpretation has offered as the last word on the subject.[68] Nearly all such readings end up searching for the links between Saigō's agenda in 1873 and his motivation in 1877, assuming that seikanron and the Satsuma rebellion are necessarily connected, simply because Saigō was involved in both. Only rarely does one find interpretations that view the dispute and its aftermath in the context of other historical events at the time. Yet these rare and adventuresome approaches actually make the most sense, chiefly because this sort of contextual perspective offers the only way to see the seikanron crisis for what it most obviously and importantly was: a power struggle within the evolving Meiji oligarchy.

On the surface, the seikanron episode looks like an argument about whether Japan's leaders should make war on Korea, or secure their political position in Japan. That is, it looks like a quarrel over mutually exclusive priorities, and so historians have identified the two sides in the dispute as a group advocating overseas military action (*gaiseiha*), and a group calling for domestic consolidation (*naijiha*). Not surprisingly, Saigō is held to speak for the gaiseiha, which is made up mostly of members of the caretaker government, while Ōkubo speaks for the naijiha, which is composed of those who went abroad with Iwakura. In this reading, those who had been overseas and had seen how much Japan would have to change to achieve parity with the West were aware that ambitious military adventures were simply beyond Japan's capacity, and therefore out of the question, regardless of their desirability.

This last point is important to bear in mind: at no time during the dispute did anyone question Japan's right to dictate terms to Korea. On the contrary, at the heart of the controversy was the unspoken assumption that Korea was in the wrong because it was refusing to grant Japan the recognition and the rights it deserved by virtue of its own developmental and geopolitical needs, whose validity was assumed to be self-evident. Thus Korea deserved whatever happened to it, and the only problem was to figure out what that should be.[69]

Many historians, having come this far in their analyses, have postulated that the dispute was therefore not an argument about priorities, but one about timing: invade Korea first, or catch up to the West first? The timing question assumes that everyone in the government agreed that Japan should force itself on Korea, and disagreed only about when that should happen. It is tantalizing as an explanation because, as we saw above, within three years after the government split over sending Saigō to negotiate with the Koreans, Japan had indeed forced itself on them, and had achieved without a war what members of the gaiseiha presumably had hoped to achieve by provoking a war.

Both the question of priorities and that of timing were important in bringing on the seikanron crisis, and when the issue was settled, those for whom the council's decision was the wrong one left Tokyo. Some, like Ōkuma Shigenobu and Itagaki Taisuke, went back to their native provinces and took the first steps toward creating political parties, hoping to get themselves back inside the government from which they had just been squeezed out. Others, like Etō Shinpei and Maebara Issei, returned to their homelands and then rose up in rebellion, likewise hoping to reclaim positions of influence for themselves in the government, only by less pacific means. Meanwhile, with all significant opposition removed from the scene, those who stayed in Tokyo were at liberty to redefine the national agenda however they saw fit, and to implement it without interference from political opponents.

In the end, the issue that was settled by the outcome of the seikanron crisis was not just whether to seek glory in Korea or to put the domestic house in order, nor was it which of those two goals ought to be pursued first, though of course both sets of questions were important, and were settled. The central questions were: who would make those decisions, and in pursuit of what national agenda. The answers provided by the outcome were all in favor of the members of the Iwakura group, most particularly Ōkubo and his political proteges, who soon came to dominate the national government to a degree unimagined by any shogun.

To put the point in different terms, everyone who joined in the coalition of forces that overthrew the Tokugawa was motivated by a vision of what Japan's future should be, but no one had the time before 1868 to worry much about the differences among those visions. Once the threat from the Tokugawa was eliminated, it was only a matter of time before those differing visions came into conflict. In my reading of the Korea dispute, it is most essentially that contest of visions, up for settlement at last, and it did resolve the question of whose vision was going to inform Japan's agenda, at least in the short run. Such conflicts of vision are characteristic of all major political transitions where a long-standing order is removed so that it can be replaced by something else as yet not clearly defined or understood.[70]

This means that the dispute was not a contest between Saigō and Ōkubo, and that what was at stake was not the fate of the samurai. Thus it also means that Saigō's involvement in the episode, while terribly important to him for his own reasons, was not very important in deciding the outcome and its significance for national politics. It means, finally, that seikanron, or something very much like it, would have occurred sooner or later, serving as a mechanism to resolve the conflicting visions of Meiji Japan's leaders and leave only one of them in effect. It does not mean, necessarily, that anyone involved in the dispute at the time understood that this was what was going on, though I suspect that Ōkubo did understand. If he did, then that helps to explain why his view of things prevailed, and why he so quickly came to dominate the government once the seikanron matter was settled.

The episode's significance in Japan's modern history, then, is different from its significance in Saigō's life. Yet if I have found an acceptable way to characterize its import for Japan's development, I still need to explain what it meant for Saigō, and what he hoped to achieve through his involvement in it. Notice, first, that there is no mention of Korea in Saigō's writings until barely two weeks before it comes to dominate the government's agenda. That is, Saigō's position on Korea, even when we see it for the first time, has not been uppermost in his mind prior to that point. Rather, he articulates his position in response to that of Itagaki only after the latter forces Korea to the top of the government's list of concerns. As I have pointed out, some scholars believe that Saigō may have begun thinking about Korea as a possible solution for the problem of samurai unrest as early as the middle of 1872,[71] but if we are bound by the evidence available, he did not consider it important enough to comment on it until the summer of 1873. And if that is the case, then it would be difficult to sustain the argument made by some that the eruption of the seikanron crisis was the final manifestation of a dream of conquest Saigō had been harboring for a long time.

Regardless of when he finally started thinking about Korea, the question that has always dominated the conflict of interpretations is: what did he want to do there? Because he said it in so many words himself, I think Saigō probably did see action in Korea as a way to release some of the pressure building up among samurai in Japan. At the same time, it is important to note that he said this to Itagaki, who would have found it appealing, and who therefore would support him in the council. He said just the opposite to Sanjō, who would not support him in the council unless it were clear that an immediate outbreak of hostilities was not what Saigō hoped for.[72] Thus, however serviceable Korea might have appeared as a safety valve for domestic samurai unrest, it does not follow that Saigō found it desirable, and there is not enough evidence to settle this point. Going by the available evidence, it appears that Saigō figured out whose support he must have in order to carry the council in his favor, and then told those people what he knew they would need to hear in order to give him that support.

The passages from Saigō I have quoted above are sufficient to show that, even if he did want to see Japanese military action in Korea, he wanted it to come only after every effort to find a solution by diplomacy had been tried and proven inadequate. He speaks repeatedly of resorting to force only after other events have established that the Koreans deserve nothing better than force, and only after Korean intransigence has ruled out the possibility of friendship between the two countries. In his 10/17 deposition to the council, he goes so far as to assert that Japan's original aim toward Korea has always been to establish a 'firm friendship.'[73]

If Saigō could knowingly commit Satsuma to mutually exclusive obligations in alliances with Chōshū and with Tosa, as we saw earlier, or if he could deliberately tell Itagaki and Sanjō contradictory things simply because he knew they needed to hear them, then it is quite possible that he also could speak of a firm friendship with Korea when he meant nothing of the kind. Moreover it is possible, as many scholars have argued, that if Saigō was willing to die in Korea in order to give Japan a suitable pretext for military action, then he must have wanted that action pretty desperately himself.

These are not unreasonable conclusions to reach if one looks only at the documents of 1873, but there is other evidence, and it points in a different direction. That evidence suggests, in short, that what Saigō hoped to achieve in Korea was what he already had achieved in Chōshū in 1864, and in Edo in 1868, and what he had probably hoped to achieve in Kyoto as early as 1862. Certain elements are consistent in Saigō's approaches to all of these episodes, and they become more conspicuous as success in one experiment leads to confidence in the outcome of the next, and to refinement of the overall formula. That formula runs as follows.

First he agrees that there is a deadlock, and that a solution is essential, but that the behavior of the other party is unacceptable, rendering a solution impossible; therefore some sort of retaliation seems called for. He then argues that one who resorts to violence without first exhausting more reasonable and less disruptive solutions lowers himself to the same level of moral bankruptcy as the opponent whose behavior he seeks to correct. To protect the righteousness of the aggrieved party, Saigō insists that talk must come before force, and he offers to do the talking himself. He approaches representatives of the other party with the assumption that their view of the situation is valid, whether he agrees with it or not. In other words, he suspends judgement and takes his opponent's position seriously. More importantly, he approaches his opponent alone and unarmed, and he makes it clear that finding a solution through discussion is so important to him that he is willing to die trying it. His willingness to die is nothing more than the final proof of his own sincerity. If all goes well, the opponent will be won over by Saigō's candor and sincerity, and the deadlock will be resolved peacefully and to everyone's satisfaction. If the opponent is really as bad as everyone says, on the other hand, then he will kill the mediator, thus demonstrating for all to see that he deserves to be punished.

The consistency with which these elements come up in Saigō's proposals for the use of this approach, together with their faithful reappearance in his arguments about Korea, suggest that what he hoped to achieve there was, like what he had achieved at earlier

154

moments of crisis, a mutually acceptable negotiated settlement that would give both parties more or less what they wanted and would also eliminate the need for violence. It is not difficult to show that this sort of formula would have appealed to Saigō.

In Saigō's understanding of Confucianism – which he learned as a child in the last days of the Tokugawa world and then adapted to his own needs as an adult in exile – the relationship between humanity and Heaven is the most important element of all, and the only way to test the character of that relationship is through action. What Heaven wants in human affairs, however, is not violence and disorder but their opposites, tranquility and orderliness. Accordingly, every effort must be made to behave so as to avoid the former condition and to bring about and perpetuate the latter one. Not surprisingly, the formula for mediation Saigō developed after returning from the exile where he put all these ideas together would have had the effect of achieving exactly those results.

Certainly it is possible to take a cynical perspective. One can view this formula as nothing more than a sort of sting, an elaborate subterfuge with which to entrap one's opponent and force him to provide one with a pretext for an attack. It probably would work remarkably well at provoking the other fellow to strike the first blow so that one could then go ahead and do what one already had meant to do in any case. But even in light of what looks very much like deliberate double dealing on more than one occasion during Saigō's life, it is difficult to imagine him being so cynical as to advocate an approach like this one merely as a means of provocation. It simply seems out of character, and if one can say nothing else about Saigō after a careful review of the whole record of his life, it is that he did not act out of character.

Whatever the case may be, Saigō did not get to do what he wanted to do in Korea, and so he left the government and went back to Kagoshima, where he spent the remaining four years of his life. During those four years, relations between Kagoshima and Tokyo grew progressively more strained, until those in Kagoshima finally rose up in rebellion. It is the task of the next chapter to examine how that came about, and where Saigō fits into it.

· 7 ·

Collision Course in
Kagoshima,
1873–77

During the last four years of Saigō's life, government leaders in
Tokyo and Kagoshima travelled with hardening determination
along opposing courses until they collided in 1877. Leaders in
Tokyo were attempting to create a centralized national government; those in Kagoshima sought to perpetuate as much as they
could of the local autonomy they remembered from the regime
of the Tokugawa. In practice, the requirements of those two
sets of goals were mutually exclusive.

Saigō did not play any direct role in this process; after his
defeat by Ōkubo in the council meetings on Korea in 1873, he
was not personally on a collision course with anyone. No doubt
he was disappointed at the outcome of the seikanron dispute,
but he had done his best and then had moved on, placing that
problem behind him.[1] Others in Kagoshima were not as willing
as he was to accept defeat gracefully, and he was drawn into
their confrontation with Tokyo largely against his will, by forces
beyond his control. When the collision finally occurred, Saigō
had the misfortune to get caught in the middle.

Already by 1864, thanks to his accomplishments in Chōshū
and to his reputation throughout Japan, Saigō's image had grown
larger than his reality. By the time he returned to Kagoshima in
1873, he had already become that empty vessel he continues to
be today. To the degree that he believed his personal choices
were constrained by his obligations to those who depended on
him, he was no longer in control of his own life. What he wanted
to do with the rest of it had ceased to be a factor in the outcome;
his future now lay in the hands of others, who would fill him
with meanings and purposes of their own.

Toward the final drama:
1873–6

When Saigō left Tokyo in the autumn of 1873, Kirino Toshiaki went with him. Over the next few days, some four hundred members of the imperial guard, together with considerable numbers of former gōshi from the metropolitan police force, also resigned their positions and left for Kagoshima. These men were led by Shinohara Kunimoto, who had rejected a direct appeal from the emperor to remain at his post. In their wake, the government was reorganized, and Ōkubo consolidated the position he had won through his victory in the seikanron dispute. With the creation of the Home Ministry (*naimushō*) on 1873/11/ 10, his power was secure.[2] In the midst of this process, Iwakura expressed concern to Ōkubo about what Saigō might do next, but Ōkubo assured him he had nothing to fear.[3] Some commentators agree with Ōkubo's judgement, while others do not.

According to Tamamuro Taijō, Saigō intended from the moment he resigned to raise an army and overthrow the government.[4] Tamamuro reports that Saigō met with Itagaki just before he left Tokyo, and that Itagaki asked him to join in a new movement to create a popular assembly. Saigō replied that he was done with debates, and that he would now employ other means to correct the government's errors.[5] Inoue Kiyoshi also repeats this story, but disagrees with Tamamuro that it is sufficient to establish Saigō's intent to rebel, simply because it would have been out of character for Saigō to rise in arms against the government of the emperor.[6] Inoue's evidence comes from several poems Saigō wrote near the time of his resignation, in which he appears to express satisfaction that he had done all he could to get the government off to the right start, and that posterity would remember him kindly.[7] As Inoue sees it, these poems establish that Saigō meant to retire to private life.[8]

There is another story like the one about Itagaki, according to which Saigō stopped in Osaka on his way home and met with Saishō Atsushi, another old friend from Kagoshima. When asked by Saishō what had happened in Tokyo and what might be likely to happen next, Saigō told him to ask Ōkubo, since the government was in his hands now.[9] As in Inoue's reading of his poems, Saigō in this anecdote appears to have accepted Ōkubo's victory, and to have put the matter behind him. The difficulty with anecdotes about Saigō, needless to say, is that there are hundreds of them, all presumably of unquestionable authority because they come from eyewitnesses, and all unreliable because they cannot be corroborated from other evidence.[10]

In any event, when Saigō got home he did not stay in Kagoshima for very long, but proceeded to the countryside, just as he had done in 1869. There he began once again to spend his time working the land, hunting, fishing, and seeking relief for his physical discomforts in the waters of his favorite hot springs.[11] Barring the discovery of compelling new evidence to the contrary, one may infer that these were the activities he looked forward to enjoying for the rest of his life. Of course, one may also infer, as some have done, that Saigō's withdrawal to the countryside was only a ruse, meant to lull the suspicions of those against whom he was plotting rebellion. If the withdrawal itself were the only evidence available, there would be no way to evaluate the relative merits of these two conclusions. As the following discussion shows, however, there is other material which, if not conclusive, is at least suggestive enough to tip the scales toward the former judgement.[12]

Despite his eagerness for a respite from the stressful uncertainties of national politics, Saigō was not to be allowed the retirement he hoped for, because Kagoshima was full of angry samurai who assumed he would protect their interests.[13] Little had changed in Kagoshima during Saigō's years in Tokyo. Despite the removal of formal status distinctions among samurai after 1868, former monbatsu and lower samurai still hated one another. Hisamitsu, still outraged by Saigō's behavior, continued to grumble and make accusations, doing nothing to help ease the animosities between upper and lower samurai. Determined to protect their traditional prerogatives, the samurai in control of Kagoshima's government ignored the steady stream of reform notices coming from Tokyo, and instead continued to create new institutions to preserve old customs and mores.[14] All of this had begun soon after Saigō's departure for Tokyo.

On 1871/8/23, Ōyama Tsunayoshi, who had begun his official career early in the 1850s as a tea server in the castle, was named to the senior executive office in Kagoshima (*gondaisanji*). He rose steadily after that, and on 1874/10/5 became Kagoshima's first governor (*kenrei*). From then until his dismissal by Tokyo on 1877/3/17, he remained at the center of Kagoshima politics, working tirelessly to prevent the erosion of local traditions and the absorption of Kagoshima by the centralization process.[15] Few others in Kagoshima after 1873 did more than Ōyama to open the path toward rebellion and encourage others to head down it.

After Saigō's return, Ōyama tried to reinforce his own position by appropriating Saigō's symbolic power. This strategy did not succeed, however, because Saigō did not trust Ōyama. The two had known each other since childhood; Ōyama had introduced Saigō to the varied pleasures of Edo in 1854, and had joined in the abortive second plot to murder Okada Yura after Nariakira's last surviving son died two years later. In recent years, however, this youthful intimacy had waned. In 1873 Saigō questioned Ōyama's integrity in a letter to his uncle. But Ōyama had lost Saigō's trust primarily through his failure to support Saigō at a critical moment. He shared Hisamitsu's disgust with the reforms of the Meiji government, and instead of coming to Saigō's defense against Hisamitsu's incessant criticisms, he took a neutral position and refused to commit himself either way. Given Saigō's feelings about Hisamitsu, and his vivid memories of how other supposed friends had betrayed him to Hisamitsu in 1862, he could hardly have viewed Ōyama's attitude in the 1870s as anything less than another betrayal.[16]

Thus by the end of 1873 it was not likely that Saigō would be eager to work closely with Ōyama on anything. However, by then Kagoshima was crawling with disgruntled samurai, and it was clear to Saigō that something must be done to channel all of that destructive energy and keep it under control, so he agreed with Ōyama about the advisability of creating a system of private schools (*Shigakkō*) as a way to bring some order and discipline to the lives of these young men. The Shigakkō system began to take shape in the middle of 1874, and Saigō evidently played no more than a peripheral part in the process, but it was not the first school for young samurai whose creation he had supported.[17]

After the conclusion of the Tōhoku campaigns in 1869, the court had issued rewards (*shōten*) to a number of political and military leaders, including honorary stipends to be paid annually for life. Among those rewarded in Kagoshima, Saigō received 2,000 *koku*, and Ōkubo got 1,800. Komatsu Tatewaki, Iwashita Masahira, Yoshii Tomozane, and Ijichi Masaharu each received 1,000, while Ōyama got 800, and others received equal or smaller sums, including 200 koku for Kirino.[18] Saigō was not eager to accept a material reward for things he would have done in any case out of a sense of duty. Moreover, he was not alone in his belief that it was those who had died in the Meiji civil war who should have been rewarded, and that to give those rewards instead to others who had not made the ultimate sacrifice would be an insult to the dead.[19]

Together with Ōkubo and a number of others, Saigō applied his reward to the establishment of a school called the Shugijuku in Tokyo. Located in Kōjimachi, it opened its doors in 1873/6. In the school's charter, Saigō declared that there could be no more appropriate way to use the reward money than to support an academy that would honor the memory of those who had died and help prepare the living to follow their noble example.[20] When Saigō left Tokyo this school closed, but it was then reopened in Kagoshima, now under the name Shōten Gakkō, with the purpose of training local children in foreign languages and Western learning. Saigō continued to contribute the entire 2,000 koku of his reward in support of this school for the rest of his life. Ōkubo also continued giving his 1,800 each year until 1876, when he transferred the funds to the home ministry budget.[21]

Some commentators have suggested that the opening of this school was the first step in the creation of the Shigakkō system, but it appears to have been totally unrelated to that enterprise. The evidence suggests that the Shigakkō system was not Saigō's idea, nor was it a project in which he had invested much interest. If the Shigakkō system was only a means to conceal the creation of a private army whose purpose was to overthrow the Tokyo government, then it is intriguing that Ōkubo helped to support the growth of that army almost until the eve of its rebellion.

The Shigakkō system in its mature form included a number of loosely interconnected operations. The core of the system consisted of two institutions: an infantry school (*jūtai gakkō*) under the command of Shinohara Kunimoto, and an artillery school (*hōtai gakkō*) under Murata Shinpachi, both located adjacent to the castle in the heart of Kagoshima and enrolling together about a thousand regular pupils.[22] In time a branch school was set up in each rural district. Pupils came to Kagoshima from these branches in rotation to receive training at the main schools, and all central and local offices of the civil government eventually came to be staffed by Shigakkō officers. Besides the Shōten Gakkō, which was incorporated into the system under Shinohara's direction, there was another facility outside of Kagoshima called the Yoshino Kaikonsha, devoted to the study of agriculture, husbandry, and land reclamation.[23] It was here that Saigō appears to have spent most of his time between 1873 and 1877, and it was in the work going on here that he seems to have been most interested.[24]

The formal connection between the Yoshino Kaikonsha and the Shigakkō system is not clear. It may have been another branch school, fully integral to the system, in which case there is some small justification in arguing that Saigō was involved in the activities that led to the rebellion, however indirectly. It may also have had no connection at all, except in the minds of Saigō scholars who have assumed that, because he eventually led the rebellion, everything else he was involved in prior to that must be connected. It seems to be an assumption like this that allows some scholars to discuss the Yoshino Kaikonsha as if it strengthened the case against Saigō, and keeps them from realizing that it might actually weaken it.

In 1875, Saigō's cousin Ōyama Iwao invited him to go to Europe to observe the developing tensions between France and Prussia. This may have been the first step in an attempt to draw Saigō back into the government, but it failed. On 1875/4/5, Saigō wrote Ōyama and declined his invitation, explaining that a major undertaking would keep him in Kagoshima for the rest of the year (*tōnen wa daisaku ni shikakari*).[25] Evidently Saigō was referring here to the Yoshino project. Later in the same letter, he added:

> I've now turned completely into a farmer, and I'm studying diligently. It was really difficult for me at first, but now I can easily spade up one or two plots of ground for cultivation in a day. I've grown accustomed to eating potatoes and soup made from bean curd dregs (*okara*) and none of this causes me any difficulty.

About three weeks later, Saigō wrote to his brother Kohei in Kagoshima about paying the workmen for construction done at Yoshino, and on 6/19 he wrote to Shinohara to order a large quantity of hand tools, and discussed the sale of his house in Kagoshima.[26]

To judge from these details, Saigō was not only spending most of his time at Yoshino; he had made arrangements eventually to take up permanent residence there. And even when he was not turning over the ground at Yoshino, he did not frequent the city. Instead he spent all his time at the hot springs, or out in the mountains with his dogs. On 1875/8/11 he wrote to Shinohara from Shiratori hot spring to say that his mail henceforth would be delivered to Shinohara's residence, and he should open it all and inform Saigō of anything important.[27] On 8/31, he wrote again to Shinohara, thanking him for a recent letter, and adding that in the mountains where he was he had only his dogs for company.[28]

Many of Saigō's letters in these years contain comments on aspects of the national situation, suggesting that even if he had no further desire to be involved in it personally, he still had not lost interest altogether. He was especially concerned about the problem with Taiwan, as he had been earlier, and he supported the dispatch of a body of Kagoshima troops to join the expeditionary force led by his brother Tsugumichi in 1874. Yet there is a tone almost of detachment in these letters, and they convey a general mood of light-heartedness and enthusiasm such as he had not shown since the more innocent and optimistic days of the early 1850s. It is tempting to conclude that he was finally content with life, perhaps for the first time since before Nariakira's death. There is no explicit evidence to refute the claims of Tamamurō Taijō and others that Saigō used these years to build the Shigakkō into a rebel army,[29] but the overall impression produced by these letters is that of a man wholly absorbed in the pursuit of private work and leisure, and not at all that of a bitter malcontent plotting rebellion and waiting for his chance to strike back at his former colleagues in Tokyo.[30] Yet if Saigō was not plotting rebellion, there is little doubt that others were.

To play out this farce in combat:
1876–7

Saigō may have been able to relieve his personal frustrations by losing himself in the distractions of agrarian life, but in Kagoshima, angry samurai had no such recourse. The curriculum of the Shigakkō was taken up largely by military training, with a foundation in the Confucian classics. The daily routines were reminiscent of those in the gōjū kyōiku, the neighborhood education system that had given Saigō and his playmates their first formal training in how to be Satsuma samurai. Under the watchful eyes of Kirino, Shinohara, Murata, and Ōyama, the new

162

generation of Kagoshima samurai daily grew more restless and resolutely opposed to the Meiji government. Reluctant to provoke a violent response, Ōkubo and his colleagues in Tokyo left Kagoshima alone, in spite of angry charges of favoritism from Kido and others.[31] But the steady erosion of samurai privilege legislated by the Meiji government only fed the anger of Kagoshima's leaders and their pupils, and by the middle of 1876 the question was no longer whether they would act, but only when.

In the spring of 1875, the first assembly of prefectural governors convened under Kido's leadership, and Ōyama attended. But the very idea of such a body, with the limits on local autonomy and initiative it entailed, was distasteful to him, and he obstructed its proceedings repeatedly by dissenting from consensus and refusing to take part in plenary votes.[32] The only important effect of such behavior was to anger Kido, who repeatedly accused Ōkubo and the government of allowing Kagoshima to exempt itself from the standardization and subordination to which all other prefectural governments had long since agreed. Concern about Kagoshima and about what Saigō might be planning was widespread in Tokyo, and late in 1876 Ōkubo finally took some action.

Like Ōyama, Ōkubo had begun his public career as a tea server in the castle when barely out of adolescence, and so the two men had ties running back to childhood. Ōkubo now summoned Ōyama to Tokyo and pleaded with him to take whatever steps were needed to bring Kagoshima into line with the national norm.[33] However, Ōyama was unwilling to cooperate, warning that the situation in Kagoshima was too volatile to tamper with. In reply to Ōkubo's entreaties, he said that if his service and that of his subordinates was not satisfactory, they would all be willing to resign. In effect, he warned Ōkubo that either Kagoshima could be allowed to proceed under its separatist rule or the central government could intervene and force changes from above. In the latter case, however, there would be no cooperation from Kagoshima, and quite likely a good deal of direct obstruction.

Either leave us alone, hinted Ōyama, or be ready to face unpleasant consequences. Unwilling to challenge Ōyama directly and risk the outcome he hinted at, Ōkubo sent a subordinate named Hayashi Yūko to Kagoshima to collect accurate information on what was happening there. During the final month of 1876, Hayashi examined the workings of the Kagoshima government from top to bottom. His report, submitted early in 1877, made it clear that nothing short of direct and sustained intervention from Tokyo was likely to change the situation, or alter the course on which Kagoshima's leaders had set themselves.[34]

In fact, by the time Hayashi was able to report to Ōkubo, the situation in Kagoshima had already become critical. In the early 1870s, the Tokyo government had established a network of garrisons and arsenals throughout Japan to help discourage local defiance of its policies. The garrison nearest to Kagoshima was in the city of Kumamoto, but one of the largest stockpiles of weapons and ammunition in the country was located in Kagoshima itself, in a group of army and navy arsenals. The Tokyo government had decided to remove temptation from beneath the very noses of the malcontents in Kagoshima, and had sent ships there to transfer the contents of those arsenals to Osaka. But the angry young men of the Shigakkō, already eager to challenge Tokyo and primed for just this sort of provocation, could hardly permit such a move to go unchallenged. On 1877/1/29-31, and again on 2/1-2, groups of youths attacked the arsenals and carried off large quantities of weapons and ammunition. There is nothing to indicate whose idea this was, or whether it was spontaneous or premeditated,[35] but the consequences were unmistakable: Kagoshima was now in open rebellion, and had challenged the central government's right to rule.

While these events were unfolding, Saigō was on a hunting trip at Konejime, far down toward the tip of the Ōsumi peninsula, across the bay from Kagoshima, and apparently he knew nothing of what had happened. He learned of the attacks on the arsenals on 2/1 from his brother Kohei, and hurried back to Kagoshima. There, on 2/7, he reportedly told Ōyama that he believed he could have prevented the outburst if he been in the city at the time, but now that the young men had their blood up and their rebellion was underway, there could be no persuading them to turn back.[36] There is only one fragment of evidence to suggest what was in Saigō's mind at this moment, and like so many others, it is too ambiguous to be conclusive.

Following Etō Shinpei's uprising in Saga in 1874, and the harsh punishments meted out to its leaders by Ōkubo after its suppression, there had been no other resorts to violence by groups of samurai for about two years. Then, on 1876/10/24, a group calling itself the League of the Divine Wind (*Shinpūren*) attacked the headquarters of the Kumamoto garrison. After that,

other groups of samurai rose in rapid succession, in the old
Kyushu han of Akitsuki on 10/27, and in Chōshū's old castle
town of Hagi on 10/28. Soon the rebel fever had spread to
Kagoshima as well. The young men of the Shigakkō were eager
to rise in rebellion, but Kirino and their other leaders were
reluctant to take any action without approval from Saigō.[37] As
usual, he was not in the city at the time, but at Hinatayama, and
was therefore unavailable for comment.

During the month after this series of uprisings, he wrote to
Katsura and made the following comment in reply to a suggestion
that he should return to Kagoshima:

> If I were to hurry back to the city now, I suspect that the
> young men there would become uncontrollable. I certainly do
> not intend to let anyone see me behaving intemperately,
> especially not now. No doubt, if I were to go into action,
> it would astonish the entire country (*tenka odorokubeki no
> koto*)[38]

Those who believe Saigō was plotting rebellion welcome this
comment as containing all the proof they need. According to
them, what Saigō means here is that as soon as Kagoshima's
young men set eyes on him their rebellious spirit would have
become irresistible, and that was precisely what he wanted, but
he was not yet ready to make that move. When he finally did,
however, discontented people all over Japan would rise up to
follow him. Those who argue that Saigō had no plans for rebellion read this comment the other way: because the young men
of Kagoshima would become uncontrollable at the mere sight of
Saigō, and because that was the one thing he did not want to
happen, he would go nowhere near the city. If he were to raise
the standard of revolt, people all over Japan would be shocked
in disbelief at such behavior in one of whom they had expected
nothing of the kind. In other words, this statement is a perfect
example of the difficulty surrounding nearly all of the key evidence about Saigō: it is so amenable to mutually exclusive interpretations that it is of practically no value at all.

Whatever Saigō meant by this statement, the die was cast for
him now. When he got back to Kagoshima, he learned that a
large number of former gōshi from the Tokyo police, led by
Nakahara Hisao, had been arrested in and around the city, and
had confessed that they had been sent there by Ōkubo and
Kawaji Toshiyoshi to spread confusion and dissent in the ranks

of the Shigakkō and to murder Saigō.³⁹ There is a strong likelihood that the confessions of Nakahara and the others were extracted by torture, and so their reliability is doubtful, but what matters is that Saigō believed there was a plot against his life, and that Ōkubo had been involved in planning it. Thus he consented to become the leader of the rebel army, intending to lead the troops to Tokyo and to confront Ōkubo. In addition to a natural desire to have the truth from his boyhood friend, Saigō was motivated by a powerful sense of obligation to the young samurai who had brought on the rebellion. He had supported the creation of the Shigakkō system as a way to build their character, but he had failed to keep them from attacking the arsenals. It was now his responsibility to take charge of the rebellion they had begun in the belief that he would lead them once they were in motion.

These motives are consistent with Saigō's character and his beliefs, and so they are not difficult to infer from the circumstances surrounding the outbreak of the rebellion, but there are other aspects of what the rebel army intended to do that also deserve attention. We should recall that at the time of his death in 1858, Nariakira was apparently planning to lead a large military force to the capital, denounce the abuses of the government, and demand appropriate reforms, relying on the combined incentives of an open appeal to morality and an implied threat of force to induce cooperation. He had sent Saigō to Kyoto with instructions on how to prepare the way for this move, and so Saigō probably knew more about it than anyone else. Nariakira had not lived to carry out his plans, but his half-brother Hisamitsu had succeeded in exactly the same set of maneuvers in 1862, bringing about the first major reforms in bakufu social control institutions in over two centuries. It appears that Saigō now meant to try the same thing once more, and whether it had any chance of success or not, at least we need not think it remarkable that he expected it would work. It is also worth noting that, as conceived by Nariakira and carried out by Hisamitsu, this strategy had not required the use of violence, but rather had succeeded in part through the implied threat of violence. That too was something that would have appealed to Saigō.

After some rather difficult strategy sessions, the rebel army left Kagoshima on 1877/2/15, in the midst of what was reportedly the first heavy snowfall in the city in fifty years. Saigō's fiftieth birthday had passed only a few weeks earlier.⁴⁰ Saigō's brother

Kohei had wanted to send the main part of the army to capture Nagasaki, crush the relief sent from the Kumamoto garrison, and then go on northward to seize Fukuoka and Shimonoseki as a prelude to a combined land and sea advance on Tokyo. Given the resources of the national government, even this strategy probably would not have worked, but later events did prove it to have been the most appropriate one, because it was through Shimonoseki, Fukuoka, and Nagasaki that government reinforcements eventually converged on the Satsuma forces to overwhelm them and break the seige of Kumamoto. Others in the army's leadership rejected Kohei's proposals, apparently in part because they were devious and therefore dishonorable for samurai, and in part because they believed that the Kumamoto garrison would turn and run at the first sight of the Satsuma army.[41]

As events soon demonstrated, investing Kumamoto was the strategy most assuredly guaranteed to bring disaster to the rebels, because, thanks to the determination of the Kumamoto commander, Tani Kanjō, it tied them down and kept them busy long enough for the government to muster reinforcements in numbers too large for the rebel army to resist. The turning point in the rebellion came soon after the withdrawal from Kumamoto, in a series of bitterly fought battles at Tabaruzaka in central Kyushu. After meeting defeat there, the army fought a prolonged series of tactical retreats throughout southern Kyushu. Saigō and the remnants of what at its peak had been an army of more than 30,000 men returned to Kagoshima on 9/1 and took up fortified positions on the heights of Shiroyama, a range of low hills running behind the castle in the center of the city. On 9/24, government forces launched an all-out attack on the heights and destroyed most of what was left of the army.

Saigō had been hiding in an earthen cave located in a narrow ravine called Iwasakidani on the northeast side of Shiroyama. On the morning of the government assault, he set off down the ravine to meet his fate, accompanied by Kirino, Murata, Katsura Hisatake, Beppu Shinsuke, and a few others. A little over halfway down the slope, a bullet caught him in his right thigh and passed through his pelvis. According to the tradition, he dropped to the ground, turned to Beppu, and said, 'Shinsuke, right about here ought to be good enough. Please do the honor of beheading me.' (*Shinsuke-don, kokora hen de yōka. Kaishaku o tanomōsu.*). He then composed himself, faced in the direction of the imperial palace, and solemnly sliced open his abdomen before Beppu's blow fell. This story makes for thrilling theater, and has been a vital element in the growth of the Saigō image since his death. Almost certainly it did not happen.

Given the nature of the bullet wound, it is highly unlikely that Saigō would have been physically capable of all this activity. On the contrary, if he did not go promptly into shock from the pain and the trauma, he probably lost consciousness quickly from loss of blood. In any case there is no evidence of any abdominal wound of the sort the suicide ritual would have caused. The official autopsy report on Saigō's body (*itai kensa sho*) is terse and to the point:

> Saigō Takamori
> Clothing: Light yellow striped unlined kimono. Dark blue
>   leggings.
> Wounds: Head separated from body. Bullet wound from right
>   hip passing through to left femur. Old sword wound in
>   right ulna. Dropsy of the scrotum.[42]

Saigō's last recorded utterance was a brief note dated 9/22 which he ordered circulated to the defenders of Shiroyama.[43] He told his troops that they were about to go into battle for the last time. And he urged them all to resolve to die bravely, so that no shame would tarnish their memories later.

There is no conclusive evidence to establish that Saigō either planned or instigated the Satsuma rebellion. The men most evidently responsible for that were his immediate followers, Kirino, Shinohara, Murata, and a dozen or so others in the command echelons of the Shigakkō. They fomented the rebellion because of the resentments they still harbored about Korea and about the central government's gradual destruction of the samurai class. They were supported administratively, if not encouraged actively, by Ōyama Tsunayoshi and others in the Kagoshima government, whose feelings about the destruction of the samurai were aggravated by their refusal to accept the absorption of Kagoshima's traditional autonomy and its sense of uniqueness into the faceless uniformity of centralized government.

As with Etō Shinpei in Saga, or with Maebara Issei in Hagi, in Kagoshima it was men who rebelled, but there is a sense in which the Satsuma rebellion was not just men in revolt, but a whole society, a whole way of life fighting desperately for survival. Like the Confederate armies under Lee's leadership in the American Civil War, the Satsuma rebel army ultimately fought to preserve a particular kind of world, without which a particular kind of society could not survive. What was finally at stake for these rebels was not Japanese feudalism, or even the samurai class itself. It was personal identity, which could not continue to exist and function outside of the world in which and from which it derived its meaning.

If Saigō was not guilty of rebellion, he was nevertheless at least partly responsible for it. The concentration of samurai resentment in Kagoshima was a given about which no one could have done very much. Saigō may have believed that the institutional framework provided by the Shigakkō system would constrain the angry samurai and make them easier to control, so that their energies could be drained off gradually through hard physical training, ethical reflection, and the eventual adoption of an agrarian way of life. In other words, it is likely that Saigō hoped eventually to convert the remnants of the samurai into farmers. But the organization of so many angry men into military units allowed them to believe they might yet have a chance to fight for the preservation of the social identities their own actions between 1866 and 1869 had so tragically and ironically rendered obsolete. Whether Saigō intended it or not, the Shigakkō system did evolve into a rebel army, and even Saigō ought to have been insightful enough to realize how easily that might happen.

Given that realization, he could have put more of his attention into helping Kagoshima's samurai work through the transition from Tokugawa to Meiji, and particularly into helping them craft new identities for themselves out of the remnants of their former world. This sort of transformation is apparently what he expected the Yoshino Kaikonsha to help facilitate, but he missed the chance to make that happen by choosing to spend so much of his time away from Kagoshima, where his attention was needed, and where in his absence other men acted according to what they thought were his wishes and eventually unleashed a force none of them could control.

It may be that, even if Saigō had no intention of rebelling himself, he had no objection if others wanted to do so. He could have justified such an uprising as an appropriate response to the corrupt behavior of government officials in Tokyo, perhaps even understanding it as the punishment of Heaven that such corruption sooner or later always calls forth. It may also be that the matter was completely out of Saigō's hands because Ōkubo was determined to provoke Kagoshima into open rebellion so that he could suppress it all the more decisively.[44] The removal of government ordnance from Kagoshima, and the sending of Nakahara and his fellow spies to Kagoshima, were nothing if not overtly provocative. At a minimum, there is a good chance that, like Saigō, Ōkubo could have done more to prevent the rebellion, and therefore sinned primarily by omission rather than by commission

In the end, regardless of what it meant for Saigō or even for Ōkubo, the significance of the Satsuma rebellion for Japanese history is analogous to that of the seikanron crisis: it represents a stage in the conversion of a loosely centralized state characterized by strong local autonomy into a highly centralized one featuring uniform hierarchies of institutional and functional specialization, one in which the legitimate use of force and the distribution of administrative authority are monopolized by the central government. Thus, it is highly likely that a rebellion like the one in Satsuma would have occurred at some point in the consolidation of the Meiji state, whether in Satsuma or somewhere else.

There is a widespread belief, shared alike by apologists and detractors of Saigō, that the rebellion was a direct response to the defeat of the proposal to punish Korea, and might not have happened if supporters of that proposal had gotten their way. This is possible, certainly, but it is not necessary to make this connection. Given the stakes as they were understood by leaders in Kagoshima, it is equally possible that the rebellion would have occurred even if Saigō had gone to Korea and had involved the samurai in a war there. No matter what the fate of the samurai under the Meiji government, sooner or later the problem of how to balance the central government's demand for a monopoly on political initiative and the local government's claim to some degree of residual autonomy would have come up for solution. Given the reluctance of Kagoshima's leaders to surrender their autonomy, that solution almost certainly would have involved some kind of violent confrontation. It might not have been as large as the Satsuma rebellion was, because under diferent circumstances there might not have been as many former samurai outside of Satsuma who felt their identities threatened. But people are often reluctant to give up their lifelong sense of themselves without a fight, and it was that sense of self that Kagoshima's samurai felt they were about to lose. It was not directly imperiled by anything, but it was tightly interwoven with institutions, customs, and mores that were directly in peril under the agenda of the Meiji government, so the net effect was the same.

Thus in the end it was two ways of life, two ways of organizing political space, that collided in Kagoshima. If the results had been different, what we now understand as modern Japan would have been obliged to wait a while longer before beginning to emerge from the ruins of the Tokugawa world, whose last defenders, ironically, were the very same Kagoshima samurai who had played the central role in its destruction.

Aftermath

And so it was done. Near the end of his second exile, early in 1864, Saigō had hinted that he might be interested in getting involved in national politics once again, so as 'to play out the remainder of this farce in combat.'[45] If it was his own life that he referred to as a kyōgen at that time, it was in his final moments on Shiroyama that he brought closure to it at last. It was probably not the end he had imagined for himself, but with that closure, he had passed into a realm where he no longer would have to worry about Hisamitsu's anger, or about his conflicting obligations to samurai and to peasants, to the Shimazu and to the emperor, to public and private morality, or to principle and practicality. The death about which he had often mused, and which had been denied him several times already, was finally his, and his lifelong service to Nariakira was at an end. His personal drama was finished, and now there was nothing left to restrain the growth of his image; unfortunately for Ōkubo, there was one drama demanded by that image that had yet to be played out.

Early on the morning of 1878/5/14, Ōkubo was accosted by a group of samurai from Kanazawa as he made his way through Shimizudani near the imperial palace.[46] They pulled him from his carriage and with a few swift sword strokes put an end to his life. In the manifesto they wrote to explain their actions, they denounced him as a traitor to the samurai and to the traditional Japanese values they saw embodied in Saigō.[47] These men had wanted to join in the Satsuma rebellion, but had not been able to get to Kyushu in time. Now they had come to Tokyo and had confronted Ōkubo, as Saigō had meant to do, though surely not at all in the way he had intended.

There is some irony in the fact that the man who discovered Ōkubo's body was Saigō's brother Tsugumichi; the central irony in Ōkubo's death is that it was probably the last thing Saigō would have wanted. Yet the requirements of his image, much more than of the man behind them, had rendered it necessary. In the minds of Ōkubo's killers, the Great Saigō demanded revenge, and therefore Ōkubo had to die. Thus the life of Saigō the man was over, and the life of Saigō the image could now begin.

EPILOGUE
Reality and Image: Saigō Takamori in Japanese History

I began this study of Saigō Takamori with a discussion of his image, of some of its more interesting manifestations, and of some of the functions it performs in the Japanese imagination today, but my central purpose has been to reconstruct as much as I could of the historical Saigō from the clues he has left in his own words and deeds. I wanted to do this in order to provide an accurate account of the career of one of the most widely known and admired figures in Japanese history, but we may also use that account to establish a baseline against which to evaluate the image of the man as it has evolved in the Japanese imagination since his death.

What becomes clear in the end is that there is little factual basis for most of the enduring elements of the Saigō legend. The verifiable details of his life and his character are clear, even if there are not as many of them as we would like to have. Moreover, the human portrait they reveal is impressive enough in its own right, without any need to make it more impressive by enlarging it to legendary proportions. Except for an occasional fleeting sense of recognition, the verifiable historical portrait is not a very good match for any of the starkly one-sided images of Saigō that appear so consistently in Japanese literary and historical works. In short, judging from the historical record, there is no Great Saigō, either as great hero or as great villain, except in the Japanese popular imagination.

There are two questions we can raise by way of conclusion. First, where do we find correspondence or the lack of it between the historical Saigō and his various images in legend and popular mythology? Where does fact leave off and fancy begin? Second, what can we say about the image itself, about its origins, its dimensions, and its remarkable vitality for so many Japanese?

To begin with the most enduring and widely accepted aspect of the legend, it seems clear that Saigō was no military genius, nor was he the great swordsman many would like to believe he was. The means to achieve such distinctions were readily available to him in the world of his youth, had he chosen to take advantage of them. Like many other localities in early modern Japan, Satsuma had its own style of swordsmanship, a sort of headlong frontal attack that nullified more subtle and refined styles and overwhelmed through its sheer dynamism. Likewise a number of Satsuma's hanshu over the centuries were exceptionally capable military leaders, as were many of their senior vassals. Both traditions were well established and both were perpetuated in Satsuma's folklore and in its education system. Any Satsuma samurai who wished to do so could find capable instructors to train him in either of these traditions, and help him evolve into a formidable swordsman or a clever tactician. But Saigō did not take advantage of such opportunities, and made neither of these traditions his own, except as conceptual ideals that helped to shape his identity as a Shimazu vassal. Moreover, it seems clear that his lack of extensive practical knowledge or accomplishment in martial arts arose chiefly from a simple lack of interest. His passions lay elsewhere, and so the first thing we can say is that it has made no sense for various groups of Japanese militarists over the years to have adopted Saigō as their heroic ideal. They have made him into something he never was, for reasons of their own, responding not to his reality but only to one of his many images.

The same must be said of his image as a great pacifist and humanitarian. There are good grounds for concluding that his temperament was not especially bellicose, but it takes more than a simple lack of warlike inclinations to make one a pacifist. Certainly Saigō preferred to resolve conflicts without violence when he could, but he never hesitated to advocate the violent solution when circumstances seemed to call for it. His preference was not for the peaceful solution at any cost, but rather for the one that was most appropriate to the situation, as would have been consistent with the Confucian insistence on rectifying the fit between name and reality (*ch'ing ming*). When forced to fight, he fought, as in the Chōshū attack on the imperial palace in 1863, and in the military campaigns of the civil war of 1868–69. In the same way, he sanctioned others' use of force even when he was not directly involved, as with his support for the military expedition to Taiwan in 1874. His conspicuous condemnation of the use of force in the Kang Hwa incident in 1874 arose not from any disapproval of force itself, but rather from his belief that, in that particular instance, it not only was not necessary, but was in fact a source of shame for Japan's leaders, who could have achieved the ends they sought through peaceful means.

Through his service in rural administration, he came to have great sympathy for the peasants and their plight, and when he was in exile in the southern islands between 1859 and 1864 he labored unstintingly to improve their lot. But his motive was not some belief in the universal worth and dignity of all humans, or in their uniform and equal right to any particular thing, in spite of his famous injunction to revere Heaven and love human-kind (*keiten aijin*). Rather, he was afraid that the samurai in charge of the peasants might be jeopardizing their own moral integrity, and that of Japanese society, through such lapses as venality and lack of respect for their social responsibilities. His attitude grew less from humanitarian or egalitarian motives than from a keen sense of the social hierarchy and the kinds of behavior required of individuals by virtue of their places in that hierarchy. Highly normative in its ethical requirements, his posi-tion on relations between social classes and the individuals in them is best understood as elitist, which is exactly as it should be for a member of the dominant class in a society organized according to clear and rigid hierarchical values. To call him the last of the true samurai, as many Japanese do, is thus not to discover in him some pure paradigm of the samurai type, but merely to acknowledge that he was precisely what his Confucian upbringing as a samurai's son had made him: a typical samurai, no different from thousands of others.

For most of his life, Saigō had a taste for certain kinds of literary activity, and was quite accomplished in his own way, but there is nothing to suggest that he was the seminal thinker some of his apologists have found. He liked to read, and to adapt the ideas of others to his personal needs, but he produced few ideas of his own. He put great effort into learning Chinese poetic forms, but for the most part his poetry is too prosaic to be really inspiring. Most of his poems are little more than mechanical exercises in form and just a bit too affected in their images. As we would put it today, they seem sophomoric.[1] However much he may have wanted to be an accomplished poet, it appears he lacked the talent for it, if not the vision.

In calligraphy, Saigō excelled, and a good number of his

works have survived. Many find his brushwork too heavy and assertive to be esthetically pleasing, but no one questions his absolute mastery of the brush.[2] He perfected his calligraphic style during his exile on Okinoerabujima, where he also worked hard at mastering the rules of Chinese poetry, and in both forms of expression he had the guidance of his fellow exile, Kawaguchi Seppō, who apparently influenced him a good deal. Noting the striking similarity of their styles, some have claimed that much of what is now regarded as Saigō's calligraphy was actually done by Kawaguchi after Saigō's death, and sold to help the Saigō family make ends meet during the twelve years of disgrace and hardship before Saigō was exonerated and restored to his former rank and status in the general pardon issued to mark the adoption of the Meiji constitution in 1889. These claims are unsubstantiated, and Saigō apologists vehemently deny that Kawaguchi produced forgeries of Saigō's work. Even if that vehemence reflects nothing so much as their own need to believe in the authenticity of all of the works attributed to Saigō, it is nevertheless interesting to note that works of calligraphy believed to have come from Saigō's brush evidently commanded prices high enough to make a significant contribution to the family income, even during the years when their ostensible author was officially condemned as a traitor.

Both Saigō's calligraphy and his poetry are replete with barely contained emotional energy, and together they give the impression of a man so full of feeling that there could have been little room left for systematic intellectual activity. In fact, in the memorials, petitions, and other writings where Saigō's thought is most readily discernible, we find little to persuade us that he was an original thinker, or even a very imaginative one. If he had a clear preference among the intellectual traditions available in nineteenth century Japan, it was for the formula of inherent goodness expressed spontaneously in unmediated action, as developed by Japanese thinkers from the ideas of the Chinese Neo-Confucianist Wang Yang-ming.[3] His notion of 'hidden virtue' (*intoku*) – of goodness as a personal and private quality not meant for discussion but only for expression in action – would have made sense to Wang Yang-ming, and the same applies to his habit of judging the worthiness of samurai administrators by their deeds rather than their words.

The intellectual orthodoxy in Satsuma for most of its history was derived, as elsewhere in Japan, chiefly from the more reflective and analytical approach originating with Chu Hsi, and Saigō would have imbibed the elements of this formulation in his education as a matter of course, whether he found it especially attractive or not.[4] During his lifetime, fortunately, there was enough official tolerance of heterodox schools of thought within Satsuma so that there would have been nothing to keep him from choosing whatever intellectual system he found most satisfying. He explored freely in the writings of Chinese and Japanese thinkers, particularly the various Neo-Confucians, and not only the classical authors, but also some from his own time, including Fukuzawa Yukichi, whose ideas were nothing if not radically different from those of traditional thinkers.[5] Despite his wide exposure, however, it appears that Saigō's tastes changed little, and throughout his life he retained the basic orientation he had absorbed in his childhood education.

We may gain some sense of the limits of his mental agility by considering his performance in a semantic problem that he and many others had to confront in the second half of the nineteenth century. Throughout the long process that led from Tokugawa to Meiji, Japanese thinkers employed a limited and unchanging set of terms to express their evolving ideas about a constantly changing set of realities. From the late 1700s through the 1840s, they used those terms to discuss what they might do to restore the failing Tokugawa order to its former vigor. In the 1850s and 1860s they used the same terms to talk about how they would dismantle the old order, which they now understood to have outlived its usefulness. Then, in the 1870s and after, they continued to use the same terms to describe the outlines of the new order they proposed to build on the cleared ground where the old one had so recently stood. Because the realities changed dramatically while the vocabulary stayed the same, many in Japan, including Saigō, eventually came to a moment of rude awakening, when they realized that the world in which they found themselves bore no resemblance to the one they had always referred to with their terms. Those who were unable to reconcile the new realities with the traditional vocabulary faced varying degrees of what we can only call cognitive dissonance.

To illustrate what this meant in practice, we may examine two terms that Saigō used often in his writings, just as many of his contemporaries did. One of them is *kokka*, meaning roughly 'the country.' The other is *tenka*, meaning 'the realm.' During most of the Tokugawa period, the term kokka customarily referred to the daimyo domain (the han), its institutions, and its people. The referent was concrete and finite. In contrast, tenka meant the imperial realm, and it referred to a conceptual space infused with moral value, understood as everything, whether material or spiritual, that fell under the authority of the emperor. The kokka, while largely autonomous in relation to the Tokugawa government in Edo, was a constituent part of the tenka, and as such, it was subordinate to the will of the imperial court in Kyoto. The two terms, like the two entities they named, depended on each other for key elements of their meaning and their significance.

Like his contemporaries, Saigō grew up understanding these terms to mean just these things, and it is essential to note that his personal sense of morality depended importantly, even if not decisively, on the relationship between kokka and tenka, because it was in the space defined by the two terms that morality was operative for him. By the late 1860s, however, while everyone continued to use these same two terms, the referent for kokka had changed from the domain to the entire nation of Japan, a new idea that might be more or less comprehensible geographically, but that was not likely to make much sense as the abstraction it was in the minds of the Westerners from whom the Japanese learned the ideas of the nation-state and nationalism. Getting through these difficult intellectual waters without upset meant being able to convert the referent of kokka from the traditional daimyo territory to this new concept of the nation, and then readjusting the moral relationship between kokka and tenka. For if kokka had hitherto been defined largely in terms of its relation to tenka, and it now meant something new and different, then what became of the traditional meaning and entailments of tenka?

Those who came through the turbulent early years of Meiji and emerged as the leaders of the new Japan after the 1870s did so in part by virtue of their ability to make this intellectual reallocation of meaning. Those who were unable to make that reallocation either died in military confrontations with the new government or sank into confused obscurity. If the former fate had not befallen Saigō in 1877, there is little doubt that the latter would have claimed him before long.[6]

Saigō's own ethical philosophy of Heaven shows clear connections to Mencius, revolving as it does around the idea of Heaven's mandate, or will, as manifested in the balance of harmony and chaos in the realm. In all of his writings, he accepts Tokugawa Japan's social hierarchy without apology, implying if not actually stating that while the peasants are the flesh and bones of the body politic, and must be cared for attentively by their rulers, that care is in effect no different from what one would give to any beast of burden or domesticated animal. One does not abuse one's horse, or cow, or dog, and likewise one must not abuse the peasants. To do so is bad not so much because it hurts them, although that is important, as because it impairs their productive capacity, and thus jeopardizes one's own material security, as well as one's own righteousness and benevolence. It is expressly not bad because it deprives the peasants of their own ethical prerogatives; for Saigō they have none, except derivatively, through their function as barometric indicators of Heaven's pleasure or displeasure. Only the members of the ruling class, the samurai, are bound by ethical norms, because only they are capable of ethical choices.

The decisive nexus in Saigō's view of ethics is the moment of choice. The samurai who chooses to act in accordance with the principles of right conduct ordained by Heaven, as codified by Confucius and Mencius, perpetuates the harmony of the realm. The one who follows his own baser inclinations in pursuit of social or material betterment violates those principles, and brings chaos into human affairs by not acting in keeping with the requirements of his social position. The secular world remains in harmony only as long as everything in it follows the will of Heaven, and the proper function of each element in the system is determined by its place in relation to other elements, a place ordained by Heaven. But only the samurai, as the ethical care-takers of the society, can alter the balance. Through acts of choice, they can maintain righteousness and harmony throughout the realm. Or they can lead the world away from Heaven's will and replace harmony with chaos. Thus it is incumbent on them to keep faith with Heaven, and by following its dictates to perpetuate the cosmically ordained social order. For Saigō, all of the emphasis falls on acts – on the expression of character in deeds.

No doubt Saigō accepted influences from a wide variety of thinkers, though the most important of them, as pointed out earlier, was Satō Issai, whose reformulations of Wang Yang-ming's ideas were especially appealing to him. In the end, what-ever the sources of his philosophical orientation, the essential point is that his own intellectual activity was overwhelmingly

179

adaptive rather than synthetic or creative. Even at its most idio-syncratic, Saigō's thought is still quite clearly a patchwork of other people's ideas, and not a fabric of his own design.

Yet if Saigō was not remarkable as either a fighter or a thinker, that does not mean that there was nothing remarkable about him. On the contrary, he seems to have been quite competent in a number of areas. For example, all the evidence suggests that he had both the taste and the talent to be a capable administrator, and that, contrary to the most widely accepted image of the ideal samurai, he was good at computation, and felt more at home with an abacus in his hands than a sword. In the same way, it seems clear that he was a good teacher, and that he liked working with young children. At any rate, his service as a teacher is one of the things that is remembered about him with striking consistency in every place where he spent any amount of time.

In addition to these talents, he seems in particular to have had a natural aptitude for conciliation and conflict resolution, based on an ability to present difficult issues to opposing parties in the simplest of terms, and to persuade others to accept compromise, through a combination of straightforward argument and tremendous personal sincerity. It must have been very diffi-cult to say no to Saigō, not because he could manipulate ideas and argue his way past any objection, but simply because it was impossible to doubt the sincerity of one who so obviously meant exactly what he said. The passion he brought to his work as a mediator would have made him easy to trust and difficult to resist, even if one were determined beforehand to prevail against him.

It may be significant that the men who influenced him the most were evidently much like him. Shimazu Nariakira, Fujita Tōko, Hashimoto Sanai, Gesshō, and Katsu Kaishū: all of these men were direct and forceful, unimpressed by dissimulation or sophistry, clear in their beliefs, and utterly convinced of the correctness of their views. They differed from Saigō chiefly in being politically more sophisticated, intellectually more agile, and conceptually less dependent on formulas, which Saigō seems to have found the most satisfying way of expressing the truths he embraced. Lacking these qualities in like degree, but quick to recognize the kindred spirit in the personal style they all seem to have shared, Saigō would have been more or less at the mercy of such men. By the same token, of course, anyone who lacked the direct and forceful character Saigō shared with these others

– and that would include a great many of those who came into contact with him – would have been equally at his mercy. It may well be that when Saigō went into Chōshū in 1864, he prevailed not so much because his propositions made sense to those he confronted, as simply because they suddenly found themselves overwhelmed by the force of his determination, and agreed with him in spite of themselves. The same was likely true of his success in persuading the imperial army command to accept the surrender of Edo in 1868, and to spare the life of Yoshinobu.

Saigō's style of negotiating may have been much like the Satsuma style of swordplay: the sudden frontal rush that negated all defenses by its unexpected dynamism. It may even be that his success as a mediator had less to do with his talents of persuasion than with the fact that he was relentless, so that his opponents gave in not out of consent but simply from exhaustion. And of course we must not discount the likelihood that Saigō's mere physical presence gave his arguments added effect. A full head taller than the average nineteenth century Japanese, and a good deal more massive as well, Saigō in many cases could have cowed others simply by walking into a room, or by rising to his feet to tower above a circle of seated men. One does not try to argue with a tidal wave, or with an avalanche; likewise, perhaps, one did not try to argue with Saigō.

As the foregoing discussion indicates, it is not difficult to produce a coherent and intelligible portrait of Saigō – one that clearly delineates his strengths and weaknesses and gives a reliable sense of who he was – but it is difficult to make that portrait match any of the ones that have appeared as images in Japan since his death. Tenuously based though some of them are in the facts of his life, those images have come almost entirely out of the fancifully embroidered recollections of others. It is clear from what his contemporaries have said about him that he left a deep and unforgettable impression on everyone who met him. As early in his political career as 1859, when he left Kagoshima for his first exile, his reputation already had begun to precede him wherever he went, and his name had acquired a certain amuletic power among the politically active in all parts of Japan. After his death, as his aging former associates recalled the good old days and Saigō's place in them, edited out of memory whatever was unattractive and enlarged what was most appealing, and then passed this artificial portrait on to others who never knew him, his reputation could only continue to grow beyond the boundaries of his reality.

This in itself goes some way toward accounting for his reputation after his death, and for the seductive power of his image in the minds of so many Japanese today. Yet for all their devotion to his image and its allure, most Japanese seem to have difficulty spelling out exactly what they find so estimable in Saigō's character. 'He was the purest of Japanese,' they may say, or 'He was the last of the true samurai,' but they are usually unable to specify what these statements mean. As I suggested in the introduction, the images evoked by statements such as these are filled with emotional power in part because they are fuzzy. Detailed descriptions of the admirable elements of Saigō's character are rare, and when pressed for specifics, many Japanese seem to find it easier to say what Saigō means to them by spelling out what he does not mean. Interestingly enough, they do this most frequently by contrasting him with his boyhood friend, Ōkubo Toshimichi, and in fact the differences between the two men, both in fact and in fancy, are instructive.

Unlike Saigō, Ōkubo has never become the subject of elaborate imagery. In the Japanese mind, he has never been more than what he was in life: an exceptionally able politician who played a vital role in the Tokugawa-Meiji transition and in the early emergence of the Meiji state. Many Japanese admire Ōkubo for his achievements, and readily acknowledge his political genius, but few of them seem eager to regard him as a good example of what it means to be Japanese. He seems to be a little too pragmatic, too cold, and too rational to be appealing. He was exceptionally well suited to become the chief architect of the new polity that both he and Saigō did much to create, but that in itself is one of the reasons why Japanese find him less appealing than Saigō.[7]

Unlike Saigō, he was also able to reallocate his construals of kokka and tenka, which initially had meant the same things to him as they did to Saigō, and to embrace their new referents. In fact, no one did more than Ōkubo to imagine new referents for those two terms, and then to realize them in preliminary form. But as with other aspects of Ōkubo's character, the ability to make this sort of semantic shift without any difficulty seems to be among the things that make him suspect in Japanese eyes, just as the lack of that ability in Saigō adds to his appeal.

No one in Satsuma did more than Saigō and Ōkubo to bring

the Tokugawa world to an end, but they responded to the results differently. Intimate friends at the beginning of the process, they were fated to end as bitter opponents, confronting each other across a chasm of conceptual difference that they had created for themselves out of their differing responses to change and its consequences. The NHK version of their lives, as constructed from Shiba Ryōtarō's historical fiction for the television audience, concentrates on these things – what they learned as they grew up in Kagoshima, how their friendship evolved as they became men, how circumstances then pulled them in opposite directions, and how, in the end, the two friends became enemies, less by personal inclination than because of the demands of their respective opinions about the proper course of early Meiji politics. Their letters to each other during their period of closest cooperation in the 1860s make it clear that they were intimate, and that they held each other in great esteem, yet to compare them as grown men it is difficult to understand what they had in common, and equally difficult to imagine how they might have become friends.

Saigō was deliberate, quiet, evidently somewhat shy and self-conscious, and thus probably uncomfortable in social situations; Ōkubo was quick-witted, articulate, not troubled by ambiguities, and very good at manipulating variables to his own advantage. Saigō viewed human life in terms of a morality based on simple and absolute distinctions, and judged others unsparingly in terms of those distinctions; Ōkubo appears not to have been much encumbered by questions of morality, and to have been motivated wholly by practical concerns. Perhaps most importantly, Saigō appears to have been committed to the values embodied in and sanctioned by traditional society, and to have been willing to see that society vanish only if some way could be found to keep its values alive; Ōkubo seems not to have cared much about the values themselves, but to have been determined to preserve the polity of which traditional society was but one possible expression among many, and to bring Japan out of what he viewed as its traditional backwardness and into the world of the industrial revolution, regardless of the social cost.

Thus each man was the opposite of the other: Ōkubo embodied just those qualities that Saigō was bound to find most distasteful, while Saigō was all that Ōkubo would have found impractical and dangerously out of date. People who differ in these ways do not often find common ground, especially not of the sort required for lifelong friendships. Yet the evidence indicates that they were friends, and that it was their ability to work together smoothly, each one compensating for the other's weaknesses, that enabled them to play such important roles in the transition from Tokugawa to Meiji. This image of their friendship captures the popular imagination today, because it appears that they worked closely together and achieved remarkable things through cooperation based on trust and a shared vision of a better Japan, only to end up in bitter opposition. There is a sense of love's labors lost that adds poignancy and makes their shared story irresistible as theater, and that probably accounts in part for the success of the NHK television series. But there is also a sense in the popular view of their association that, whatever caused the loss of love, the fault was all with Ōkubo, and not at all with Saigō. If only Ōkubo had had more of the qualities that make Saigō so appealing, we infer, things need not have turned out as they did.

The tone that comes through most consistently when Japanese speak about Saigō and Ōkubo together is one of wistfulness, and of a regretful acceptance of the way things are, blended with a nostalgic yearning for the way they ought to be. Ōkubo represents the world as it is, where hard-headed pragmatism and the Machiavellian pursuit of rationally defined goals offer the only guarantees of success. Saigō represents the world as it ought to be, where soft-hearted sentiment and simple moral distinctions make it possible for people to care about each other without concern for the stakes, and to interact with mutual support in the pursuit of the common good. In this simple polarization, sincerity, friendship, and honor are what we ought to have, while cynicism, duplicity, and pragmatism are what we do have. Such intangible qualities as these, however much they may be based on real differences between two very different real men, become inflated into universal and uncomplicated truths about human nature, and about the condition of the modern Japanese polity. In that form, they characterize the idealized difference between Saigō and Ōkubo in the Japanese imagination, and help make it possible for Saigō's image to function as it does.

It is important to bear in mind that this ritual of contrasting Saigō and Ōkubo does not function primarily to tell us anything about Ōkubo, or about the friendship between the two men. It does both things explicitly, but it does them in order to highlight certain aspects of Saigō through their contrasts with their opposites in Ōkubo, aspects that might not be so easy to point out with affirmations about Saigō himself. It is striking how many Japanese have chosen this technique to convey their views about Saigō to me in the numerous conversations that have unfolded when I have told them of my interest in him. It is equally striking how many Japanese have simply volunteered their views, without any inquiry or encouragement from me.

This tendency to offer unsolicited statements about Saigō may reflect a more generalized desire, occasionally expressed by former Prime Minister Nakasone Yasuhiro, to be understood (*rikai sarete hoshii*). Such culture-based generalizations are risky, of course, but what is noteworthy about this phenomenon is that I have not often observed it when other things were under discussion. My Japanese friends and acquaintances do not usually seem eager to volunteer explanations of bilateral trade friction, for example, or the relationship between Japanese art and Zen Buddhism, or the motives behind the attack on Pearl Harbor. Most of them are quite willing to talk about these things, certainly, but usually not until asked. What I find impressive is how many of them are eager to tell me about Saigō, almost as if they were always on the lookout for opportunities to talk about this man, of whom they seem to feel so much while they know so little. Informed of my research, even at first meeting, many Japanese immediately have repeated their favorite anecdotes about Saigō, or have offered some grand statement about the Japanese, illustrated with some bit of information about him. Understand Saigō, they tell me, and you will understand Japan. Other foreigners have had similar experiences, to judge from what they tell me, even when they had no interest in Saigō, nor even any idea of who he was.

In the end, what is most intriguing is the numbers of Japanese who do not seem to care very much about how little demonstrable correspondence there is between the historically verifiable Saigō Takamori of the primary evidence and the legendary Great Saigō of the popular imagination. This is not a paradox. We have enough of those about Japan already. But it is a fascinating illustration of the power of images. The question that remains is, what are the qualities in Saigō that make his image so powerful?

As I suggested at the beginning of this study, the best answer may be that Saigō offers, first of all, some especially appealing personal characteristics, such as sincerity, integrity, simplicity, and selflessness. To top it all off, there is utter fidelity not only to friends and subordinates, but even to a hopelessly lost cause. If

Ivan Morris is correct about the nobility of failure in Japanese culture, then no one exhibits it more vividly than Saigō.[8] In addition, he seems to embody in his value system the most fundamental, definitive, and highly prized elements of traditional Japanese culture. These things are easy to admire in anyone, but in him they are combined with ambiguities and reinforced by a lack of conclusive data about very tantalizing questions. Did he want to invade Korea, or not? Did he take the first fateful steps that led Japan into the dark valley of the Pacific War, or not? Did he lead a rebellion against the very government he had helped to create, or not? Does he combine in a single person the paradigms of perfect loyalty and perfect betrayal, or not?

If it is true that symbols derive their power chiefly from their ambiguity, then it is thanks to the combined effect of Saigō's potent and irreducible ambiguities that he becomes the empty symbolic vessel I described in the introduction. With superficial qualities that make him instantly recognizable as a Japanese, he is nevertheless sufficiently empty of any fixed inner meaning of his own, so that he can be adapted to stand for almost anything the Japanese in search of a symbol might want, filled with whatever meaning is called for at the moment.

If that is the case, then his persistence for over a hundred years as one of the most reliable sources of content for the ongoing conversation among the Japanese about themselves and their collective meaning is only the opening sequence in an endless drama of immortality. Given that much, it follows, finally, that the real importance of Saigō Takamori is less the role he played in the creation of the Meiji state and the birth of modern Japan than it is the role he continues to play in the imaginations of Japanese today, and what we can learn about them from that.

GLOSSARY:
Key Persons, Places, and Terms

Aikana (1837–1902)   Saigō's first wife, a native of the village of Tatsugō on Ōshima island, where Saigō stayed during his first exile, 1859–62.

Aizu han   A Tokugawa collateral domain located in present-day Yamagata Prefecture; it became the rallying point for pro-Tokugawa resistance to the Meiji Restoration.

Aki han   An ōzama daimyo domain centered around present-day Hiroshima; it jōined the Satsuma-Chōshū ōbaku alliance in 1867.

Ansei purge (1859–60)   A purge conducted by the bakufu great councillor (tairō) Ii Naosuke to remove from power all who had opposed his policies in the shogunal succession and trade treaty disputes of 1858.

Arima Shinshichi (1825–62)   A Satsuma samurai; renowned for his learning, an influential member of the Seichūgumi, and later a leader of the extremist anti-foreign faction; killed at the Teradaya in Kyoto.

bakkaku   A generic term, analogous to 'the government' in English, denoting the Tokugawa bakufu bureaucracy.

bakufu   Originally, a military field headquarters; after 1600, the government of the Tokugawa family.

bakuhan seidō   The loosely centralized system of bakufu bureaucracy and autonomous daimyo domains that governed Japan, 1600–1868.

bakumatsu   The final years of the Tokugawa bakufu, usually from either the 1830s or the 1850s to 1868, depending on whether one dates the period from the Tenpō reform era (as most Japanese historians do) or from the arrival of Commodore Perry and other Western representatives (as most Western historians do).

Beppu Shinsuke (1847–77)   A Satsuma samurai; a command grade officer in the Shigakkō system; took his own life after performing kaishaku (beheading) for Saigō at the end of the Satsuma rebellion.

Bunka purge (1808–9)   The forced removal from office by the former hanshu, Shimazu Shigehide, of han government officials appointed by his son, hanshu Shimazu Narinobu, after Narinobu committed Satsuma to nostalgic reforms contrary to Shigehide's intentions.

chiji   Chief executives of the former han during the late 1860s; functional precursors of the prefectural governors (kenrei) established after 1871.

Chōshū han   A tōzama daimyo domain located in present-day Yamaguchi

Prefecture; initially a stronghold of sonnō jōi sentiment; later, with Satsuma, a leader of the anti-bakufu movement in the 1860s.

daimyo The lord and fief holder of the Tokugawa period quasi-feudal domain.

daimyo council(s) A series of efforts between 1864 and 1868 to create a special quasi-legislative body composed of powerful daimyo, to formulate policy through deliberation and to advise the court; based on the assumption that some vestige of Tokugawa power could be preserved even after the destruction of the bakufu and the bakuhan system.

dajōkan A temporary council of state based on classical Japanese institutions, created immediately after the ōsei fukko coup d'etat in 1868, soon replaced by a more elaborate system.

Date Munenari (1818–92) The hanshu of Uwajima; one of four daimyo who attempted to realize the kōbu gattai agenda, then tried to establish conciliar leadership for the court.

Dazaifu In ancient Japan, a satellite office of the central government, located in northern Kyushu near the present-day city of Fukuoka; later the site of the confinement of Sanjō Sanetomi and other young loyalist court nobles, as arranged by Saigō in the 1864 Chōshū settlement.

Echigo A province in Tōhoku, scene of some of the fiercest fighting in the Meiji civil war.

Etō Shinpei (1834–74) A Saga samurai; member of the caretaker government, 1871–3, and seikanron advocate; resigned at the same time as Saigō; led a samurai rebellion in Saga, 1873; executed by the government on Ōkubo's orders.

Fujita Tōko (1806–55) A Mito samurai and Confucian thinker; influential in developing sonnō jōi ideology; exerted important influence on Saigō; died in the great earthquake of 1855.

Fukui han A Tokugawa collateral domain located in present-day Fukui Prefecture.

Fukuoka han An ōzama daimyo domain located in present-day Fukuoka Prefecture.

gaiseiha That faction of the Meiji government identified with seikanron; centered around Saigō, it includes most of those in the caretaker government of 1871–3, in particular Etō Shinpei, Gotō Shōjirō, and Itagaki Taisuke. (Cf. naijiha)

Gesshō (1813–58) A Kyoto imperial loyalist monk affiliated with the Kiyomizu Temple and with the Konoe family; influenced Saigō importantly, and jōined in suicide pact with him in 1858.

Go-shinpei The early name for the imperial guard created with samurai from Satsuma, Chōshū, and Tosa to protect the government in case of armed opposition to the haihan chiken initiative (see Konoe-hyō).

Godai Tomoatsu (1835–85) A Satsuma samurai; studied in England, served as a go-between in negotiations with English representatives, later became a powerful industrialist.

gōjū kyōiku A system of neighborhood education for sons of lower ranking samurai in Kagōshima; emphasis on physical training and memorization of Confucian ethical norms, especially loyalty, duty, and sincerity; important early influence on Saigō and other Satsuma samurai.

gōshi   A type of samurai, holding a status created in Satsuma during the sixteenth century as a form of reward for loyal military service; lowest ranking of all Satsuma samurai, in principle confined to the countryside, and traditionally subjected to discrimination by castle town samurai. The term is generic, literally meaning 'rural samurai,' but the social type it identified was different in each han where gōshi existed. For example, gōshi in Satsuma were altogether different in origin, status, and socio-economic character from gōshi in Tosa.

Gotō Shōjirō (1838–97)   A Tosa samurai; worked with Saigō and others to form the Satsuma-Tosa alliance in 1867; persuaded Tosa hanshu to ask Yoshinobu to surrender his power to the court; later tried to save the Tokugawa family from destruction.

habu   A poisonous snake much like a cobra, indigenous to all of the Amami Islands except Okinoerabu.

Hagi   The original castle town of Chōshū han, and home to most of the important Chōshū samurai.

haihan chiken   A political initiative taken in 1871 as an early step in the conversion of Tokugawa institutions to centralized government; means 'abolition of domains and establishment of prefectures.'

han   A Tokugawa period domain or fief.

hanseki hōkan   A political initiative taken in 1869 by Satsuma, Chōshū, Tosa, and Saga, involving the return to court control of han lands and peoples formerly subject to the hanshu.

hanshu   (*see* **daimyo**)

Hashimoto Sanai (1834–59)   A Fukui samurai close to the hanshu and instrumental in han reforms; a progressive thinker, he worked with Saigō during the political struggles of 1858, and influenced Saigō importantly; executed by Ii Naosuke during the Ansei purge.

hatamoto   The direct hereditary household vassals of the Tokugawa.

Hirano Kuniomi (1828–64)   A Fukuoka samurai; rescued Saigō from drowning in 1858; advocated sonnō jōi, and later died in an uprising at Ikuno, near Osaka.

Hitotsubashi Yoshinobu (1837–1913)   The fifteenth and last of the Tokugawa shogun, 1866–7; one of the most resourceful and capable politicians of the bakumatsu period.

Hyōgo   Present-day Kobe City.

Hyūga   A traditional province corresponding roughly to present-day Miyazaki Prefecture.

Ii Naosuke (1815–60)   A Tokugawa vassal daimyo; became great councillor in 1858 and forcibly ended both the treaty approval and the shogunal succession disputes; murdered in 1860 by loyalist samurai from Mito and Satsuma.

Itagaki Taisuke (1837–1919)   A Tosa samurai; active in the ōbaku movement; later a vocal advocate of action against Korea; left the government in 1873 and created Japan's first political party.

Itō Hirobumi (1841–1909) A Chōshū samurai; initially close to Kido, later among Ōkubo's most important proteges; eventually became the most important figure in the later Meiji government, playing a key role in the drafting of the Meiji constitution and other events, including most of the early steps in the Japanese absorption of Korea.

Iwakuni han A Chōshū collateral domain through whose hanshu Saigō conducted the initial negotiations for the 1864 settlement of the bakufu punitive campaign against Chōshū.

Iwakura Tomomi (1825–83) A junior court noble, expelled from the court in the early 1860s but later, with Ōkubo, the chief planner of the ōsei fukko coup and a leading figure in the early Meiji government.

Iwashita Masahira (1827–1900) A Satsuma samurai, who worked closely with other han leaders in setting up the ōsei fukko coup.

Kaei purge (1849–50) The forced removal from office by hanshu Shimazu Narioki of samurai suspected of plotting to murder his concubine Okada Yura.

Kagoshima Castle town of Satsuma han, the domain of the Shimazu.

kaikoku A political term of the bakumatsu era; it means 'open country' and implies full diplomatic and economic interaction with the Western nations.

Kajiyamachi A residential district in Kagoshima reserved for koshōgumi families, and the boyhood home of Saigō, Ōkubo, and many others who became prominent in either the early or the later Meiji period.

kakkyō A concept devised by bakumatsu thinkers; it means 'local self-sufficiency' and suggests an arrangement where each han is politically and economically independent from all others.

kannushi A Shintō priest; a category defined by Saigō as having the mission of indoctrinating local communities in the meaning and importance of Shintō rituals.

karō The senior vassals under a daimyo; means 'house elder.' Equivalent at the domain level to the rōjū of the bakufu.

karōza The highest governing body in a han, immediately beneath the hanshu and composed of karō; means 'council of elders.'

Katsu Kaishū (1823–99) A bakufu vassal, who played a key role in the early development of Japanese naval technology and institutions, and influenced Saigō importantly.

Katsura Hisatake (1830–77) A high-ranking Satsuma samurai, among Saigō's most intimate confidantes, who jōined in the Satsuma rebellion and took his own life after Saigō's death.

Kawaguchi Seppō (1818–90) A Satsuma samurai, whom Saigō came to know on Okinoerabu; influenced Saigō's poetry and his calligraphy, and helped care for his family after his death.

Kawaji Toshiyoshi (1836–79) A Satsuma samurai, who organized and headed the first Tokyo police force, and was suspected of plotting with Ōkubo to have Saigō murdered.

kenrei A prefectural governor under the Meiji system (see chiji).

Kido Takayoshi (1833–77) A Chōshū samurai; initially a sonnō jōi activist, later a key political leader; associated with Saigō and Ōkubo as one of the 'three heroes' of the Meiji Restoration.

Kikkawa Kenmotsu (1829–96) The hanshu of the Chōshū collateral han of Iwakuni; worked with Saigō to negotiate the settlement of the first bakufu campaign against Chōshū.

Kirino Toshiaki (1838–77) A Satsuma gōshi close to Saigō; renowed among bakumatsu activists for his mastery of the sword; later a high ranking official in the Shigakkō system, and one of the main instigators of the Satsuma rebellion.

Koba Dennai (1817–91) A Satsuma samurai and close confidante of Saigō; the chief official on Ōshima during Saigō's exile there; later in charge of Satsuma's Osaka residence.

kōbu gattai A bakumatsu political strategy aimed at creating a coalition of bakufu and court and supported chiefly by Satsuma, Fukui, Tosa, and Uwajima; abandoned as unworkable after 1865; means 'union of court and bakufu.'

Kōchi The castle town of Tosa han, the domain of the Yamauchi.

kōgi seitai A bakumatsu political concept envisioning a legislative body as the central organ of the Japanese government, predicated on free discussion among all elites; means 'political structure based on deliberation of public affairs.'

Kogoshō An annex building within the imperial palace compound in Kyoto; scene of initial policy conference after ōsei fukko coup.

kokka A political concept usually rendered as 'state' in English; for most bakumatsu users it referred to the polity of the han, and did not come to refer to the polity of the Japanese nation until the later Meiji period.

koku A unit of dry measure, equivalent to roughly 4.95 bushels, and used chiefly to measure rice.

kokutai A political concept given currency by Mito thinkers and usually rendered as 'national polity' in English; literally it means 'the body of the country,' and its implication in ideological formulations is 'national essence.' Thus it overlaps with the term kokusui, customarily rendered 'national essence.'

Komatsu Tatewaki (1835–1903) A high-ranking Satsuma samurai; Hisamitsu's chief agent in Kyoto and elsewhere during the bakumatsu period, he worked closely with Saigō and Ōkubo; played an important role in local reforms in Kagoshima after 1868.

Konoe Tadahiro (1808–98) A high-ranking court noble; the head of a family with long-standing ties to the Shimazu, he played a vital role in helping Saigō and others gain access to the court during the bakumatsu period.

Konoe-hyō The later name for the imperial guard (see Go-shinpei).

koshōgumi The lowest stratum of the castle town samurai hierarchy in Kagōshima, outnumbering higher ranking samurai by about ten to one;

most members of the bakumatsu political group were of this rank, including Saigō and Ōkubo.

Kumamoto The castle town of Kumamoto han, and headquarters of the early Meiji Kumamoto garrison, which became the target of the Satsuma rebel army.

Kuroda Kiyotaka (1840–1900) A Satsuma samurai and boyhood friend of Saigō and Ōkubo; performed vital services at several points during the bakumatsu period, and later became a powerful figure in the Meiji government.

Kuroda Kiyotsuna (1830–1917) A Satsuma samurai; brother of Kuroda Kiyotaka.

Kuwana han A Tokugawa collateral han loyal to Yoshinobu during the bakumatsu period, later joined with Aizu as the nucleus of Tokugawa partisan resistance in 1868.

kyōwa seiji A political concept predicated on free and open discussion in government; connotes 'republican government.'

Maebara Issei (1834–76) A Chōshū samurai; a member of the early Meiji government and a supporter of seikanron, he resigned in 1873 and led a brief rebellion in Hagi in 1876.

Matsudaira Shungaku (1828–80) Hanshu of Fukui, and a leader in the daimyo councils.

Matsudaira Katamori (1835–93) Hanshu of Aizu, and leader of Tokugawa loyalist resistance after 1868.

Matsukata Masayoshi (1835–1924) A Satsuma samurai, later minister of finance and prime minister.

Mito With Owari and Kii one of the three original Tokugawa direct collateral houses, and most influential of the three; scene of important Tenpō era reforms, vital intellectual activities, and customarily regarded as the birthplace of sonnō jōi activism.

monbatsu A generic term referring to all of the highest ranking samurai status groups in Kagoshima; dominated local politics until 1869, then abolished in reforms; means 'titled faction.'

Mōri Yoshichika (1819–71) Hanshu of Chōshū.

Murata Shinpachi (1836–77) A Satsuma samurai and close friend of Saigō; later a high official in the Shigakkō system and an instigator of the 1877 rebellion; took his own life after Saigō's death.

naijiha That faction of the Meiji government opposed to seikanron and favoring internal consolidation as the most urgent national priority after 1871; included mostly members of the Iwakura mission of 1871–3, especially Iwakura, Ōkubo, and Kido. (Cf. gaiseiha)

naiyū gaikan A Chinese political concept; a steady increase of domestic troubles (naiyū) and external dangers (gaikan) indicates that the regime in power, through loss of virtue, has lost the right to rule conferred by Heaven and is about to fall.

Nakahara Hisao (?) A Satsuma gōshi, initially a member of the Tokyo police, later the leader of a group of spies sent to Kagoshima to collect information on the Shigakkō system and accused of plotting to murder Saigō.

Nakaoka Shintarō (1838–67) A Tosa samurai closely associated with Sakamoto Ryōma, and murdered with him by bakufu agents at the Teradaya Inn just prior to the ōsei fukko coup d'etat.

Namamugi A small village between Tokyo and Yokohama; scene of an incident in 1862 in which Hisamitsu's escorts murdered one British citizen and injured two others; became the pretext for the inconclusive British punitive action against Kagoshima in 1863.

Okada Yura (1795–1866) A concubine of the Satsuma hanshu Shimazu Narioki, and mother of Hisamitsu.

Okinoerabujima A small island in the Amami group just north of Okinawa; site of most of Saigō's second exile.

Ōkubo Toshimichi (1830–78) A Satsuma samurai and boyhood friend of Saigō; central in the ōsei fukko coup d'etat and the most powerful figure in the Meiji government during the last five yaers of his life, from the time of the seikanron crisis until his murder by disgruntled former samurai.

Ōkuma Shigenobu (1838–1922) A Saga samurai who resigned with Saigō and others in 1873, created one of Japan's early political parties, and became important in the later Meiji government.

Ōmura Masujiro (1824–69) A Chōshū samurai and military leader, first conceptualized the modern army later created by his protege, Yamagata Aritomo; antagonized Saigō during the suppression of Tokugawa loyalist resistance in Edo in 1868.

ōsei fukko Chinese political concept used as the justification for the overthrow of the Tokugawa; means 'restoration of rule by the emperor as of old.'

Ōshima The largest island in the Amami group and site of Saigō's first exile, 1859–62.

Ōshima Shōsha A mercantile enterprise created in the 1870s by leaders in Kagoshima with Saigō's support; based on the earlier Satsuma sugar monopoly in the Ōshima islands, its purpose was to provide new sources of income to pay samurai stipends in Kagoshima.

Ōsumi A traditional province in southern Kyushu, equivalent to the eastern half of Satsuma-han, and of present-day Kagoshima Prefecture.

Owari With Mito and Kii, one of the three original Tokugawa direct collateral houses.

Ōyama Iwao (1842–1916) A Satsuma samurai, cousin to Saigō, and later an important Meiji military leader.

Ōyama Tsunayoshi (1825–77) A Satsuma samurai, boyhood friend to Saigō and Ōkubo; later Kagoshima's first governor and one of those responsible for the 1877 rebellion.

rusu seifu A caretaker group left in charge of national affairs during the absence of the Iwakura mission, 1871–73; included Saigō, Sanjō Sanetomi, Etō Shinpei, Itagaki Taisuke, Yamagata Aritomo, and others.

ryō A gold coin serving as the basis of Tokugawa period currency.

Saga A tōzama domain in northern Kyushu; among the first in Japan to begin modernizing reforms, later a member of the anti-bakufu coalition.

Saigō Kohei (1847–77) Third and youngest of Saigō's brothers; fought against Tokugawa partisans in 1868 and then died in the 1877 rebellion.

Saigō Shingo (*see* **Saigō Tsugumichi**)

Saigō Kikujirō (1861–1928) Saigō's oldest son, born to Aikana on Ōshima; later a mayor of Kyoto.

Saigō Kichibei (1806–52) Saigō's father.

Saigō Kichijirō (1833–68) Oldest of Saigō's brothers; looked after the family in the 1850s and 1860s; died fighting Tokugawa partisans in Echigo.

Saigō Tsugumichi (1843–1902) Second of Saigō's brothers; close to Ōkubo and Yamagata, and later an important Meiji military leader.

Sakamoto Ryōma (1835–67) A Tosa samurai, originally a gōshi; instrumental in helping to arrange the Satsuma-Chōshū alliance of 1866.

Sakoda Taji'emon (1786–1855) A Satsuma samurai in charge of rural administration in the 1850s; exerted important influences on the development of Saigō's ideas about rural government.

sakoku A term customarily applied to Japan under Tokugawa rule, implying complete isolation from the outside world; means 'closed country.'

sangi A high government office under the early Meiji system; means 'participating in deliberations.'

sanji A high government office under the early post–1868 Kagōshima government; means 'participating in affairs.'

Sanjō Sanetomi (1837–91) A young court noble in the 1860s associated with Chōshū extremists; fled Kyoto when Chōshū forces were driven from the city in 1863; remained under guard at Dazaifu until after 1868; later a key member of the early Meiji government, in charge of the caretaker government, 1871–3.

sankin kōtai A system under which all daimyo made regular trips to Edo to pay homage to the shogun; the key social control mechanism of the bakuhan system; effectively abolished in 1862.

sansei A high government office after 1868; means 'participating in government.'

Satō Issai (1772–1859) A Confucian thinker advocating the teachings of the Chinese Neo-Confucianist Wang Yang-ming; his ideas influenced Saigō's thought importantly.

Satsuma A tōzama domain in southern Kyushu, hereditary fief of the Shimazu family from 1185 through 1868; named for a traditional province corresponding to the western portion of the han, and making up its largest part.

Seichūgumi A name adopted by Kagoshima's young samurai activist group; means 'the league of the sincere and loyal.'

seikanron A term customarily identified with early Meiji imperialism and debated in the crisis of 1873; means 'the proposal to punish Korea.'

Glossary

seinan sensō The Satsuma rebellion of 1877; means 'the war in the southwest.'

senkyōshi (see also kannushi) A religious official conceived by Saigō to help the government indoctrinate the masses; means 'missionary,' or 'proselytizer.'

Shigakkō A set of educational and military institutions created in Kagoshima after 1873 to train local samurai, based on earlier reforms in 1869, and eventually the source of the 1877 rebellion; means 'private school.'

Shigeno Yasutsugu (1827–1910) A Satsuma samurai living on Ōshima during Saigō's first exile there, and thus a source of important anecdotes; later a central figure in the influential Kyoto School of Japanese historians.

Shimazu Hisamitsu (1817–87) Half-brother to the hanshu Nariakira by Narioki and his concubine Okada Yura; father to the last hanshu Tadayoshi, and the most powerful figure in Kagoshima from 1858 through 1866.

Shimazu Tadayoshi (1840–97) Son of Hisamitsu and the last hanshu of Satsuma, 1858–69.

Shimazu Nariakira (1809–58) Son of Narioki and hanshu of Satsuma, 1852–58; aggressive modernizing reformer and imaginative politician; among the most important of those who influenced Saigō's political development.

Shimazu Narioki (1791–59) Son of Narinobu and hanshu of Satsuma, 1809–52; overseer of Tenpō reforms under Zusho Hirosato, and initiator of the Kaei purge.

Shimonoseki A port city in Chōshū, located on the narrow straits separating western Honshu from northern Kyushu.

Shinagawa Yajirō (1843–1900) A Chōshū samurai who worked with Ōkubo and Iwakura in planning the ōsei fukko coup d'etat.

Shinohara Kunimoto (1836–77) A Satsuma samurai, member of the early imperial guard, later a high official in the Shigakkō system and instigator of the 1877 rebellion.

shizoku A generic term coined by Meiji leaders to cover all former samurai regardless of rank; means 'military family.'

shizoku hanran A series of armed uprisings involving mostly former samurai between 1874 and 1877; means 'samurai uprising.'

shōgun The senior official of the Tokugawa government; designated by the emperor as his official proxy.

Shōnai A Tokugawa vassal domain in the Tōhoku region, involved in the Tokugawa partisan coalition, and treated favorably by Saigō after its surrender in 1868.

Soejima Taneomi (1828–1905) A Saga samurai, and early Meiji foreign minister; left the government in 1873.

sonnō jōi The slogan of imperial loyalist expulsionists in the 1860s; means 'revere the emperor and expel the barbarian.'

195

tairō The senior post in the Tokugawa government under the shogun, only filled in times of crisis; means 'great councillor.'

taisei hōkan A political move proposed by Yamauchi Yōdō and carrried out by Tokugawa Yoshinobu in 1867, in which he formally surrendered his right to rule the country as the emperor's proxy, hoping thereby to retain his rights as head of the Tokugawa family.

Takasugi Shinsaku (1839–67) A Chōshū samurai and important leader in that han's bakumatsu politics.

tenka A Chinese political concept implying 'the realm presided over by the emperor'; means 'under Heaven.'

Tenpō reforms A series of administrative and fiscal reforms conducted in many han between the late eighteenth and early nineteenth centuries; customarily viewed in Japan as the first set of events in the bakumatsu period.

Teradaya An inn located in the city of Fushimi near Kyoto; site of the battle between Seichūgumi members in 1862, and later of the murder of Sakamoto Ryōma and Nakaoka Shintarō.

Terajima Munenori (1832–93) A Satsuma samurai important in bakumatsu relationships with England and other powers, later a high official of the Meiji government.

tōbaku A term employed by anti-bakufu forces, and ambiguous because written in two different ways that are pronounced identically; in one formulation, it means 'admonish (strike) the bakufu'; in the other, it means 'overthrow (topple) the bakufu.'

Tōhoku A Japanese geographical region encompassing the northeastern half of the main island of Honshu.

Tokugawa Iemochi (Yoshitomi; 1846–66) Heir apparent of Kii han, which with Mito and Owari was one of the three original direct Tokugawa collateral houses; in 1858, the strongest claimant by blood to succeed as shogun, and so appointed under Ii Naosuke's direction.

Tokugawa Nariaki (1800–60) Hanshu of Mito and father of Hitotsubashi Yoshinobu.

Tokugawa Yoshinobu (*see* **Hitotsubashi Yoshinobu**)

Tokugawa Yoshikatsu (1824–83) Hanshu of Owari and commander of the first Chōshū punitive campaign.

Tokunoshima An island in the Amami group, where Saigō stayed briefly at the beginning of his second exile.

Tosa A tōzama domain on Shikoku, and a key participant in bakumatsu politics.

tōzama A daimyo considered 'outside' the direct Tokugawa vassal network because he did not proclaim his fealty to the Tokugawa family until after Tokugawa Ieyasu achieved national dominance at the battle of Sekigahara in 1600; normally excluded from politics and government appointment in the bakufu.

Tsuchimochi Masateru (1835–?) A native of Okinoerabu island, in charge of Saigō during his exile there.

Uwajima A tōzama domain in Shikoku.

Glossary

Yamagata Aritomo (1838–1922) A Chōshū samurai active in the bakumatsu period and later among the most powerful men in the Meiji government, as both creator of the modern army and prime minister.

Yamaguchi An alternate castle town in Chōshū.

Yamauchi Yōdō (1827–72) Hanshu of Tosa; initially involved with Hisamitsu and others in efforts to realize kōbu gattai; later a supporter of Yoshinobu and efforts to preserve Tokugawa prerogatives.

NOTES

Introduction

1. Cf. Shiba Ryōtarō, *Tobu ga gotoku*, Tokyo, 1975. Also included in the NHK script were story elements from *Bakumatsu*, Tokyo, 1963, *Yotte sōrō*, Tokyo, 1965, and *Saigo no shōgun*, Tokyo, 1967. For discussion of Shiba and his work, cf. '*Tobu ga gotoku* to Saigō Takamori,' a special issue of *Bungei shunjū derakusu* for 197/1/1.
2. Ivan Morris, 'The Apotheosis of Saigō the Great,' in *The Nobility of Failure*, London, 1975. This is the only rigorous treatment of Saigō in English, and it relies heavily on the work of Sakamoto Moriaki, whose father was imprisoned for fighting in the Satsuma rebellion. The son poured a great deal of energy into exonerating Saigō, hoping, one assumes, to clear the father's name in the process. Most of the secondary writing on Saigō in Japan is like this, arising not from a desire to make sense of Saigō, but from other motives that often have very little to do with Saigō himself.
3. For an English study of Ōkubo's career, cf. Iwata Masakazu, *Ōkubo Toschimichi, The Bismarck of Japan*, Berkeley and LA, 1964.
4. The writings of Sakamoto Moriaki, mentioned above, are among the more elaborate recent examples of the tendency to blame Ōkubo for everything that went wrong in Saigō's life.
5. Cf. Charles L. Yates, 'Meiji kokka no keisei to Saigō Takamori,' in *Nenpō: Kindai Nihon kenkyū*, #14, October, 1992.
6. Morris, *The Nobility of Failure*, 218.
7. Only about five hundred of Saigō's letters are known to exist, together with a couple of hundred Chinese poems, a handful of memorials, and a few odds and ends. The most recent attempt at a complete collection is *Saigō Takamori zenshū*, 6 vols., Tokyo, 1980.
8. Having made this assertion several times, I ought to offer some support for it, but that would oblige me to cite examples from the entire narrative tradition on Saigō, and in any case my purpose here is not

198

Notes

primarily to validate claims about the reliability of Japanese scholarship on Saigō, but rather to move from that problem to some reflections on the forces preventing consensus among scholars. My Japanese readers will know what I mean, simply from their familiarity with the ongoing debate. I must ask my readers elsewhere to bear with me.

9. Cf. Carol Gluck, *Japan's Modern Myths*, Princeton, 1985. She mentions Saigō on page 24.

10. Gluck, *Japan's Modern Myths*, 249 and 257.

11. Morris begins 'The Apotheosis of Saigō the Great' with a discussion of the Ueno monument, thereby associating himself with others whose main task has been to create an emotionally satisfying image of Saigō.

12. Cf. STZ VI: 524–25 for bibliographical data on collections of nishiki-e portraying Saigō and his times. Especially valuable is Konishi Shirō, *Nishiki-e bakumatsu Meiji no rekishi*, 12 vols., Tokyo, 1977, esp. vols. 7, *Shizoku hanran*, and 8, *Seinan sensō*.

13. To judge from the examples Morris gives us in *The Nobility of Failure*, more than one Japanese hero has been widely believed to have escaped death and gone into hiding in some distant land, there to bide his time until the right moment comes for him to return to Japan and finish whatever heroic work his enemies had interrupted. According to Ikai Takaaki, one of Saigō's most recent biographers, the rumor that Saigō had been transformed into a heavenly body began circulating within days of his death, helped in no small part by the presence of Mars in the night sky at the time. Ikai also reports that within a year after the defeat of the Satsuma forces, newspaper stories had convinced many people that Saigō had escaped abroad and was in hiding somewhere. Cf. Ikai Takaaki, *Saigō Takamori: Seinan sensō e no michi*, Tokyo, 1992, 2–6. A good example of Saigō represented in nishiki-e as a survivor is in Ōzaki Hotsuki, *Nishiki-e Nihon no rekishi*, Tokyo, 1982, *Saigō Takamori to meiji jidai*, 90–1, where we see Saigō and three of his close associates debarking from Russian crown prince Nikolai's vessel during the latter's state visit to Japan in 1891. Cf. this same work, 88–9 and 96, for examples of Saigō as vengeful ghost and as heavenly phenomenon. Further examples are in Asukai Masamichi, *Saigō Takamori*, Tokyo, 1978, 70–3.

14. Cf. Ōzaki, *Saigō Takamori to Meiji jidai*, 92–93, for examples of kabuki prints.

15. For examples, cf. Konishi, *Nishiki-e bakumatsu Meiji no rekishi*, vol. 7, 1–7.

16. One of these uniforms is on display in the private memorial museum for Saigō (*Nanshū Kenshōkan*) in Kagoshima. If nothing else, it establishes beyond question that Saigō was an unusually large man, and would not look the least bit out of place in a line-up of today's heaviest *sumo* champions. Some illustrations of Saigō's clothing, along with a well-known portrait of him in uniform, may be found in Kaionji Chōgorō et al, *Botsugo hyakunen Saigō Takamori sono eidai naru shōgai*, Tokyo, 1977, 3, 6–7, 12, and 14–15.

17. One of Nagayama's photographs is reproduced in Kaionji Chōgorō et al, *Botsugo hyakunen Saigō Takamori*, 74, along with those of two other men at one time thought to be Saigō.
18. Cf. Marius Jansen, *Sakamoto Ryōma and the Meiji Restoration*, Princeton, 1961. Like Saigō, Sakamoto was converted into a television image by NHK, in its mini-series for 1968. Also, and probably not coincidentally, the basis for that series was another multi-volume novel by Shiba Ryōtarō, *Ryōma ga yuku*, Tokyo, 1963.
19. Cf. for example *Taiyō* magazine for 1978/4/12, 73, where the celebrity Tatsuda Yū, caricatured to look strangely like Saigō, cheerfully urges us to buy a National refrigerator-freezer. Representations of Saigō turn up routinely in advertising for special tour packages offered by Japan Rail, particularly in Ueno station. And of course Saigō is a popular image in advertisements for *shōchū*, the speciality liquor of southern Kyushu and the Ryūkyū islands.
20. For bibliography on Saigō, cf. STZ VI: 449–534, and Nonaka Keigo, comp. and ed., *Saigō Takamori kankei bunken kaidai mokuroku kō*, Matsuyama-shi, 1970 (enlarged 1978, revised and enlarged 1979). Both works list over 1,500 entries, giving an average of fifteen new items published about Saigō every year since his death in 1877.
21. Inoue Kiyoshi insists on the importance of the exile, and my interpretation of that period and its impact on Saigō owes much to Inoue's analysis. Cf. Inoue, I: 72–133.
22. This is not to say that my self image is in no way at stake in my portrayal of Saigō; but it is at stake in different ways from those that matter to the Japanese.

1 · *Saigō's Childhood in Satsuma,*
1827–59

1. The following account of Satsuma is necessarily brief. For a more detailed discussion of the events and issues presented here, cf. Diss, 34–104. Detailed information on references and sources for Satsuma's history may be found in both the narrative and the notes there. The source of the first reference is the *Kagoshima kenshi*, in five volumes. For primary sources, the best single collection is *Kagoshima ken shiryō*, which approached 30 volumes as of 1993.
2. Some Japanese sources give 1185 as the year of Koremune's appointment. I have chosen to follow Robert Sakai, in the essay cited in note 4 below. Contemporary accounts of Yoritomo's career and campaigns are in the *Heiki monogatari* and the *Azuma kagami*. There is a large body of detailed scholarly treatment in English. Cf. the works of Jeffrey P. Mass: *Warrior Government in Early Medieval Japan*, New Haven and London, 1974; *The Kamakura Bakufu*, Stanford, 1976; *The Development of Kamakura Rule, 1180–1250*, Stanford, 1979; and *Court*

and *Bakufu in Japan*, New Haven and London, 1982. Also valuable
is Jeffrey P. Mass and John W. Hall, eds., *Medieval Japan*, New Haven
and London, 1974.

3. The best known contemporary account of Hideyoshi's career is the
Taiheiki. For a scholarly English treatment, cf. Mary Elizabeth Berry,
Hideyoshi, Cambridge, MA and London, 1982.

4. Various aspects of late sixteenth and early seventeenth century Japan
are examined in George Elison and Bardwell L. Smith, *Warlords, Art-
ists, and Commoners*, Honolulu, 1981. Also cf. John W. Hall, *Government and Local Power in Japan, 500 to 1700*, Princeton, 1966, and
John W. Hall and Marius B. Jansen, eds., *Studies in the Institutional
History of Early Modern Japan*, Princeton, 1968. Especially valuable
in the latter publication is Robert Sakai, 'The Consolidation of
Power in Satsuma-han,' 131–9, which gives more detail on the events
summarized here.

5. Satsuma was one of the few *han* which included a class of rural samurai
(*gōshi*) among its samurai population. Barely more than peasants with
swords, Satsuma's gōshi traced their origins back to the sixteenth
century, when they were given samurai status as a reward for their
service in Shimazu military campaigns. Because they were so numerous, the overall proportion of samurai in Satsuma was higher than in
any other place in Tokugawa Japan, with a ratio of about one samurai
for every three commoners.

6. The *ryō*, a flat hammered oblong of gold, was the basic unit of currency
throughout the Tokugawa period. Its value fluctuated, declining toward
the end of the period as a result of inflation caused by currency
revaluations and systematic debasement of the alloy. The weight ranged
from just under eighteen ounces in 1601 to just over three in 1860,
but the average was around thirteen ounces, and approximately seventy
percent of that was gold. At 1990 gold prices, one of these coins would
be worth between four and five thousand dollars, which would put
Satsuma's debt at the beginning of the nineteenth century in the vicinity
of a quarter of a billion dollars. In a time when national budgets are
calculated in trillions of dollars, and even local budgets are in the
hundreds of millions, this may seem like a paltry sum. For the average
Japanese in 1800, it would have been incomprehensibly large.

7. Samurai status groups and numbers of households in Satsuma in the
nineteenth century were as follows.

    direct Shimazu relatives, or collateral houses:
      ichimon   4 houses
    senior vassals, or titled samurai (*monbatsu*):
      isshōmochi   17 houses
      isshōmochi kaku   41 houses
      yoriai   54 houses
      yoriai nami   10 houses
    junior vassals, or lower samurai (*heishi/hirazamurai*):
      koban   760 houses

shinban	24 houses
koshōgumi	3,914 houses
marginal and rural samurai:	
sotsu/ashigaru	undetermined
gōshi	undetermined

Numbers of marginal and rural households are not recorded with any precision in the documents, but they probably numbered somewhere betweem 10,000 and 20,000, all told.

8. Ōkubo was among the first of Meiji Japan's leaders to receive scholarly attention in the West. Cf. Iwata Masakazu, *Ōkubo Tochimichi, The Bismarck of Japan*, Berkeley and Los Angeles, 1964.

9. OT den I: 33–42.

10. For a list of those in the activist group, known as the Seichūgumi, cf. Kenshi III: 292–4. Narioki's victims in the Kaei purge are listed in Kenshi II: 284–7. The victims of Shigehide's Bunka purge are listed in Kuroda Yasuo, 'Satsuma han Bunka hōtō jiken to sono rekishiteki haikei,' *Kyushu bunkashi kenkyūjo kiyō*, #19, 1974. The three lists have enough surnames in common to raise tantalizing questions about the possibility of a growing and ever more widely shared group consciousness.

11. DSZ III: 67–68. The narrative biography that makes up most of the third volume of the 1923 *Dai Saigō zenshū*, the first attempt at a complete collection of Saigō's writings, contains as much detail as one could want. The source for its narrative cliches is Katsuda Magoya's 1895 work, *Saigō Takamori den*, which is less detailed but seems to be the locus classicus for all the most durable elements of the biographical tradition.

12. DSZ III: 67–8. According to the autopsy report on Saigō's corpse, there was an old sword wound in the right arm. Cf. Tamamuro Taijō, *Saigō Takamori*, Tokyo, 1960, 194. If Saigō really was a master of martial arts, he ought to have given the sword cut rather than receiving it, and turning his attention to scholarship would have been no sacrifice because he already would have taken martial arts as far as he could. However, these inconsistencies seem not to trouble those who view Saigō in the ideal terms outlined here.

13. Inoue I: 154. Also cf. STZ II: 37–9, where Saigō expresses horror after his first direct experience of combat.

14. Tōgō Saneharu, *Saigō Takamori*, Kagoshima, 1984, 2.

15. STZ I: 19–23. Ōkubo Toshimichi's oldest existing letter is on the same subject, reinforcing the impression that the practice of supplementing income by working plots of land was not uncommon among koshōgumi. For Ōkubo's letter, cf. STZ loc. cit., and OTM I: 1–4.

16. DSZ III: 65.

17. DSZ III: 65.

18. DSZ III: 98–9.

19. DSZ III: 73–4. Also cf. OT den O: 10–18.

Notes

20. Space does not permit a lengthy discussion of the gōjū kyōiku here. For a more detailed discussion, cf. Diss, 109–14.
21. STZ I: 21; DSZ III: 73.
22. Inoue I: 38; DSZ III: 109–10.
23. Inoue I: 18–25; DSZ III: 69–71.
24. Inoue I: 19; DSZ III: 69–71.
25. DSZ III: 108.
26. STZ I: 71–7. For a modern secondary account of the conditions discussed by Saigō in this memorial, cf. Kanbashi Norimasa, 'Satsuma han gōshi nōmin no teikō undō,' *Nihonsji kenkyū*, #30.
27. STZ I: 26–8.
28. DSZ III: 111–12; Inoue I: 42.
29. DSZ III: 123–35.
30. STZ I: 57–60.
31. STZ I: 31–3.
32. STZ I: 50–1.
33. Ibid.
34. STZ I: 31–3. This is the first clear glimpse we get of what was later to evolve into a rather intolerant strain of prudery.
35. STZ I: 55–6.
36. STZ I: 38–9. Also cf. DSZ III: 116–18, and Nakamura Tokugorō, *Shimazu Nariakira kō*, Tokyo, 1933, 43.
37. Ibid.
38. DSZ III: 116–20.
39. Cf. Tokutomi Iichirō, *Kinsei Nihon kokuminshi*, Tokyo, 1960–71, vol. 30, 333. Also, Ikeda Toshihiko, *Shimazu Nariakira kō den*, Tokyo, 1954, 101–2.
40. DSZ III: 116–20.
41. For a fuller discussion, cf. Diss, 131–3.
42. DSZ III: 133–7; Inoue I: 55.
43. Inoue I: 54; Nakamura, *Nariakira*, 129–31.
44. For more detailed accounts in English of the treaty and succession issues, cf. W. G. Beasley, *The Meiji Restoration*, Stanford, 1972, 87–116; Conrad Totman, *The Collapse of the Tokugawa Bakufu*, Honolulu, 1980, xx–xxi; and Paul Akamatsu, *Meiji 1868*, New York, 1972, 92–127. Also, cf. Peter Booth Wiley, *Yankees in the Land of the Gods*, New York, 1990.
45. Nakamura, *Nariakira*, 110–18; Ikeda, *Nariakira*, 204–5, 377–80; Kenshi III: 267–71.
46. Nakamura, *Nariakira*, 315–16; Ikeda, *Nariakira*, 380–84; Kenshi III: 271.
47. DSZ III: 160.
48. DSZ III: 161–91; Inoue I: 58–66.
49. Kenshi III: 248–9.
50. STZ V: 615–34; DSZ III: 185–91; Kenshi III: 278; OT den I: 10–4.
51. STZ I: 131–3.
52. STZ I: 135–40.

53. Inoue I: 66.
54. Inoue I: 69–70.

2 · *Exile and Intellectual Growth*
1859–64

1. Among the most authoritative of these is Nobori Shōmu, *Saigō Takamori gokuchūki,* Tokyo, 1977.
2. Inoue I: iii.
3. The attribution of Saigō's obesity to filariasis is, of course, speculation on my part. His autopsy report notes a dropsical scrotum, one of the most common symptoms of elephantiasis, which is caused by a filaria worm vectored by some mosquitoes and endemic to all the Amami islands. Cf. Tamamuro, *Saigō Takamori,* 194. In a conversation in 1984, Dr. Joyce Carey, a Kyoto physician, agreed that filariasis is probably the most logical explanation for Saigō's obesity in later life.
4. Ivan Morris, in 'Apotheosis," 228, notes that Saigō 'was endowed with huge testicles.' His source for this statement is Tanaka Sōgorō, *Saigō Takamori,* Tokyo, 1958, 1. Tanaka's Japanese is *'idai naru kōgan,'* which may be translated as 'testicles of heroic proportions.' The observation, like so many concerning Saigō, tells us more about its author than about its subject.
5. STZ I: 141–4. During the winter months it rains almost incessantly in these islands, as a number of lifelong residents assured me when I visited there in December, 1984.
6. Ketōjin is a derogatory term with the literal meaning of 'hairy Chink.' For Saigō, it connoted not only the ethnic slur but probably also a view of the islanders as barely human. This attitude was common among Kagoshima samurai, many of whom had done tours of administrative duty in the islands. Saigō would have learned it routinely during his childhood, much as racist attitudes are learned by children today.
7. STZ I: 150–1.
8. STZ I: 146–9.
9. STZ I: 171–3.
10. Ibid.
11. Inoue I: 83.
12. STZ I: 141–4.
13. Nobori, *Gokuchūki,* 34–5, 38–9; DSZ III: 207.
14. For some examples, cf. Nobori, *Gokuchūki,* especially 51–6; also cf. Inoue I: 87–8. These passages relate the story of Saigō's confrontation with Sagara Kakubei, the same man who had made the proposal for a new land survey to which Saigō responded in the 1856 memorial summarized in Chapter 1.
15. STZ I: 159–63.
16. STZ I: 150–1, 159–63.

17. STZ I: 154–55, 159–63, 172.
18. STZ I: 160, 164–6.
19. STZ I: 51–4.
20. STZ I: 59. In this letter Saigō uses the phrase 'Land of the Gods' (*shinshū*) to refer to japan.
21. STZ I: 167–8.
22. Nobori, *Gokuchūki*, 56–8; DSZ III: 215–20.
23. STZ I: 171. Shōchū is a clear liquor resembling vodka, and made from potatoes, barley, or other raw materials. It has traditionally been the drink of choice in the Amami islands and southern Kyushu.
24. For a more detailed account of the material presented in the following paragraphs, cf. Diss, 161–74.
25. SHKJ I: 32–5.
26. DSZ III: 212–15; OT den I: 123–26; Kenshi III: 288–90.
27. STZ I: 183–203. This is the longest of Saigō's surviving letters, and the only one in which he speaks frankly and in detail about his motives. The following account of his collision with Hisamitsu is based primarily on this letter. A modern Japanese rendering of the letter is in Nobori, *Gokuchūki*, 105–16. For secondary narratives, cf. DSZ III: 235–45; OT den I: 222–8; Kenshi III: 315–18. Especially interesting is Mōri Toshihiko, *Meiji ishin seijishi jōsetsu*, Tokyo, 1967, to date the longest sustained examination of Satsuma's political conduct in the 1860s.
28. It appears that Saigō was in fact the only person of consequence in Kagoshima with enough experience of politics at the national level to understand what was going on. If this is the case, then we must be impressed at how quickly others in Satsuma went from total naivete to the impressive political sophistication they exhibited after 1866.
29. As we will see later on, this was one of Saigō's favorite tactics when things did not go his way. There is no doubt that Saigō loved the hot springs, and visited them whenever he could, but on a number of occasions his associates were obliged to go and retrieve him from some hot spring where he had gone to sulk.
30. For the account from here, cf. DSZ III: 245–72; OT den I: 233–49; Kenshi III: 315–26.
31. STZ I: 192.
32. STZ I: 193.
33. DSZ III: 269–70.
34. STZ I: 202–3.
35. STZ I: 215–18.
36. STZ I: 207.
37. Ibid.
38. STZ I: 226.
39. When I visited Wadomari in the winter of 1984, this cage had just been rebuilt by the city government in reinforced concrete, as part of a new municipal park and Saigō memorial. Nowhere else in Japan is Saigō's memory more alive today than in Wadomari.

40. A municpal election campaign was going on when I vivisted Wadomari, and the local newspaper had given the candidates space to outline their programs. One of them introduced himself by pointing out that his ancestors had been among Saigō's pupils.
41. STZ I: 215–18.
42. STZ I: 261.
43. STZ I: 247.
44. STZ I: 251. One wonders whether the 'kyōgen' Saigō refers to here is his own life or the course of political events in Japan.
45. Cf. Diss, 197–225; Totman, *Collapse*, 3–147; Albert M. Craig, *Choshu in the Meiji Restoration*, Cambridge, MA, 1961, 167–231.
46. The recorded sources for Saigō's thought are nearly all aphoristic in form. Besides his excerpts from Satō Issai, they consist of posthumous teachings (*ikun*) and other short collections of statements attributed to him (*ikyō*), precisely as the *Analects* are attributed to Confucius. Only the Satō excerpts are actually in Saigō's own hand. The others have been assembled from notes taken by his pupils. Besides these writings, one should also consult his Chinese poems (*kanshi*), and his memorials. All are collected in various volumes of STZ.
47. For this and the following two statements, cf. STZ IV: 179, 206, 223. Also cf. Inoue I: 125–33.
48. STZ I: 271.
49. If this is an accurate picture of Saigō's outlook, then it may also suggest that he would have been automatically suspicious of anyone who was especially good at manipulating words, and few of his contemporaries have better established reputations for such facility than his boyhood friend Ōkubo Toshimichi.
50. DSZ III: 192.
51. Robert Jay Lifton, *Death in Life: Survivors of Hiroshima*, New York, 1968.
52. Quoted in Inoue I: 68. This is the same Shigeno Yasutsugu who later gained fame as the founder of the Kyoto school of Japanese historians.
53. Morris, 'Apotheosis,' 231, 234–5.
54. If Saigō was simply insane, as many believe, then there is no need to look further for an explanation of his behavior, because anything he might have done would make sense in its own insane way. I am not satisfied with this approach. If Saigō was insane, then he bears no responsibility for his choices, and he becomes uninteresting.
55. Cf. *Yohito yaku daitai*, *Magiri yokome yaku daitai*, and *Shasō shōshi-shō*, STZ I: 263–71. Also cf. Nobori, *Gokuchūki*, 204–7. The outline of Saigō's ideas given here draws from all three of these texts.
56. STZ I: 272–8.

3 · The Rise to Leadership
1864–5

1. For a more detailed narrative of the following summary, cf. Diss, 197–215. Detail on Hisamitsu's activities between 1860 and 1864 is in SHKJ I: 32–322, II: 1–320. For more detail from the perspectives of Saigō and Ōkubo, cf. DSZ III: 205–319; OT den I: 174–552.
2. On the bakufu's reform of 1862 and subsequent events summarized here, cf. Totman, *Collapse*, 3–125.
3. Marius B. Jansen, *Sakamoto Ryōma in the Meiji Restoration*, Princeton, 1961, gives a good account of Yamauchi Yōdō's contributions to the coalition movement. The other men in this group have yet to be studied in depth, except as they appear in Totman, *Collapse*, and in W. G. Beasley, *The Meiji Restoration*, Stanford, 1972. Also cf. Conrad Totman, 'Tokugawa Yoshinobu and *Kobugattai*: A Study of Political Inadequacy,' *Monumenta Nipponica*, #30: 4.
4. On the bankruptcy of kōbu gattai, cf. Mōri, *Meiji ishin seijishi jōsetsu*, 137.
5. DSZ III: 324–25; OT den I: 551–2; Kenshi III: 377–9.
6. For accounts of Chōshū and the development of sonnō jōi activities, cf. Albert M. Craig, *Chōshū in the Meiji Restoration*, Cambridge, MA, 1961; Thomas M. Huber, *The Revolutionary Origins of Modern Japan*, Stanford, 1981.
7. Totman, *Collapse*, describes the Mito uprising and argues that it came close to destroying the bakufu, 108–22.
8. STZ I: 283–6. '*Izure henran aimatsu hoka gozanaku sōrō.*'
9. DSZ III: 321–5 summarizes the period immediately after Saigō's arrival in Kyoto.
10. DSZ III: 314–23; Kenshi III: 378. With the promotion conferred by Hisamitsu on 1864/4/8, Saigō rose from koshōgumi to shinban, crossing the Satsuma status barrier from low- to middle-ranking samurai.
11. Between 1864 and 1868, Saigō wrote over 100 letters to Ōkubo, who was himself equally prolific. Cf. STZ I: 287–473, II: 52–505; OTM I: 207–468, II: 1–151.
12. STZ I: 283–6.
13. STZ I: 287–91.
14. STZ I: 283–6.
15. Cf. STZ I: 367–9, 370–4, 375–7, 382–5, 386–92. The bakufu had begun talking about punishing Chōshū in 1864/2.
16. SHKJ II: 201–8, 223–4.
17. Saigō's report of this incident is at STZ I: 307–10, 314–18.
18. STZ I: 309–10, 314–18.
19. STZ I: 292–4, 300–1, 304–5, 307–10.
20. STZ I: 310.
21. STZ I: 314–18.
22. STZ I: 326–20.

23. STZ I: 340–9; DSZ III: 334–6.
24. STZ I: 331–5, 340–9.
25. STZ I: 337–8.
26. STZ I: 337–8, 349.
27. STZ I: 359–61; DSZ III: 327–45 gives a description of the battle.
28. STZ I: 33–5, 37–9.
29. STZ I: 354–66, 370–4.
30. STZ I: 371.
31. STZ I: 375–7.
32. STZ I: 382–5.
33. STZ I: 253–4, 260–2. This notion of kakkyō was widespread at the time, and was articulated by some of Chōshū's most influential voices as well, including Takasugi Shinsaku.
34. STZ I: 384–5, 396–7.
35. STZ I: 396–403 gives Saigō's account of the meeting with Katsu. For narrative, cf. DSZ III: 351–5. On Katsu, cf. William Steele, 'Katsu Kaishū and the collapse of the Tokugawa Bakufu,' Harvard doctoral dissertation, 1976.
36. STZ I: 399.
37. STZ I: 404–5.
38. Inoue I: 162–3 discusses this new awakening on Saigō's part.
39. STZ I: 408.
40. STZ I: 408.
41. STZ I: 416.
42. STZ I: 408–9, 417–22. 'Jitsu ni komari iri sōrō shidai.'
43. STZ I: 416.
44. Totman, *Collapse*, 136.
45. STZ I: 416; Kenshi III: 390–4; Inoue I: 164.
46. STZ I: 425–6, 434–7.
47. STZ I: 438–40.
48. STZ I: 444–6; DSZ III: 355–72.
49. STZ I: 466.
50. STZ I: 460–3. Also cf. Inoue I: 163–7; DSZ III: 355–72; Kenshi III: 389–97.
52. Inoue I: 165. Literally, he had 'placed his red heart in the belly of the other' (*Akai kokoro wo hito no hara no naka ni oku*).
53. Inoue I: 168.
54. STZ II: 25; DSZ III: 372–3. Saigō's first wife, it will be recalled, had divorced him in 1854. His second wife, Aikana, was an islander and a commoner, and so their marriage had no legal status.
55. STZ I: 426; VI: 548–9.
56. Inoue I: 167.
57. OTN I: 242; DSZ III: 373–82.
58. STZ II: 31–2.
59. Cf. Inoue I: 171–4 for a summary of these events.
60. STZ II: 40–1.
61. STZ II: 50–1.

62. OTM I: 276. Ōkubo's remark is, '. . . *omoshiroki shibai ni nari mōsu beku sōrō to tanoshimi mōshi sōrō.*'

4 · *The Destruction of the Tokugawa Regime,* *1865–8*

1. Cf. Totman, *Collapse*, 269–372 for details on the activities of France and Britain.
2. Cf. Ernest Satow, *A Diplomat in Japan*, London, 1921, for a detailed account of Britain's involvement with Satsuma. Also useful is Kanbashi Norimasa, *Satsumajin to Yōroppa*, Kagoshima, 1982.
3. For discussion of two such proposals, cf. Jansen, *Sakamoto Ryōma*, 271–311, and Huber, *Revolutionary Origins*, 42–68.
4. The events of the period from 1865 to 1868 are complex, and deserve more attention than I can give them here. Cf. Inoue Isao, *Ōsei fukko*, Tokyo, 1991 for an analysis that is thorough, insightful, and thought-provoking.
5. This is not to endorse the theory of the Meiji Restoration as a lower samurai revolution (*kakyū bushi kakumei*) as in Tōyama Shigeki, *Meiji ishin*, Tokyo, 1951, rev. 1972. There are significant problems with Tōyama's analysis, chiefly because it overlooks other factors of importance, such as the role of the West. Cf. Ishii Takashi, *Meiji ishin no butai ura*, Tokyo, 1975, and Sakata Yoshio, *Meiji ishinshi*, Tokyo, 1960. Recently, scholars have applied post-modernist frameworks as well. A good example is George Wilson, *Patriots and Redeemers in Japan: Motives in the Meiji Restoration*, Chicago, 1992. All the same, most of the samurai who played important roles were of middle and lower rank, not with reference to some arbitrary nationwide standard, but within the social hierarchies of the han from which they came. Saigō's official stipend might have ranked him among the senior vassals in a smaller han, but in Satsuma it placed him at the bottom of the hierarchy, and there was never any doubt in his mind about that. We can acknowledge this fact, and even speculate usefully about its potential as a motivator, without having to accept or reject the lower samurai revolution thesis.
6. Inoue I: 167 argues that by saving Takasugi's militia units from destruction, Saigō had preserved the nucleus of the anti-bakufu movement there, and thus had completed a crucial step in clearing the ground for the Meiji Restoration.
7. Detailed English accounts of the forging of the Satsuma-Chōshū alliance may be found in Craig, *Chōshū*, 311–19, and Jansen, *Sakamoto Ryōma*, 185–222.
8. STZ II: 52–3. Saigō's phrase is '*ahō tai.*'
9. STZ II: 54–8.
10. STZ II: 67–8. His phrase is '*onozukara taore sōrō.*'

11. STZ II: 54–8, 69–72.
12. STZ II: 69–72.
13. DSZ III: 389–93; also Jansen, *Sakamoto Ryōma*, 185–222.
14. DSZ III: 417; Inoue I: 180–1.
15. DSZ III: 418.
16. The details of the Satsuma-Chōshū agreement are well known. Cf. Diss 277–78; STZ II: 111–14; DSZ III: 421–5; Kenshi III: 410–21; Jansen, *Sakamoto Ryōma*, 185–222.
17. Inoue I: 187.
18. STZ II: 89–91.
19. STZ II: 93–97.
20. STZ II: 99–100; DSZ III: 413–16.
21. STZ II: 73–5.
22. Ibid.
23. Kenshi III: 404–9; DSZ III: 395–407.
24. DSZ III: 425–7.
25. Kenshi III: 418.; DSZ III: 432–5; STZ II: 142–49.
26. STZ II: 114–16; the phrase is '*ruiran no abunaki.*'
27. STZ II: 124–6.
28. Inoue Kiyoshi, I: 188–92, sees in this insight a 'great step forward' (*daishinpō*) in Saigō's thinking, arguing that finally he had begun to see the connection between grassroots resistance (or peasant rebellion) and revolutionary change, and hinting that even Saigō offers some confirmation for Marxist theories as applied to Japan. I think Inoue goes too far, particularly when, as we have seen, Saigō had spent some years in the islands articulating a system of thought in which administrative irregularities lead inevitably to popular unrest, as a measure of Heaven's displeasure with the ruler and his subordinates.
29. Inoue I: 182–3.
30. STZ II: 124–6; DSZ III: 427–8.
31. For details, cf. Kanbashi, *Satsuma jin to Yōroppa*.
32. STZ II: 137–40; also cf. note at ibid. 142 for an outline of these reforms.
33. For details, cf. OTden II: 32–8.
34. STZ II: 142–9; the phrase reads '*on kokka no biji.*'
35. For details, cf. Totman, *Collapse*, 227–66.
36. DSZ III: 441–50.
37. STZ II: 157–61.
38. SHKJ 97–102.
39. Hisamitsu refers here to an approach sponsored primarily by Shungaku, called *kōgi seitai*, that would have brought daimyo and other elites together to create a deliberative body much like a parliament. For discussion, cf. Mikami Kazuō, *Kōbu gattai ron no kenkyū*, Tokyo, 1979, and Yamaguchi Muneyuki, *Bakumatsu seiji shisōshi kenkyū*, Tokyo, 1982.
40. STZ II: 165–8.
41. DSZ III: 457–66.

42. Kenshi III: 430.
43. STZ II: 178–83.
44. STZ II: 187–9.
45. SHKJ III: 10–17.
46. SHKJ III: 14.
47. Cf. SHKJ III: 14–47 and Diss 293–5 for details.
48. SHKJ III: 69–79.
49. STZ II: 193–7, 198–202, 203–6, and 207–9.
50. STZ II: 205–06. Note that Saigō's term is *isshin*, meaning 'to unify anew,' rather than the more familiar *ishin*, customarily rendered as 'restoration.'
51. STZ II: 208.
52. This synopsis of the formation of the Satsuma-Tosa alliance follows DSZ III: 482–93; also cf. Jansen, *Sakamoto Ryōma*, 271–317.
53. STZ II: 224; also cf. Kenshi III: 445, SHKJ III: 79–84.
54. STZ II: 217–19; also cf. ibid. 219–22 for the terms of the Satsuma-Tosa agreement.
55. STZ II: 231–6, 240–50; also cf. Jansen, *Sakamoto Ryōma*, 319–21.
56. STZ II: 249.
57. For English accounts of the various efforts to save the Tokugawa, cf. Jansen, *Sakamoto Ryōma*, 312–42, and Totman, *Collapse*, 375–415; also cf. Inoue, *Ōsei fukko*. Equally valuable, if dated, is Tokuyama Kunisaburō's biography of Shungaku, *Matsudaira Yoshinaga kō*, Fukui, 1938.
58. Kenshi III: 446; DSZ III: 521–6; STZ II: 269–70.
59. Kenshi III: 451; OTden II: 166–75.
60. STZ II: 297–8.
61. Cf. Chapter 3, note 62.
62. Cf. note 59.
63. STZ II: 374. It may be that the enthusiasm Saigō observes here arose less from feelings about the imperial army itself than from other sources of popular disquiet current at the time. Cf. Wilson, *Patriots and Redeemers*, and other authors cited therein. Given the frequent use of the term 'daimyōin' in the utterances of late Tokugawa 'world renewal' (*yōnaoshi*) demonstrations, this is the sort of evidence that appeals to those who look for millenarian tendencies in bakumatsu unrest.
64. STZ II: 297–8; also cf. Inoue II: 10–11 for discussion of 'tama' and its implications. Mitani Hiroshi has pointed out to me (personal communication, 1992/10/5) that many historians in Japan read the word '*gyoku*' rather than 'tama,' referring to the central piece on the board in Japanese chess (shōgi). Taking this piece is analogous to taking the king in Western chess. The net effect is the same either way.
65. STZ II: 277–83.
66. The texts of these orders are at STZ II: 285–9.
67. DSZ III: 526–31; OTden II: 185–99.
68. SHKJ III: 92–7; Kenshi III: 453–56.

69. Oden II: 205–22; Kenshi III: 457–60.
70. STZ II: 303–7. One recent author, writing in *President* magazine, suggests that it was Saigō who arranged the murder of Sakamoto and Nakaoka. If the taisei hōkan strategy had worked, argues this writer, it would have made possible a peaceful transition, undoubtedly based on Sakamoto's eight-point outline. For Saigō, anything short of the total military destruction of the Tokugawa would have been unacceptable, so he had to eliminate Sakamoto however he could. Bakufu vigilantes had been hunting Sakamoto for years, so all Saigō had to do was tell them where they could find him. This is a good example of the fanciful creativity some scholars bring to their interpretations of Saigō. It even has a certain persuasiveness, except that it postulates a Saigō who is not only out of character, but even inconsistent with the man this author writes about in the rest of his article. Cf. Sakamoto Katsuyoshi, 'Saigō Takamori,' in *Purejidento*, vol. 23 no. 1, January, 1985. This was a special issue of a monthly journal aimed at corporate executives, somewhat analogous to *Forbes*. Perhaps the author of this piece thought Saigō's cold practicality as portrayed here would have some hortatory value for CEOs in search of a leadership style.
71. STZ II: 309–11.
72. For a list of all appointees, cf. Inoue, *Ōsei fukko*, 331–2.
73. For summaries of this crucial meeting, cf. SHKJ III: 99–106; Kenshi III: 462–6; OTden II: 269–304; DSZ III: 548–64.
74. OTden II: 294–9; Inoue II: 52.
75. DZ III: 561.
76. For detail cf. OTden II: 305–76.
77. STZ II: 327–32.
78. OTden II: 372–6.
79. STZ II: 340–1; DSZ III: 565–7; Inoue II: 13–14.
80. Totman, *Collapse*, 379–443, gives a detailed account of Yoshinobu's decisions and the battles that followed.
81. STZ II: 349–50.
82. STZ II: 351–2.
83. STZ II: 355.
84. STZ II: 365–8. His phrase is '*toru mono toriaezu.*'
85. STZ II: 370–1. He later doubled these odds, putting the bakufu forces at ten to the emperor's one.
86. STZ II: 365–8, 373–8.
87. STZ II: 380–2.
88. STZ II: 362–3.
89. Inoue II: 93–8.
90. STZ II: 383–4.
91. STZ II: 406–7.
92. STZ II: 412–20.
93. STZ II: 436–40, 443–6; DSZ III: 599–618. For more detail, cf. Diss 319–22.
94. STZ II: 443–6.

95. STZ II: 386–7, 390–1, 462–7.

5 · *Reform and Reaction in Kagoshima,*
1868–71

1. Ōkubo's death is a major watershed in early Meiji history. Of the trio of men referred to in Japan as the 'three heroes' of the Restoration (*ishin no sanketsu*), Ōkubo was the last to die, predeceased by Saigō and by Kido Takayoshi. In more practical terms, Ōkubo was inarguably the most important individual in the early Meiji government, especially after 1873, and for a time, so it seems, one simply did not rise to power unless one was intimate with him. Cf. Tokutomi Iichirō, *Kinsei Nihon kokumin shi*, Tokyo, 1960–71, vol. 100, *Ishin sanketsu*, 1–5; also cf. Itagaki Tetsuō, 'Ishin go ni okeru Ōkubo Toshimichi no seijijō no ningen kankei,' *Shigaku zasshi*, #86: 11.
2. I will not dicuss the course of the Satsuma rebellion itself except in the broadest of terms. The military history of the rebellion has been covered elsewhere, and in any case it is of only tangential concern for an understanding of Saigō's life. Cf. Augustus Mounsey, *The Satsuma Rebellion*, London, 1879; Ernest W. Clement, 'The Saga and Satsuma Rebellions' *Transactions of the Asiatic Society of Japan*, #19: 2; and James H. Buck, 'The Satsuma Rebellion,' *Monumenta Nipponica*, #28: 4.
3. For an account of this phase of the Meiji civil war, cf. Harold Bolitho, 'The Echigo War,' *Monumenta Nipponica*, #34: 2.
4. DSZ III: 630–1.
5. The closest thing to a canonical text among Saigō apologists is the little compilation of aphorisms known as his 'posthumous teachings' (*ikun*), of which several dozen editions have appeared since his death. CF. STZ IV: 189–219. This work was compiled by a group of former samurai from Shōnai, who spent time in Kagoshima interviewing all who had known Saigō and recording what these people claimed were his most pithy remarks. Thus in its provenance it is much like the *Analects* of Confucius, and among Saigō's admirers it has at least as much authority.
6. DSZ III: 632–8.
7. STZ III: 40–1.
8. Cf. chapter 4, note 87.
9. STZ III: 25–6.
10. STZ VI: 322–3.
11. Minami Nihon shinbunsha, comp. and ed., *Kagoshima hyakunen*, 3 vols, Tokyo, 1968, vol. 1, 367–68. Katsura's family was actually a collateral branch of the Shimazu, known as the Hioki, but it appears that Katsura's own loyalties were with the lower samurai, especially after his brother's death in 1850.

12. STZ III: 27. Ijichi refers to Saigō here as 'master initiate' (*nyūdo sensei*), suggesting a Buddhist novice or a monk, which is surely the impression one would have gotten from a man with a shaven head and simple clothing such as Saigō evidently affected from this time throughout most of the rest of his life.
13. STZ III: 26.
14. OTden II: 503–8.
15. OTden II: 545–55, 564–72.
16. OTden II: 605–11.
17. OTden II: 611–18.
18. Kenshi III: 515–18.
19. Kenshi III: 519–25; DSZ III: 641–5; STZ III: 25.
20. DSZ III: 749–50.
21. Kenshi III: 526; OTden II: 631.
22. OTden II: 642–3.
23. SHKJ III: 134–48; OTden II: 649.
24. Kenshi III: 531–42.
25. Kenshi III: 543–62.
26. DSZ III: 694–7; also cf. STZ III: 98–9, 114–16, 133–4, 178, 222–3, 238–9, 242–4, 245, 247–8, 249–51, 252–3, and 254–5. All of these letters are concerned with details of the formation of the Tokyo police, and are dated from 1871/5 through 1872/4. A police officer in Tokyo once told me that a disproportionately large number of Kagoshima natives still join the Tokyo police every year.
27. For detailed discussion, cf. Kenshi III: 593–688.
28. Kenshi III: 564–92.
29. In addition to Kenshi, loc. cit., also cf. *Kagoshima hyakunen*, I: 370–90.
30. *Kagoshima hyakunen*, I: 370.
31. For one of the most articulate and outspoken recent expressions of this view, cf. Tamamuro Taijō, *Seinan sensō*, Tokyo, 1958, and *Saigō Takamori*, Tokyo, 1960. Cf. also note 33 for further comment.
32. Tamamuro, *Saigō Takamori*, is not alone in using this term.
33. It is probably the lack of conclusive evidence about Saigō's personal feelings that has allowed the controversy over the militarization of Kagoshima to remain alive for so long. As I think I have made clear, his involvement in that process was never central. However satisfying scholars such as Tamamuro may find it to lay all responsibility for these developments at Saigō's feet (cf. note 31 above) it is difficult to understand how they have so consistently managed to ignore the evidence of the reforms of 1869–70, and to avoid the conclusions to which that evidence seems to point.
34. STZ III: 64–5.
35. Cf. Diss 353–7 for further details.
36. In light of his erratic and perplexing behavior during the Tōhoku campaigns, it may be that Tokyo's leaders wanted Saigō in the government chiefly to keep him nearby, for much the same reason Lyndon Johnson is said to have offered in justification of his retention of Dean

Rusk: they would rather have him inside the tent pissing out, than outside the tent pissing in.

37. DSZ III: 668–72.
38. STZ III: 78–87.
39. STZ III: 125–8, 151–8, and 160–8.
40. STZ III: 414–16.
41. STZ III: 491–3.
42. STZ III: 78. Perhaps what had just occurred in Kagoshima prompted Saigō to make this point. In light of what happened in the 1930s, it was a prophetic caveat indeed.
43. STZ III: 79, 81–6, 160, 166–7.
44. STZ III: 112.
45. STZ III: 78, 84–5, 151–2.
46. STZ III: 78, 151–2, 168.
47. STZ III: 160–6.
48. STZ III: 166–7.
49. STZ III: 79–81, 125–8, 152–7.
50. STZ III: 78–9, 80–1, 84–5, 155–7. Ironically, the adoption of the land tax in 1873, the inflation of the currency to finance rapid military development, and the prostration of the rural economy under the deflationary policies implemented in the early 1880s, was almost exactly the sequence of events Saigō feared.
51. STZ III: 85.
52. STZ III: 86.
53. STZ III: 254–5.
54. Cf. chapter 1, note 30.
55. STZ III: 491–3. Notice that Saigō is not the least bit concerned about the rights of the women who are sold or driven into prostitution. How they got to be prostitutes is not an issue for him.
56. There is no obvious reason to reach these conclusions, beyond what seems to be suggested in Saigō's surviving remarks, both about prostitution in particular and about morally correct behavior in general. Moreover, such conclusions will not comfort those who like the image of Saigō as a sexual superman, or who subscribe to the hypothesis that he was bound to Nariakira, Gesshō, and other prominent men in his life by homosexual ties. Certainly there has been a widespread belief in Japan for a long time that Satsuma samurai had a special taste for homosexuality, but whatever the factual basis for that, it still does not follow that Saigō was promiscuous, whether homosexually or heterosexually. Ultimately, it simply does not matter, but it has been a point of lively contention in the biographical tradition for over a century now, once again telling us more about other Japanese and their views of Saigō than about Saigō himself.

6 · Hard Times and Trouble in Tokyo,
1871–3

1. DSZ III:684–7; STZ 201–2.
2. DSZ III:690–1; Inoue II:159–60; also cf. Suyama Yukio, *Tennō to guntai*, vol. 1, *Meiji hen*, Tokyo, 1985, 76–89.
3. DSZ III:692–4; STZ III:256–8.
4. Cf STZ III:4–4, 91–2, 100, 116–17, 119–21, 355, 362–3, and 363–8 for remarks Saigō made about his health, some of which are suggestive. For example, on 1873/6/19, he wrote to Sanjō that pain in his chest would keep him away from work. On 1873/6/19, he wrote to his uncle in Kagoshima that he had been quite ill recently, and that the emperor had been so concerned about it that he had placed Saigō under the care of his personal physicians, Iwasa Jun and a German named Theodore Hoffman. In addition to filariasis and its resulting obesity, which undoubtedly caused him great discomfort, he apparently also suffered from heart trouble, caused by bad diet, lack of exercise, and sheer overweight. At times he seems to have been completely incapacitated, unable to walk for extended periods, and more than once actually in peril of his life.
5. SHKJ III:143–7.
6. SHKJ III:207–42.
7. SHKJ III:245–6.
8. SHKJ III:260–2.
9. SHKJ III:262–8.
10. SHKJ III:321–4.
11. SHKJ III:381.
12. STZ III:258–84, 294–7.
13. DSZ III:705–11; SHKJ III:199–203.
14. STZ III:299–300.
15. SHKJ III:199–202; STZ III:300–2.
16. Ibid.
17. SHKJ III:343–50.
18. STZ III:318, 319–22.
19. STZ III:294–7.
20. Inoue II:165–6.
21. STZ III:202–11.
22. STZ III:213–14.
23. STZ III:173–5. Katsura took these warnings to heart, and passed them on. His family refused to release some of Saigō's letters for publication until quite recently, and these appeared in print for the first time in STZ. Cf. ibid. III:213.
24. STZ III:108–10, 112.
25. STZ III:120–3.
26. DSZ III:709–10; Inoue II:160–1.
27. STZ III:179–83.

29. STZ III:173–5.
30. STZ III:144.
31. STZ III:148.
32. Inoue II:159.
33. Inoue II:152–5.
34. STZ III:190–6.
35. STZ III:356–9.
36. Inoue II:166–7.
37. STZ III:130–1.
38. Kenshi III:692–704; DSZ III:672–4, 678–91; Inoue II:132–4, 140–1.
39. STZ III:125–8.
40. DSZ III:676–8; OTden II:850–76.
41. DSZ III:698–705; OTden III:1–61.
42. DSZ III:717; Inoue II:167.
43. For a thorough English account of the Korean issue, cf. Hilary Conroy, *The Japanese Seizure of Korea*, Philadelphia, 1960.
44. Inoue II:169; Tamamuro, *Saigō Takamori*, 129. Also cf. Yamaguchi Muneyuki, 'Bakumatsu seikanron no haikei,' in *Bakumatsu seiji shisō-shi kenkyū*, Tokyo, 1968.
45. DSZ III:713–16.
46. Inoue II:167.
47. Inoue II:167–8; STZ III:380–1; DSZ III:731–4.
48. Inoue II:171–2.
49. Inoue II:173.
50. Inoue II:170–1; DSZ III:715–31.
51. STZ III:369–70.
52. STZ III:373–5; Inoue II:174.
53. Inoue II:180–6; DSZ III:730–1; STZ III:389.
54. At this point, Saigō was staying with his brother Tsugumichi in Shibuya, where he was taking various treatments in an effort to regain and stabilize his health.
55. STZ III:371–3.
56. STZ III:385–7.
57. STZ III:386. Saigō's phrase is '*nairan o koinegau kokoro o soto ni utsushite.*'
59. STZ III:390–1.
60. The council meetings leading to the government break over Korea have been scrutinized and described repeatedly, and the search for the one overlooked and decisive detail continues today as it has ever since 1877. Conroy's account in *The Japanese Seizure of Korea* presents all the detail one needs, and is also a good statement of the standard Japanese view. For more detail, cf. Inoue II:186–97; DSZ III:735–60; OTden III:80–167; Ikai, *Saigō Takamori*, 124–78. The most exhaustive treatment in Japanese is Kokuryūkai, comp. and ed., *Seinan kiden*, 6 vols, Tokyo 1910. It contains a wealth of detail, but should be used with caution.
61. Inoue II:192–3; OTden III:117–29.

62. STZ III:423.
63. STZ III:422.
64. STZ III:424–5.
65. STZ III:414–16, 417–18.
66. STZ III:479–81; also cf. ibid. 481–3.
67. Needless to say, it is not the only one. Interpretations of the Satsuma rebellion – to take just one other example from Saigō's life – present an equally tangled snarl of conflicting views.
68. For a summary and critique of interpretations by professional historians that have elicited the most comment in recent decades, cf. Ikai, *Saigō Takamori*, 156–78.
69. Given that these were the assumptions on which Western nations most frequently operated during the nineteenth century, and that Japan had no models for foreign relations other than the behavior of those same Western nations, it is not remarkable that Japan's leaders embraced assumptions such as these. Given, in addition, the long history of ambiguous interaction between Japan and Korea, and the belief of many Japanese that they had some sort of destiny in Korea, such assumptions are even less remarkable.
70. In all of the major political transformations of recent centuries – in the United States, France, Russia, China, Viet Nam, and again in the Soviet Union, to name only a few of the most obvious – the initial turnover of power has always been followed, first by a period of busy preliminary consolidation such as we see in Japan between 1869 and 1871, and then by a major power struggle in which all visions of the future but one are pushed aside so that that one may be realized by its advocates.
71. Cf. note 36 above.
72. Cf. note 57 above.
73. Cf. note 65 above.

7 · Collison Course in Kagoshima,
1873–7

1. Inoue II:201 makes this claim also, basing it on several of Saigō's poems. Cf. note 7 below.
2. OTden III:194–206.
3. OTden III:167–70.
4. Tamamuro makes this argument in both *Saigō Takamori* and *Seinan sensō*, from somewhat different perspectives.
5. Tamamuro, *Saigō Takamori*, 140–1.
6. Inoue II:198–9. Inoue holds Kirino and Shinohara primarily responsible for the rebellion.
7. Saigō's poetry is collected in STZ IV:5–146. Some of it is quite moving, but I have avoided relying on it for support of claims about him,

partly because it is too elliptical to offer much in the way of evidence, partly because most of it is impossible to date accurately.

8. Inoue II:201. Inoue also argues, ibid. 196–7, that Saigō began showing indications of senility during his time in Tokyo.
9. DSZ III:762–3.
10. A number of these anecdotes appear in evaluations of Saigō by people who knew him, many of them public figures quite well known to later generations. Cf. STZ VI:5–207.
11. DSZ III:763–4.
12. The view of Saigō as biding his time in the countryside until conditions were right for rebellion depends heavily for its appeal on the precedent of Ōishi Kuranosuke, the leader of the famous forty-seven masterless samurai (*rōnin*), who spent two years in drunken debauchery so as to lull the suspicions of the man who had caused the destruction of their lord, and against whom they plotted their vendetta. However appealing this image may be, it is difficult to make it fit Saigō, who was neither that clever nor that deceitful, to say nothing of that patient.
13. Inoue II:198.
14. Kenshi III:729–52.
15. Kenshi III:710–28.
16. STZ III:363–8.
17. Kenshi III:866–79; DSZ III:779–86.
18. DSZ III:654–8; OTden II:713–18; STZ III:331–3. A koku is a unit of measure equivalent to just under five bushels.
19. DSZ III:658.
20. STZ III:370–1.
21. STZ III:333; OTden III:542–52; Kenshi III:872–3.
22. Nothing is left of the Shigakkō or the castle of the Shimazu now except the stone retaining walls around the lots where they once stood, a part of the castle moat, and one gate. Prefectural government offices, museums, and the prefectural library occupy the former castle grounds, and there is a monument marking the site of the Shigakkō. The pockmarks of bullets and cannon rounds scattered here and there in the otherwise undisturbed stones of the retaining walls offer the only direct reminders of what happened there in 1877.
23. Tamamuro, *Saigō Takamori*, 150–1.
24. STZ III:468–70.
25. STZ III:470–1.
26. STZ III:473–5, 475–7.
27. STZ III:435–6.
28. STZ III:442–4.
29. Tamamuro, *Saigō Takamori*, 151.
30. John Stephan reached this same conclusion while still a graduate student at Harvard, using nothing more than English and Japanese secondary materials. Cf. 'Saigō Takamori and the Satsuma Rebellion,' in *Papers on Japan*, vol. 3, Cambridge, MA, 1965.
31. OTden III:569–71; Kenshi III:856; DSZ III:809–10, 819–21.

32. Tamamuro, *Seinan sensō*, 13–14.
33. OTden III:549–99; Kenshi III:855–8; DSZ III:823–5.
34. OTden III:598–9; Kenshi III:858; DSZ III:823, 825–6.
35. Tamamuro, *Seinan sensō*, 76–9, asserts that these attacks were carefully planned in advance by Kirino, Shinohara, and Murata.
36. Tamamuro, *Seinan sensō*, 79–80.
37. DSZ III:827–8.
38. STZ III:506–7.
39. DSZ III:828–30; Kenshi III:900–23. The latter includes Nakahara's confession. Also cf. Kodera Tetsunosuke, *Seinan eki Satsugun Kōkyō-sho*, Tokyo, 1967, 8–14, for Ōyama's confession, and Mounsey, *The Satsuma Rebellion*, 275–89, for English translations of both confessions. To this day it remains impossible to ascertain whether there actually was a plot to kill Saigō or not, or whether Ōkubo had anything to do with it if it did exist. The most exhaustive recent examination of the primary materials is Kawano Hiroyoshi, *Seinan sensō tantei hiwa*, Tokyo, 1989.
40. Inoue II:221; Tamamuro, *Saigō Takamori*, 171.
41. Inoue II:222.
42. Tamamuro, *Saigō Takamori*, 194.
43. STZ III:553.
44. Fukuzawa Yukichi, in his essay *Teichū kōron*, makes just this claim, but the effect of his argument, and probably the original intent as well, is less to blame Ōkubo for the rebellion than it is to exonerate Saigō.
45. Cf. chapter 2, note 44.
46. The site of Ōkubo's death is marked today by a large stone tablet, which stands in a small park only a short walk away from the new Ōtani Hotel and the headquarters of the Japan Foundation. The site of Saigō's death, on the other hand, is known only approximately, and was probably obliterated by the construction of a highway that runs up Iwasakidani to the top of Shiroyama.
47. There is a vivid and entertaining account of these events in Tokutomi, *Kinsei Nihon kokumin shi*, vol. 100, *Meiji sanketsu*.

Epilogue

1. A fair number of Saigō's poems have been translated into English, along with the collection of aphorisms known as the *Ikun*, or 'Posthumous Teachings,' assembled by former samurai from Shōnai han. Like the poems themselves, the translations are somewhat forced and self-conscious, but they are good enough to convey a clear sense of Saigō's poetic style and attainment. Cf. Sakamoto Moriaki, *Saigō Takamori's Poems and Posthumous Words*, 1971, published in a single bilingual volume with *Fukuzama Yukichi to Ōkubo Toshimichi no tairitsu*, Tokyo, 1971.
2. The best collection of Saigō's calligraphy is in a special volume

assembled to mark the fiftieth anniversary of his death, as part of a limited edition of the *Dai Saigō zenshū*, Tokyo, 1923.

3. For an excellent interpretation of Wang Yang-ming's thought and its implications, cf. Julia Ching, *To Acquire Wisdom*, New York, 1976.
4. The best introduction to the philosophies of Chu Hsi and other Chinese thinkers is Wing-tsit Chan, *A Source Book in Chinese Philosophy*, Princeton, 1963.
5. In a letter to his cousin Ōyama Iwao written at the end of 1874, he expresses thanks for the loan of a book by Fukuzawa. He does not identify the work, but the consensus is that it was probably *Gakumon no susume* (*The Advancement of Learning*), one of Fukuzawa's most important essays. Cf. STZ III:129.
6. I have argued that after 1868 Saigō's chief desire was to retire to private life, in fact, to seek obscurity. If that is correct, then this latter fate would not have troubled him at all. Indeed, it may be that one reason why he desired to vanish from the public realm and have nothing more to do with politics was the pervasive mental exhaustion that would have resulted from the effort of abandoning his lifelong and now obsolete construal of kokka and tenka and keeping them aligned with their new and unfamiliar referents.
7. To get a better sense of why Ōkubo *was* well suited to lead the new Japan, cf. Iwata Masakazu, *Ōkubo Toshimichi, The Bismarck of Japan*, Berkeley and Los Angeles, 1964, and Albert M. Craig, 'Kido Kōin and Ōkubo Toshimichi: A Psychohistorical Analysis,' in Albert M. Craig and Donald Shively, *Personality in Japanese History*, Berkeley and Los Angles, 1970. The most accessible biography in Japanese is Mōri Toshihiko, *Ōkubo Toshimichi*, Tokyo, 1969.
8. Reading Morris' book, one cannot escape the feeling that the chapter on Saigō is the real agenda, and all of the others are not so much concerned with the characters they describe as with helping to establish and validate Morris' vision of the failed hero, so that he may apply it finally to Saigō.

BIBLIOGRAPHY

The titles listed here are those I have consulted in the preparation of this study, and represent but a fraction of the print and manuscript materials available on both Saigō and Satsuma in Japanese. Materials in English are sparse, and most of them are about Satsuma rather than Saigō.

For Saigō, the best bibliographies are 'Saigō Takamori/seinan sensō kankei bunken mokuroku,' in *Saigō Takamori zenshū*, volume 6, and Nonaka Keigō's *Saigō Takamori kankei bunken mokuroku kō*. The former list is arranged by type of material and date of publication, and includes primary and secondary sources appearing in books, manuscripts, private and public collections, periodicals, and newspapers. Nonaka's work is extensively annotated, but must be used with caution because of the author's strong apologetic bias. One cannot always accept Nonaka's judgement concerning the quality of a given source, because he tends to disapprove of those that do not confirm his understanding of Saigō.

For Satsuma, the best general bibliography is 'Satsuma han kankei jūyō bunken mokuroku,' in *Satsuma han no kōzō to tenkai*, edited by Hidemura Senzō. This list is not exhaustive, but is probably the best place to begin. The most complete listings are those compiled by the Kagōshima Prefectural Library, and published in a series of separate volumes, most of which are now out of print.

The best collections for the researcher are located in Kagōshima at the prefectural library and university, and at the Historiographical Institute of the University of Tokyo. In the United States, quite good collections can be found at such universities as Harvard, Yale, and Princeton, but easily the best is the one assembled by Robert Sakai and his colleagues at the University of Hawaii.

222

Bibliography

Materials in Japanese

Andō Hideō, *Saigō Takamori*, Tokyo: Shirakawa shoin, 1976.
Dai Nihon shiryō hensanjo, comp. and ed., *Shimazu ke monjo*, 3 vols, Tokyo: Tokyo daigaku shiryō hensanjo, 1942, 1953, 1966.
Ebihara Kiyohiro, 'Sappan Tenpōdō igo zaisei kaikaku tenmatsu sho,' in Honjō Eijirō, *Kinsei shakai keisai sōsho*, vol. 4.
Fujii Sadafumi, *Shukumei no shōgun: Tokugawa Yoshinobu*, Tokyo: Yoshikawa kōbunkan, 1983.
Fujino Tamotsu, comp. and ed., *Kyūshū kinseishi kenkyū sōsho*, 10 vols, Tokyo: Kokusho kankōkai, 1985.
——, 'Kyūshū ni okeru bakuhan ryōshū shihai no tokushitsu: tōitsu kenryoku no Kyūshū shihai to taiō,' Part 1, *Kyūshū bunkashi kenkyūjo kiyō*, #16; Part 2, *Shien*, #107.
Fujitani Toshio, 'Satsuma han no shakai sōshiki to senbai seidō,' *Nihonshi kenkyū*, £6.
Fukuzawa Yukichi, *Teichū kōron*, Tokyo: Kodansha, 1985.
Fukushima Kaneharu, ed., *Shimazu shi no kenkyū*, Tokyo: Yoshikawa kōbunkan, 1983.
Godai Natsuo, ed., *Saigō Takamori no subete*, Tokyo: Shin jinbutsu ōraisha, 1985.
Haga Tōru, *Meiji ishin to Nihonjin*, Tokyo: Kodansha, 1980.
Hamada Hisatomo, *Saigō Takamori no subete: Sono shisō to kakumei kōdō*, Tokyo: Kubo shoten, 1977.
Haraguchi Izumi, 'Satsuma han gunjiryoku no kihonteki seikaku,' in Satō and Kawachi, *Bakuhansei kokka no hōkai*.
Haraguchi Munehisa, 'Meiji rokunen seihen: Ōkubo seiken seiritsu no katei,' *Rekishi kyōiku*, 1965/2.
Haraguchi Torao, *Bakumatsu no Satsuma*, Tokyo: Chūō kōron sha, 1966.
——, ed., *Kagōshima han*, 2 vols, in *Hanpōshu*, Tokyo: Sōbunsha, 1969.
——, 'Kagōshima ken kindai nōgyō shi,' *Nihon nōgyō hattatsu shi, Bekkan jō*, Tokyo: Chūō kōron sha, 1957.
——, *Kagōshima ken no rekishi*, Tokyo: Yamakawa shuppansha, 1973.
——, *Kyū Kagōshima han chihō keizai shiryō shūsei*, 2 vols, Kagoshima: Kagoshima kenritsu tōshokan, 1950.
——, 'Sappan gōshi seikatsu no keizaiteki kiso,' in Miyamoto Matajirō, ed., *Kyūshū keizaishi kenkyu*, Tokyo: 1953.
——, 'Sappan hōken shakai no kōzō ni kansuru ichi kōsatsu,' Kagoshima: Haraguchi Torao, 1956.
——, 'Satsuma han no tōjō seidō to fumoto,' *Rekishi techō*, £8:3.
——, 'Satsuma no sato,' in Fujino, *Kyūshū kinseishi kenkyū sōsho*, vol. 8.
Hayakawa Junzaburō, *Shimazu ke shōkan shu*, Tokyo: Nihon shiseki kyōkai, 1942.
Hayashi Fusao, ed., *Dai Saigō ikun*, Tokyo: Shin jinbutsu ōraisha, 1968.
——, *Saigō Takamori*, 11 vols, Tokyo: Tokuma shoten, 1985.
Hayashi Yoshihiko, *Sappan no kyōiku to zaisei narabi gunbi*, Kagoshima: Kagoshima shi yakusho, 1939.

Saigō Takamori

—, 'Satsuma han no tōjōsei,' *Kagoshima shirin*, #1.

Hidaka Misao, *Saigō Takamori ansatsu jiken*, Tokyo: Kaibundō shoten, 1938.

Hidemura Senzō, 'Satsuma han ni okeru kyūchi no ichi kōsatsu,' *Dōshisha shogaku*, #20:1–2.

—, ed., *Satsuma han no kisō kōzō*, Tokyo: Ochanomizu shobō, 1970.

—, ed., *Satsuma han no kōzō to tenkai*, Tokyo: Tadamitsu insatsu, 1976. (Includes 'Satsuma han kankei jūyō bunken mokuroku.')

Hirano Kuniomi kenshōkai, ed. Yamaguchi Muneyuki, *Hirano Kuniomi denki oyobi ikō*, Tokyo: Zosansha, 1980.

Honjō Eijirō, ed., *Kinsei shakai keizai sōsho*, Tokyo: Kaizōsha, 1929.

Ichiki Shirō, *Shimazu Nariakira genkōroku*, Tokyo: Iwanami shoten, 1944.

Ikai Takaaki, *Saigō Takamori: Seinan sensō e no michi*, Tokyo: Iwanami shoten, 1992.

Ikeda Kiyoshi, 'Ōkubo Toshimichi ni okeru 'Kokutai aikatame ron',' *Hogaku zasshi*, #9:3–4.

Ikeda Norimasa, 'Satsuma han to Teradaya no hen,' *Nihonshi kenkyū*, £87.

Ikeda Toshihiko, *Shimazu Nariakira kō den*, Tokyo: Iwasaki Yasuhide shogakkai, 1954.

—, 'Zusho Hirosato no zaisei kaikaku to Satō Nobuhiro no *Sappan kei'i ki*,' *Kagoshima shirin*, #1–2.

Ikenami Shōtarō, *Hitokiri Hanjiro*, 2 vols, Tokyo: Kadokawa shoten, 1985.

—, *Saigō Takamori*, Tokyo: Kadokawa shoten, 1986.

Imamoto Noriaki, 'Toyotomi seiken to Shimazu shi,' in Fujino, *Kyūshū kinseishi kenkyū sōsho*, vol. 1.

Inoue Isao, *Ōsei fukko: Keiō san'nen junigatsu kokonoka no seihen*, Tokyo: Chūō kōron sha, 1991.

Inoue Kiyoshi, *Meiji ishin*, Tokyo: Chūō kōron sha, 1966.

—, *Saigō Takamori*, 2 vols, Tokyo: Chūō kōron sha, 1970.

Inuzuka Takaaki, *Satsuma han no Eikoku ryūgakusei*, Tokyo: Chūō kōron sha, 1974.

Ishii Takashi, *Meiji ishin no butai ura*, Tokyo: Iwanami shoten, 1975.

Itagaki Taisuke, 'Seinan jihen no sai ni okeru danwa oyobi yōdan suken,' *Shidankai sokkiroku*, £328.

Itagaki Tetsuo, 'Ishin go ni okeru Ōkubo Toshimichi no seijijō no ningen kankei,' *Shigaku zasshi*, £86:11.

Kagōshima daigaku kyōiku gakubu, Shakaika kenkyūshitsu, ed., *Kagoshima no rekishi to shakai*, Tokyo: Dentō to gendai sha, 1979.

Kagoshima daigaku tōshokan, *Shimazu ke kokuji ōshō shiryō*, 20 vols, unpublished manuscript. (Also at Tokyo Daigaku Shiryō Hensanjo.)

Kagoshima ken, *Kagoshima kenshi*, 5 vols, Kagoshima: Kagoshima ken, 1944.

—, *Kagoshima ken shiryō*, 26 vols as of 1986, Kagoshima: Kagoshima ken ishin shiryō hensanjo. Includes the following series:

Kyūki zatsuroku zenpen, 2 vols, 1979–80.

Kyūki zatsuroku tsuiroku, 8 vols, 1974–80.

Nariakira kō shiryō, 4 vols, 1980–5.

224

Narinobu/Narioki kō shiryō, 1 vol., 1985.

Seinan sensō, 3 vols, 1978–80.

Tadayoshi kō shiryō, 7 vols, 1974–80.

Kagoshima kenritsu tōshokan, *Kyōdō shiryō sōgō mokuroku*, Kagoshima: Kagoshima kenritsu toshōkan, 1967.

———, *Ōkubo Toshimichi kankei bunken mokuroku*, Kagoshima: Kagoshima kenritsu tōshokan, 1978.

———, *Saigō Takamori kankei tōsho shiryō mokuroku*, Kagoshima: Kagoshima kenritsu tōshokan, 1977.

Kagoshima ken shiryō kankōkai, *Kagoshima ken shiryōshū*, 8 vols, Kagoshima: Kagoshima kenritsu tōshokan, 1960.

Kagoshima ken shiryō shui kankōkai, *Kagoshima ken shiryō shūi*, 14 vols, Kagoshima: Kagoshima ken shiryō shui kankokai, 1964–74.

Kagoshima kyōiku kai, *Sappan no bunka*, Kagoshima: Kagoshima kyōiku kai, 1935.

Kagoshima shishi hensan iinkai, *Kagoshima shishi*, 3 vols, Kagoshima: Kagoshima shi, 1969–71.

Kaieda Nobuyoshi, comp. and ed., *Ishin zengo jitsu rekishi den*, 10 vols, Tokyo: Denbunsha, 1892.

Kaionji Chōgorō, *Saigō Takamori*, 9 vols, Tokyo: Gakushū kenkyūsha, 1969.

———, *Saigō Takamori*, 14 vols, Tokyo: Asahi shinbunsha, 1980.

———, *Saigō to Ōkubo*, Tokyo: Shinchōsha, 1973.

———, *Shiden Saigō Takamori*, Tokyo: Shobunsha, 1985.

Kanai Madoka, ed., *Dōkai koshuki*, Tokyo: Shin jinbutsu ōraisha, 1985.

Kanbashi Norimasa, 'Kinsei makki Satsuma han no nōgyō gijutsu to keisei,' *Shakai keizai shigaku*, #18:5.

———, 'Satsuma han,' in Kodama and Kitajima, *Shinpen monogatari hanshi*, vol. 12.

———, 'Satsuma han gōshi nōmin no teikō undō,' *Nihonshi kenkyū*, #30.

———, *Satsumajin to Yōroppa*, Kagoshima: Chōsakusha, 1982.

———, *Shimazu Shigehide*, Tokyo: Yoshikawa kōbunkan, 1980.

Kasai Sukeji, *Kinsei hankō ni okeru gakutō gakuha no kenkyū*, 2 vols, Tokyo: Yoshikawa kōbunkan, 1970.

Katsuda Magoya, *Ōkubo Toshimichi den*, 3 vols, Tokyo: Dōbunkan, 1911.

———, *Saigō Takamori den*, Tokyo: Shigensha, 1976. (Reprint of 1894 first edition.)

Kawahara Hiroshi, *Saigō densetsu: Tōyōteki jinkaku no saihakken*, Tokyo: Kodansha, 1971.

———, 'Saigō Takamori to Saigō densetsu no haikei,' *Dentō to gendai*, 1975/5.

Kawakami Masamitsu, ed., Satō Issai, *Genshi shiroku*, 4 vols, Tokyo: Kodansha, 1981.

Kawamura Hiroshi, 'Sappan ni okeru gōshi seidō no kenkyū,' *Nankoku shisō*, #1–2.

Kawano Hiroyoshi, *Seinan sensō taneti hiwa*, Tokyo: Kibisha, 1989.

Kitagawa Tetsuzo, *Satsuma no gōjū kyōiku*, Kagoshima: Kagoshima ken-ritsu tōshokan, 1972.

——, *Shimazu shiryō shū*, Tokyo: Jinbutsu ōraisha, 1966.

Kitajima Manji, ed., *Nihon keizai shi*, Tokyo: Yūhikaku, 1985.

Kodama Kota, 'Kagoshima ken no chōson seidō,' *Kagoshima shirin*, #1.

——, *Seinan kibun*, manuscript.

——, 'Seinan yūhan ron,' in Kodama and Kitajima, *Shinpen monogatari hanshi*, vol. 12.

——, and Kitajima Masamoto, eds., *Shinpen monogatari hanshi*, 12 vols, Tokyo: Shin jinbutsu ōraisha, 1977.

Kodera Tetsunosuke, comp. and ed., *Seinan no eki Satsugun kōkyōsho*, Tokyo: Yoshikawa kōbunkan, 1945.

Kokuryūkai, comp. and ed., *Seinan kiden*, 6 vols, Tokyo: Kokuryūkai, 1910.

Konishi Shirō, *Nihon zenshi*, vol. 8, *Kindai 1*, Tokyo: Tōdai shuppan kai, 1962.

Koyama Hironari, 'Bakumatsu Satsuma han no ishin undō to sono haikei,' *Saitama daigaku kiyō*, #4.

Kumatsuki Kenji, 'Sat-Chō bōeki to Shiraishi Shōichirō,' *Kyōdo*, #6.

Kuroda Yasuo, 'An'ei-Tenmei ni okeru Satsuma han no dōkō,' *Chihōshi kenkyū*, #120.

——, 'Bunka-Bunsei ki Nagasaki shōhō kakuchō wo meguru Satsuma han no kakusaku,' *Shien*, #114.

——, 'Bunka hōtō jiken go no Satsuma han,' *Shien*, #112.

——, 'Satsuma han Bunka hōtō jiken to sono rekishiteki haikei,' *Kyūshū bunkashi kenkyūjo kiyō*, #19.

——, 'Satsuma han Tenpō kaikaku makki no kyūchidaka kaisei,' *Kyūshū shigaku*, #61.

——, 'Satsuma han Tenpō kaikaku no kisoteki kenkyū, 1,' *Kyūshū bunkashi kenkyūjo kiyō*, #20.

Maeda Ichiō, 'Sakoku to Sappan bōeki,' *Keizaigaku zasshi*, #13:5.

Masamura Hiroshi, 'Saigō Takamori no shisō ni tsuite,' *Bungeika ronshū*, #7.

Matsui Masato, *Satsuma hanshū Shimazu Shigehide*, Tokyo: Honpō sho-seki, 1985.

Matsumoto Hikosaburo, *Gōjū kyōiku no kenkyū*, Tokyo: Yakumo shoten, 1943.

Matsushita Shirō, *Bakuhansei shakai to kokudaka sei*, Tokyo: Taka shobō, 1984.

——, 'Bakumatsu ni okeru Sappan no kaiun ni tsuite,' *Hisutoria*, #44–5.

——, 'Jōkashi no chigyō keitai' *Kagoshima shishi*, #1.

——, 'Sappan Tenpō kaikaku kenkyūshi no ichi mondai,' *Nihon rekishi*, #225.

Mikami Kazuō, *Kōbu gattai ron no kenkyū*, Tokyo: Ochanomizu shobō, 1976.

Miki Yasushi, *Satsuma Shimazu shi*, Tokyo: Shin jinbutsu ōraisha, 1972.

Minami Nihon shinbunsha, comp. and ed., *Kagoshima hyakunen*, 3 vols, Tokyo: Kankōsha, 1967.

Miyazaki Katsunori, 'Kyūshū ni okeru hyakushō ikki no tenkai to tokushitsu,' in Fujino, *Kyūshū kinseishi kenkyū sōsho*, vol. 9.

Momozono Eshin, 'Sappan no Shinshū kinsei ni tsuite,' *Kagoshima daigaku bunka hōkoku*, #11.

——, *Sappan Shinshū kinseishi no kenkyū*, Tokyo: Yoshikawa kōbunkan, 1983.

Momozono Yoshihisa, 'O-Yura sōdō,' in Kitajima Masamoto, ed., *Ō-ie sōdō*, Tokyo, 1970.

Mōri Toshihiko, 'Hansei kaikaku kara kōbu gattai e,' *Seiji kenkyū*, #10–11.

——, *Meiji ishin seijishi jōsetsu*, Tokyo: Miraisha, 1967.

——, *Meiji rokunen seihen*, Tokyo: Chūō kōron sha, 1979.

——, *Meiji rokunen seihen no kenkyu*, Tokyo: Yūhikaku, 1978.

——, *Ōkubo Toshimichi*, Tokyo: Chūō kōron sha, 1969.

——, 'Saigō Takamori wa seikanronsha ni arazu: Seikanron setsu no kyōmō wo tadasu,' in Godai, *Saigō Takamori no subete*.

——, 'Sappan kōbu gattai undō no ichi kōsatsu,' *Rekishi to gendai*, #1.

——, 'Satsuma han kōbu gattai undō no ichi kosatsu,' *Rekishi to gendai* #3.

Murano Moriji, 'Seinan sensō no chūritsu ha oyobi han Shigakkō ha no dōkō,' in Godai, *Saigō Takamori no subete*.

——, 'Seinan sensō to Shigakkō gunzō,' in Tanikawa Ken'ichi, ed., *Meiji no nairan*, vol. 3, Tokyo: San'ichi shobō, 1968.

Nagae Shinzō, 'Bakumatsu Sappan no kokutaiteki jikaku,' *Shigaku zasshi*, #53:1.

——, 'Satsu-Echi ryōhan bakusei kaikaku undō no hattan,' *Geirin*, #5:6.

Nakamura Tadashi, 'Nagasaki kaisho Tenpō kaikaku ki no shomondai: Sakoku taisei hōkai katei no ichi sokumen,' *Shien*, #115.

Nakamura Tokugorō, 'Gakusha toshite no Shimazu Hisamitsu kō,' *Nankoku shiso*, #3.

——, 'Sappan tōjō seidō no kenkyū,' *Rekishi chiri*, 50:2–6, 51: 6–12.

——, *Shimazu Nariakira kō*, Tokyo: Bunshoin shuppanbu, 1933.

Nanshū jinja sūhaikai, ed., *Nanshū ō itsuwa*, Kagoshima: Kagoshima ken kyōiku kai, 1945.

Nihon shiseki kyōkai, ed., *Hansei ichiran*, 2 vols, Tokyo: Nihon shiseki kyōkai, 1928.

——, *Ōkubo Toshimichi monjo*, 10 vols, Tokyo: Nihon shiseki kyōkai, 1927–9.

——, *Ōkubo Toshimichi nikki*, 2 vols, Tokyo: Nihon shiseki kyōkai, 1928.

——, *Shimazu Hisamitsu kō jikki*, 3 vols, Tokyo: Nihon shiseki kyōkai, 1978.

Nobori Shōmu, *Saigō Takamori gokuchūki*, Tokyo: Shin jinbutsu ōraisha, 1977.

Nonaka Keigō, *Saigō Takamori kankei bunken mokuroku kō*, Tokyo: Nonaka Keigō, 1970, 1979.

Okada Tesshi, 'Sappan isshomochi no shihai keitai,' *Kadai shigaku*, #7.

Okazaki Isao, *Saigō Takamori genshiroku*, Tokyo: Shin jinbutsu ōraisha, 1973.

Ōkubo Toshiaki, 'Meiji shinseikenka no Kyūshū,' in Fujino, *Kyūshū kinseishi kenkyū sōsho*, vol. 13.

——, 'Shigehide kō to Shiboruto,' *Nankoku shisō*, #1.

Ono Takeo, *Kyū Kagoshima han no kadowari seidō*, Tokyo: Teikoku nōkai, 1922.

——, *Gōshi seidō no kenkyū*, Tokyo: Oōkayama shoten, 1924.

Osatake Takeshi, *Meiji ishin*, 2 vols, Tokyo: Munetaka shobō, 1942, 1978.

Rekishigaku kenkyūkai, ed., *Meiji ishinshi kenkyū kōza*, 7 vols, Tokyo: Heibonsha, 1958, 1968.

Rikujō jieitai kita Kumamoto shūshinkai, comp., *Shinpen seinan senshi*, Tokyo: Hara shobō, 1977.

Rikkyō daigaku Nihonshi kenkyūshitsu, comp. and ed., *Ōkubo Toshimichi kankei monjo*, 5 vols, Tokyo: Yoshikawa kōbunkan, 1965–71.

Saigō Takamori, (Nihonshi sekkyōkai), *Saigō Takamori monjo*, Tokyo: Nihonshi sekkyōkai, 1923.

——, (Dai Nihon bunkō kankōkai), *Saigō Takamori shu*, Tokyo: Dai Nihon bunkō kankōkai, 1941.

——, (Dai Saigō zenshū henshū iinkai), *Dai Saigō zenshū*, 3 vols, Tokyo: Heibonsha, 1923.

——, (Saigō Takamori zenshū henshū iinkai), *Saigō Takamori zenshū*, 6 vols, Tokyo: Daiwa shobō, 1976–80.

Saigō Takamori zenshū henshū iinkai, comp. and ed., 'Saigō Takamori/ seinan sensō kankei bunken mokuroku,' in *Saigō Takamori zenshū*, vol. 6.

Sakamoto Moriaki, *Saigō Takamori: Fukuzawa Yukichi no shōgen*, Tokyo: Shin jinbutsu ōraisha, 1971.

——, *Seinan sensō no gen'in toshite no Fukuzawa Yukichi to Ōkubo Toshimichi no tairitsu*, Tokyo: Hyōgensha, 1971.

Sakata Nagayoshi, *Sappan Komatsu Tatewaki rireki*, Kagoshima: Kagoshima ken shiryō kankōkai, 1980.

Sakata Yoshio, *Meiji ishinshi*, Tokyo: Miraisha, 1960.

Sappan sōsho kankōkai, *Sappan sosho*, 2 vols, Kagoshima: Sappan sōsho kankōkai, 1907.

Satō Seizaburō, 'Ōkubo Toshimichi,' in Kamishima Jiro, ed., *Kenryoku no shisō*, vol. 10 of *Gendai Nihon shisō taikei*, Tokyo: Chikuma shobō, 1965.

Satō Shigerō, and Kawachi Hachirō, eds., *Bakuhansei kokka no hōkai*, Tokyo: Yūhikaku, 1981.

Shiba Ryōtarō, *Tobu ga gotoku*, 10 vols, Tokyo: Bungei shunjū, 1980.

Shibahara Takuji, *Meiji ishin no kenryoku kiban*, Tokyo: Ochanomizu shobō, 1965.

Shigeno Yasutsugu, *Sappan shidan shu*, Tokyo: Rekishi tōshokan, 1968.

Shimazu kōshaku ke hensanjo, *Sappan kaigun shi*, 3 vols, Tokyo: Sappan kaigun shi kankōkai, 1928–29.

——, *Shimazu Hisamitsu kō jikki*, 8 vols, Tokyo: Kokubunsha, 1910.

Bibliography

Shimazu Nariakira monjo kankōkai, *Shimazu Nariakira monjo*, 3 vols, Tokyo: Yoshikawa kōbunkan, 1959, 1963, 1969.

Shimoto Tatemitsu, 'Ōkubo Toshimichi to sono nikki,' in *Kagoshima no rekishi to shakai*.

Shin Sappan sōsho kankōkai, *Shin Sappan sōsho*, 5 vols, Kagoshima: Shin Sappan sōsho kankōkai, 1971.

Tamamuro Taijō, *Saigō Takamori*, Tokyo: Iwanami shoten, 1960.

——, *Seinan sensō*, Tokyo: Shibundō, 1958.

Tanaka Akira, *Bakumatsu no Chōshū*, Tokyo: Chūō kōron sha, 1975.

——, *Bakumatsu no hansei kaikaku*, Tokyo: Hanawa shobō, 1965.

——, 'Bakumatsu Sat-Chō bōeki no kenkyū,' *Shigaku zasshi*, #69:3–4.

——, *Meiji ishin*, Tokyo: Shogakkan, 1976.

——, *Meiji ishin seijishi kenkyū*, Tokyo: Aoki shoten, 1963.

Tanaka Sōgorō, *Saigō Takamori*, Tokyo: Yoshikawa kōbunkan, 1958.

——, *Seikanron/seinan sensō*, Tokyo: Shiroaki shuppan, 1939.

Tanemura Kanshi, 'Satsuma han ni okeru hōken ronri no shōsō,' in *Kagoshima no rekishi to shakai*.

Tōgō Saneharu, *Ōkubo Toshimichi, sono shōgai*, Kagoshima: Tōgō Saneharu, 1984.

——, *Saigō Takamori, sono shōgai*, Kagoshima: Tōgō Saneharu, 1984.

Tokutomi Iichirō, *Kinsei Nihon kokuminshi*, 100 vols, Tokyo: Jiji tsūshin sha, 1960–71.

——, *Ōkubo Kōtō sensei*, Tokyo: Minyūsha, 1927.

Tokuyama Kunisaburō, *Matsudaira Shungaku kō*, Tokyo: Kishinbō, 1937.

Tokyo daigaku shiryō hensanjo, *Ishin shiryō kōyō*, 10 vols, Tokyo: Tōdai shuppankai, 1937, 1983.

——, *Shimazu ke kokuji ōshō shiryō*, manuscript collection.

——, *Shimazu ke rekidai seidō*, manuscript collection.

Tōyama Shigeki, *Meiji ishin*, Tokyo: Iwanami shoten, 1951, 1972.

——, 'Seikanron, jiyūminkenron, hōkenron,' in Meiji shiryō kenkyū renrakukai, ed., *Kindai shisō no keisei*, vol. 10 of *Meiji shi kenkyū sōsho*, Tokyo: Ochanomizu shobō, 1959.

Tsuchiya Takao, *Hōken shakai hōkai katei no kenkyū*, Tokyo: Kōbundō, 1927.

Tsukuba Hisaharu, 'Shimazu Hisamitsu ron,' in *Kyōdō kenkyū: Meiji ishin ron*, Tokyo, 1967.

Ueda Shigeru, *Saigō Takamori no higeki*, Tokyo: Chūō kōron sha, 1983.

Uehara Kenzen, 'Han bōeki no tenkai to kōzō: Tenpō, Kōka ki ni okeru Satsuma han karamono shōhō no dōkō,' *Nihonshi kenkyū*, #115.

——, 'Kinsei kōki kōshin han ni okeru ryōshūteki kiki no kōzō: Satsuma han no ba'ai,' *Miyazaki daigaku kyōikugakubu kiyō, shakai kagaku*, #42.

——, *Sakoku to han bōeki: Satsuma han no Ryūkyū mitsu bōeki*, Tokyo: Yaedake shobō, 1981.

——, 'Satsuma han in okeru gunsei kaikaku: Kōka yon nen no "kyūchidaka kaisei" no mondai wo chūshin ni,' in Fujino, *Kyūshū kinseishi kenkyū soshō*, vol. 11.

——, 'Satsuma han ni okeru karamono shōhō no tenkai: Kaishō bōeki e no shintō,' *Shien*, #113.

——, 'Satsuma han ni okeru karamono shōhō taisei no kakuritsu katei,' *Shien*, #112.

Umeki Akihito, 'Bunkyū ki Satsuma han no fukoku kyōhei saku,' *Rekishi to gendai*, #6.

Watanabe Morihide, *Arima Shinshichi sensei denki oyobi ikō*, Tokyo: Kaigaisha, 1931.

Yamada Seisai, ed., *Saigō Nanshū ikun*, Tokyo: Iwanami shoten, 1939.

Yamada Tatsuo, *Kadowari sōshiki no hōkai katei*, Tokyo: Nōgyō sōgō kenkyūjo, 1959.

——, 'Kagoshima ken ni okeru chisō kaisei,' *Nōgyō keizai kenkyū*, #24:4.

——, *Meiji zettaishugi no kisō katei*, Tokyo: Ochanomizu shobō, 1962.

Yamaguchi Muneyuki, *Bakumatsu seiji shisōshi kenkyū*, Tokyo: Pelican sha, 1982.

——, 'Bakumatsu seikanron no haikei,' *Nihon rekishi*, #155.

——, 'Shimazu Nariakira ron: Tozama kei Hitotsubashi ha daimyo no seiji ishiki,' *Rekishigaku chirigaku nenpō*, #2.

Yamamasa Tadayoshi, 'Saigō Nanshū no nōsei shisō,' *Teikoku nōkai ho*, #18:6.

Yamamoto Hirofumi, 'Sappan Tenpō kaikaku no zentei,' *Keizai shirin*, #22:4.

——, 'Satsuma han no Tenpō kaikaku,' *Keizai shirin*, #24:3.

——, 'Satsuma han no yōshiki kōgyō,' *Keizai shirin*, #26:2.

——, 'Tenpō kaikaku go no Sappan no seijō,' *Keizai shirin*, #26:1.

——, 'Toyotomi seikenki Shimazu shi no kurairichi to gunyaku taisei,' *Shigaku zasshi*, #92:6.

Yamashita Ikuo, *Kenkyū seinan no eki*, Tokyo: San'ichi shobō, 1977.

Yoshida Katsuyoshi, 'Saigō Takamori: Sono shisōteki kōsatsu,' in *Kagoshima no rekishi to shakai*.

Yoshida Masahiko, 'Seinan yūhan to chūō seikyoku,' in Fujino, *Kyūshū kinseishi kenkyū sōsho*, vol. 13.

Yoshinaga Akira, 'Kyūshū shohan ni okeru hansei kaikaku no tenkai,' *Aichi kyōiku daigaku kenkyū hōkoku*, #30.

Materials in English

Akamatsu, Paul, *Meiji 1868: Revolution and Counterrevolution in Japan*, New York: Harper & Row, 1972.

Akita, George, *Foundations of Constitutional Government in Modern Japan, 1868–1900*, Cambrige, MA: Harvard University Press, 1967.

Battistini, Lawrence, 'The Korean Problem in the Nineteenth Century,' *Monumenta Nipponica*, #8.

Beasley, W.G., 'Counsillors of Samurai Origin in the Early Meiji Government, 1868–9,' *Bulletin of the School of Oriental and African Studies*, 1957.

Bibliography

——, 'Feudal Revenue in Japan at the Time of the Meiji Restoration,' *Journal of Asian Studies*, #19.

——, *The Meiji Restoration*, Stanford: Stanford University Press, 1972.

——, 'Politics in Satsuma, 1858–1868,' *Modern Asian Studies*, #1:1.

——, *Select Documents of Japanese Foreign Policy, 1852- 1868*, Oxford: Oxford University Press, 1955.

Bolitho, Harold, 'The Echigo War,' *Monumenta Nipponica*, #34:2.

Brown, Sidney Devere, 'Kido Takayoshi (1833–1877): Meiji Japan's Cautious Revolutionary,' *Pacific Historical Review*, #25.

——, 'Ōkubo Toshimichi and the First Home Ministry Bureaucracy: 1873–78,' in Silberman and Harootunian, *Modern Japanese Leadership*.

——, 'Ōkubo Toshimichi: His Political and Economic Policies in Early Meiji Japan,' *Journal of Asian Studies*, #21:2.

Buck, James, 'The Satsuma Rebellion of 1877,' *Monumenta Nipponica*, #28:4.

Clement, Earnest, 'The Mito Civil War,' *Transactions of the Asiatic Society of Japan*, #19:2.

——, 'The Saga and Satsuma Rebellions,' *Transactions of the Asiatic Society of Japan*, #50.

Conroy, Francis Hilary, *The Japanese Seizure of Korea, 1868- 1910: A Study of Realism and Idealism in International Relations*, Philadelphia: University of Pennsylvania Press, 1960.

Craig, Albert, *Chōshū in the Meiji Restoration*, Cambridge, MA: Harvard University Press, 1961.

——, 'Kido Kōin and Ōkubo Toshimichi: A Psychohistorical Analysis,' in Craig and Shively, *Personality in Japanese History*.

——, 'The Restoration Movement in Chōshū,' in Hall and Jansen, *Studies in the Institutional History of Early Modern Japan*.

——, and Donald Shively, eds, *Personality in Japanese History*, Berkeley and Los Angeles: University of California Press, 1970.

Daniels, Gordon, 'The Japanese Civil War (1868): A British View,' *Modern Asian Studies*, #1:3.

Fairbank, John, *The Chinese World Order*, Cambridge, MA: Harvard University Press, 1968.

Flershem, Robert and Yoshiko, 'Nakano Family Documents: Satsuma-Chōshū Trade, 1856–66,' *Monumenta Nipponica*, #25:1.

Furukawa Tesshi, 'Saigō Takamori,' trans. Iwanaga Kuni, *Philosophical Studies of Japan*, #8.

Gubbins, John, 'Hideyoshi and the Satsuma Clan in the Sixteenth Century,' *Transactions of the Asiatic Society of Japan*, #8:1.

Hall, John Whitney, and Sakata Yoshio, 'The Motivation of Political Leadership in the Meiji Restoration,' *Journal of Asian Studies*, #16:1.

——, and Marius B. Jansen, eds, *Studies in the Institutional History of Early Modern Japan*, Princeton: Princeton University Press, 1968.

Huber, Thomas, *The Revolutionary Origins of Modern Japan*, Stanford: Stanford University Press, 1981.

Iwata Masakazu, *Ōkubo Toshimichi: The Bismark of Japan*, Berkeley and Los Angeles: University of California Press, 1964.

Jansen, Marius B., *Sakamoto Ryōma and the Meiji Restoration*, Stanford: Stanford University Press, 1971.

Kirk, Russell, *The Conservative Mind*, 7th ed., Chicago: Gateway, 1986.

Lamberti, Matthew, 'Tokugawa Nariaki and the Japanese Imperial Institution,' *Harvard Journal of Asian Studies*, #32.

Lee, Edwin, 'The Kazunomiya Marriage: Alliance between the Court and the Bakufu,' *Monumenta Nipponica*, #22:2.

Lifton, Robert Jay, *Death in Life: Survivors of Hiroshima*, New York: Vintage, 1968.

McWilliams, Wayne, 'Soejima Taneomi: Statesman of Early Meiji Japan, 1868–74,' unpublished doctoral dissertation, University of Kansas, 1973.

Matsui Masato, 'Shimazu Shigehide 1745–1833: A Case Study of Daimyo Leadership,' unpublished doctoral dissertation, University of Hawaii, 1975.

Matsumoto Sannosuke, 'The Significance of Nationalism in Modern Japanese Thought: Some Theoretical Problems,' trans. Kano Tsutomu, *Journal of Asian Studies*, #31:4

Mayo, Marlene, 'The Korean Crisis of 1873 and Early Meiji Foreign Policy,' *Journal of Asian Studies*, #31:4.

——, 'Rationality in the Meiji Restoration: The Iwakura Embassy,' in Silberman and Harootunian, *Modern Japanese Leadership*.

Moore, Ray, 'Samurai Discontent and Social Mobility in the Late Tokugawa Period,' *Monumenta Nipponica*, #26:1.

Morris, Ivan, *The Nobility of Failure: Tragic Heroes in the History of Japan*, London: Martin Secker & Warburg, 1975.

Motoyama Yukihiko, 'The Political Thought of the Late Mito School,' *Philosophical Studies of Japan*, #11.

Mounsey, Augustus, *The Satsuma Rebellion*, London: John Murray, 1879.

Mushanokōji Saneatsu, trans. and adapt. Sakamoto Moriaki, *Great Saigō: The Life of Takamori Saigō*, Tokyo: Kaitakusha, 1942.

Nock, Elizabeth, 'The Satsuma Rebellion of 1877: Letters of John Capen Hubbard,' *Far Eastern Quarterly*, #7:4.

Palais, James B. *Politics and Policy in Traditional Korea*, Cambridge, MA: Harvard University Press, 1975.

Sakai, Robert K., 'The Consolidation of Power in Satsuma han,' in Hall and Jansen, *Studies in the Institutional History of Early Modern Japan*.

——, 'Feudal Society and Modern Leadership in Satsuma han,' *Journal of Asian Studies*, #16:3.

——, 'Landholding in Satsuma, 1868–77,' *Studies on Asia*, Omaha: University of Nebraska Press, 1963.

——, 'The Satsuma-Ryūkyū Trade and the Tokugawa Seclusion Policy,' *Journal of Asian Studies*, #23:3.

——, 'Shimazu Nariakira and the Emergence of National Leadership in Satsuma,' in Craig and Shively, *Personality in Japanese History*.

——, and Haraguchi Torao et al, trans. and ed., *The Status System and Social Organization in Satsuma: A Translation of the Shūmon Tefuda Aratame Jōmoku*, Tokyo: University of Tokyo Press, 1975.

——, 'The Ryūkyū Islands as a Fief of Satsuma,' in Fairbank, *The Chinese World Order*.

Sakihara Mitsugu, 'Ryūkyū's Tribute-tax to Satsuma during the Tokugawa Period,' *Modern Asian Studies*, #6:3.

——, 'The Significance of Ryūkyū in Satsuma Finances during the Tokugawa Period,' unpublished doctoral dissertation, University of Hawaii, 1971.

Satow, Ernest, *A Diplomat in Japan*, London: Seely, Service and Company, 1921.

Silberman, Bernard and Harry Harootunian, eds, *Modern Japanese Leadership: Transition and Change*, Tucson: University of Arizona Press, 1966.

Steele, William, 'Against the Restoration: Katsu Kaishū's Attempt to Reinstate the Tokugawa Family,' *Monumenta Nipponica*, #36.

——, 'Katsu Kaishū and the Collapse of the Tokugawa Bakufu,' unpublished doctoral dissertation, Harvard University, 1976.

Stephan, John, 'Saigō Takamori and the Satsuma Rebellion,' in *Papers on Japan*, vol. 3, Cambridge, MA: Harvard University Press, 1965.

Totman, Conrad, *The Collapse of the Tokugawa Bakufu, 1862–68*, Honolulu: University Press of Hawaii, 1980.

——, 'Ethnicity in the Meiji Restoration,' *Monumenta Nipponica*, #37:3.

——, 'From Sakoku to Kaikoku: The Transformation of Foreign Policy Attitudes, 1853–68,' *Monumenta Nipponica*, #35:1.

——, 'Fudai Daimyo and the Collapse of the Tokugawa Bakufu,' *Journal of Asian Studies*, #34:3.

——, 'Political Reconciliation in the Tokugawa Bakufu: Abe Masahiro and Tokugawa Nariaki, 1844–52,' in Craig and Shively, *Personality in Japanese History*.

——, 'Political Succession in the Tokugawa Bakufu: Abe Masahiro's Rise to Power, 1843–1845,' *Harvard Journal of Asian Studies*, #26.

——, *Politics in the Tokugawa Bakufu, 1600–1843*, Cambridge, MA: Harvard University Press, 1967.

——, 'The Struggle for Control of the Shogunate (1853–58),' *Papers on Japan*, vol. 1, Cambridge, MA: Harvard University Press, 1961.

——, 'Tokugawa Yoshinobu and *Kōbugattai*: A Study of Political Inadequacy,' *Monumenta Nipponica*, #30:4.

Umegaki Michiō, 'Centralization and Local Politics: The First Decade of Japan's Nation-building,' unpublished doctoral dissertation, Princeton University, 1978.

Wakabayashi, Bob Tadashi, *Anti-Foreignism and Western Learning in Early Modern Japan*, Cambridge, MA: Harvard University Press, 1986.

Wilson, Robert, *Genesis of the Meiji Government in Japan, 1868–1871*, Berkeley and Los Angeles: University of California Press, 1957.

Wilson, George M., 'The Bakumatsu Intellectual in Action: Hashimoto

Sanai in the Political Crisis of 1858,' in Craig and Shively, *Personality in Japanese History.*

——, *Patriots and Redeemers in Japan: Motives in the Meiji Restoration*, Chicago: University of Chicago Press, 1992.

Yates, Charles L., 'Meiji kokka no keisei to Saigō Takamori,' *Nenpō: Kindai Nihon kenkyū*, #14, October, 1992.

——, 'Restoration and Rebellion in Satsuma: The Life of Saigō Takamori, 1827–77,' unpublished doctoral dissertation, Princeton University, 1987.

——, 'Saigō Takamori in the Emergence of Meiji Japan,' *Modern Asian Studies*, ?

Index

Index

Index

Index

101, 115, 116, 123–9, 136; problem of evidence 4, 23, 26; relationship with Nariakira 32, 37, 78; relationship with Ōkubo 25, 66, 83, 182–5; resignation as commander of the imperial guard (*Konoe tōtoku*) 148; resignation as general of the army (*rikugun taishō*) 148; resignation from government 147–8; scholarly controversy 3, 4, 12, 150*ff*, 158, 162, 165, 212, 214; suicide attempt with Gesshō 8, 37–8, 40, 57; suicide legend 11, 167–8; Ueno monument 7, 111, 199; views on foreign relations 127, 149, 162; views on morality, ethics, and virtue 40, 51, 53, 56–61, 76, 79, 80, 84, 87, 88, 108, 112, 114, 116, 124, 128, 131, 145–6, 154, 171, 175, 178, 183, 184, 215; views on personal integrity 29, 30, 33, 40, 45, 52, 53, 56, 57, 61, 68, 69, 70, 76, 79, 88, 125–6, 128, 156, 159, 166, 169, 175, 215; views on religion 126–7; views on rural enterprise and administration 27–30, 58–61, 124, 126–7, 131, 139, 158, 160–1, 162, 169, 175; views on tradition 30, 33, 125, 127, 138, 179, 183

Saigō Tsugumichi 9, 24, 52, 55, 144, 172, 217

Saisho Atsushi 157

Sakamoto Moriaki 198

Sakamoto Ryōma 10, 80, 84, 86, 89, 90, 97, 103, 212

Sakoda Taji'emon 27–8, 44

samurai class, fate of 127, 130, 137, 138, 139, 141, 142, 152, 168, 170

samurai stipends, disposition of 124, 138, 142

Sanjō Sanetomi 79, 110, 128, 142–7, 153, 216

Satō Issai 56, 58, 179, 206

Satow, Ernest 94, 98–9

Satsuma: direct trade with China 19, 20; factional politics 22, 31, 34, 48, 50, 74, 100, 103, 110, 113, 118, 136; geographic isolation 16; *Hayatō* 16; Mita residence 105, 112; rebellion (1877) 3, 4, 8, 9, 10, 11, 13, 24, 120, 123, 150, 155, 170–1, 213, 218; reform 17–22, 47, 91, 110, 112, 116–24, 131, 143; relations with Britain 91–3, 99; relationship to Chōshū 65, 67, 70, 71, 73, 74, 80, 84, 85, 88, 94, 99; status system and inequality 16–22, 48, 50, 83, 96, 97, 113, 117–20, 133, 134, 158,

207; Tenpō reform 18; traditional values 16, 26, 111; young samurai 22, 45, 48

Satsuma-Chōshū alliance 80–1, 209, 210

Satsuma-Tosa alliance 97, 98, 100, 211

Seichūgumi 25, 49, 50, 52, 202

seikanron see Korea, debate on

seinan sensō see Satsuma, rebellion (1877)

Sendai 107

Shiba Ryōtarō 1, 2, 7, 183

Shigakkō see private schools

Shigeno Yasutsugu 57, 206

Shimazu, military accomplishments 15, 16

Shimazu family 15, 16, 119, 138, 139, 171

Shimazu Hisamitsu 19, 34, 36, 47–53, 62, 64, 66, 69, 75, 83, 86, 91, 92, 95*ff*, 118, 131–5, 139, 141, 142, 158, 166, 171, 205, 207, 210

Shimazu Nariakira 19, 20, 33–5, 37, 45, 47, 49, 62, 74, 78, 113, 115, 116, 120, 133, 143, 159, 162, 166, 171, 180, 215

Shimazu Narinobu 18, 21

Shimazu Narioki 18, 21, 33, 34, 47, 48, 202

Shimazu Shigehide 17, 18, 20, 21, 45, 202

Shimazu-shō 15

Shimazu Tadayoshi 34, 47, 48, 49, 87, 88, 91, 106–7, 118, 119, 123, 133, 135, 141

Shimonoseki 50–1, 64, 72, 77, 81, 88, 167

Shinpūren (League of the Divine Wind) 164

Shinagawa Yajirō 97, 98, 100, 101

Shinohara Kunimoto 121, 122, 123, 143, 149, 157, 160–2, 168, 218, 220

Shiroyama 167–8, 171, 220

shizoku see samurai class

Shōgitai 107, 111, 113

shogun, succession dispute 34–6

Shōnai 105, 112, 213

Shugijuku 160

Soejima Taneomi 143, 144, 146

sonnō jōi (and expulsionism) 55, 64, 65, 66, 71, 75, 93, 102, 207

Tabaruzaka, battle of 167

taisei hōkan 97–9, 100, 102, 212

Taiwan 144, 147, 162, 174

Takasugi Shinsaku 77, 79, 81, 208, 209

Tamamuro Taijō 157, 162, 214

Tani Kanjō 167

Tatsugō 39, 42, 46

tenka 88, 89, 90, 93, 96, 177–8, 182, 221

Teradaya 51, 52, 103

Terajima Munenori 92

Toba-Fushimi 100, 101, 106, 112, 113

Index